Garden to Desert

A Walk Through the Book of Genesis

by David Deckard

Hope this is good!

Copyright © 2016 David Deckard

All rights reserved.

ISBN-10:
0692654763
ISBN-13:
978-0692654767

Cover Photo Copyright © 2016 Rosanna Cartwright, All rights reserved

Book of Genesis taken from the Holy Bible, New International Version®, NIV® Copyright © 1973, 1978, 1984, 2011 by Biblica, Inc.® Used by permission. All rights reserved worldwide.

Scriptures taken from the Holy Bible, New International Version®, NIV®. Copyright © 1973, 1978, 1984, 2011 by Biblica, Inc.™ Used by permission of Zondervan. All rights reserved worldwide. www.zondervan.com The "NIV" and "New International Version" are trademarks registered in the United States Patent and Trademark Office by Biblica, Inc.™

DEDICATION

To all who have put up with me in churches, Bible Studies, at seminary, and at Blazersedge.com. Especially to Careen, Derek, and Ali for sparing the time to make this possible.

ACKNOWLEDGEMENTS

Thank you to Kelly AuCoin, to my family, to Jennifer, Phil M., John, Carla, Katherine, Terry Fretheim, Diane Jacobsen, and all those who have spent blessed hours in deep theological discussion with me over the years. (Also to those people who say such stupid things in God's name that the anger you've caused has kept my desire to do this burning. See? God uses you too.) And finally, to the people of the Genesee Lutheran Parish and Washington Lutheran Church who have spent years in Bible Study with me that inspired and refined these thoughts. This is as much your book as it is mine.

CONTENTS

	Foreword	vii
	Introduction	xi
1	The Foundation	Pg 1
2	The Fall	Pg 57
3	Life After Eden	Pg 76
4	Stories of Abraham	Pg 102
5	Isaac and His Sons	Pg 171
6	Joseph and His Brothers	Pg 236
	Epilogue	Pg 317

FOREWORD BY KELLY AUCOIN
"PASTOR TIM" OF THE FX NETWORK SHOW, "THE AMERICANS"

I'm an actor, and one of my current gigs is the recurring role Pastor Tim on the FX show, The Americans. In other words, I'm not a pastor but I play one on TV (Dave gave me that line when he pitched me on the idea of writing this forward. I'm annoyed I didn't think of it. I mean, come on, it was RIGHT THERE! Damn, you're good Deckard…). The show is about Cold War era Soviet spies posing as regular suburban parents with two, unsuspecting children. Over the past three seasons, my character's arc has centered around the daughter of these spies. She finds a father figure in Pastor Tim and a community in the church. Naturally her Soviet parents find this unsettling.

I'm proud and extremely lucky to be on The Americans. It's a great show, and the writing is spectacular. One thing I found unique in the first script I read, and remains one of the things I love most about the story, is that there is no suggestion that Pastor Tim has any nefarious or unsettling motives. He isn't using god, or the church, as some sort of crutch, or to hide some deep, dark secret. Neither is he an evangelical hard-liner, preaching exclusion or hate. If Kevin Bacon wanted to dance in his town, by golly, that'd be just fine. There was even a scene last season in which Pastor Tim tried to convince the (Soviet spy) father to accompany his daughter and the church group on a trip to help build a school in Kenya. His pitch included the disclaimer that "these trips can be really light on the whole GOD thing," and they shared a laugh. The guy is self-aware, willing to engage in the world as it is, including people who may not share his views.

This approach still seems almost radical to me. When was the last time you saw a person of the cloth portrayed this way, not as a mere plot device or blanket representation of a pre-conceived agenda? It's especially remarkable for a spy show, where one might expect to see one dimensional characters advancing plot and little else.

Pastor Tim is tantalizing, because, although I am not a religious person (pretty much agnostic), I find negative storytelling about religion and clergy prevalent and tiresome. One of the show's creators once told me that the character was, in part, inspired by his father, a progressive, politically active Rabbi. Yet in early writers' meetings about Pastor Tim's arc, he had to ban the word "cult" from the room.

He and I connected over this. We both remembered a different time, where religious leaders were not viewed as monolithic or portrayed as such. Their backgrounds, political leanings, and stories brought texture, if not meaning, to daily life.

I grew up in a political family. From 1974-1992 my father was a US Congressman from Oregon. During the 70's and 80's our lives were pretty evenly split between Washington DC and our home state. I have very clear memories of activist, engaged church groups, and of my father traveling the state engaging progressive congregations. He was (and remains) a liberal Democrat, but many of his most ardent supporters came from religious communities. Not everyone agreed on everything, but they found common ground and the discourse was civil, if sometimes "energetic".

When I read The Americans script, I liked that my character was a good man who cared about people and the world. Pastor Tim was a guy I recognized. He was political, but like so many of the church-going folk I knew from my dad's campaigns, his politics ran towards the populist. (In one episode he was dragged to jail for protesting nuclear arms proliferation.) But his populism stemmed from compassion for others. In a pivotal moment in an early script, Tim was met with the aggressive menace of, and potential violence from, one of the principle characters. He met the challenge with openness and grace. That reaction, completely lacking in any sort of guile, saved him and maybe even left a mark on the psyche of this principle character who was grappling with a crisis of conscience and, in his own way, faith.

Despite this nuanced character portrayal, the blogosphere was convinced on sight that Pastor Tim was nefarious. Part of this may be the wig I wear. It's been described more than once as "creepy". I can't really argue; it's sort of strawberry blonde, wavy…basically a Dazed-And-Confused-Era-Matthew McConaughey looking number (unfortunately minus the McConaughey mug). Influenced by hairstyle or not, some viewers felt an immediate, universal mistrust of the guy. The most popular theory was that I was going to turn out to be a pedophile (which to my relief is not the case). Others debated that I was a KGB operative or an FBI agent. For the record, I can neither confirm nor deny these last two possibilities (or FX will have to kill you), but it was sort of amazing that the only option that never seemed to get serious consideration was that Pastor Tim was, you know, just a decent pastor…a pretty normal human being just like the rest of us.

As the character has developed I've argued that even a person of deep faith has to be normal in many ways, otherwise how will other people connect with that faith? Pastors can have a sense of humor. They can be Star Wars fans. Maybe they even like sports!

Which leads me, finally, to the connection between all this and Dave Deckard.

I am a huge Portland Trail Blazers fan. Early on, my dad and I bonded over basketball and the Blazers. I grew up pestering him for stories from his All-State High School playing career (Ask me sometime about how Les AuCoin's Redmond High team broke the 4th quarter surprise man-to-man defense of highly-favored Pendleton!) He routinely drilled me on free throws in our driveway and I became my high school team's designated free throw shooter my junior year. My dad made it to, probably, 75% of my high school games. I'm still not sure how he managed that with Congressman's schedule, but there he was, night after night, signaling from the stands that I wasn't using my knees on my shot or my elbow or follow-through were off.

In Washington D.C., Dad took me to games at the Capitol Centre whenever the Blazers came to town to play the Bullets. One of my most vivid, and crushing, early memories was when I watched Bill Walton and Maurice Lucas lose to Wes Unseld, Elvin Hayes, and Bobby Dandridge. But we reveled in the little bit of home that seemed to follow us to the Big City whenever the Blazers played. When they won the NBA championship in 1977? Forget about it.

I can still recite, verbatim, Bill Schonely's radio call of the last five seconds of the championship-deciding game and I will still talk with anyone about my Blazers, anytime, anywhere. Sadly, living in Brooklyn, NY, I rarely have the opportunity. But some eight or nine years ago, I stumbled onto Blazer's Edge, Dave's terrific website dedicated to the Trail Blazers. It is a forum where fans of all stripes drop in to discuss and debate their team. And it's an unusually civil place. There are some wonderful weirdos who contribute regularly and there can be heated disagreements, but, unlike most other sports sites I've run across, things always remain respectful. Surprisingly in this day and age, you'll often find people on Blazer's Edge thoroughly debating a subject and ultimately shifting their position based on a well-written argument someone has made. The phrase "I see your point" is almost shockingly prevalent.

The way Dave's website brings people together sometimes reminds me of those old church meetings on the campaign trail. Lots of very different people create community around a common idea, be it the best way to solve the problems of a basketball team, or a city, state, or country. The fact that a man (who happens to be a pastor) runs the site, and that the site itself builds great community without being stereotypically religious, gives me fuel to maintain Pastor Tim as a well-rounded character.

I know a pastor who totally geeks out about basketball. I'm sorry, but you can't tell me that if you have religion in your life, you're automatically the kind of shorthand proselytizer we commonly portray on TV. One "outside" interest, like, say, maintaining a website for thousands of people to meet and obsess about the Portland Trailblazers, opens the possibility of more. Faith takes many forms.

I am grateful to Dave, and to Blazer's Edge…first and foremost for the community and connection to my home and one of my obsessions, but also for helping me to find a little more nuance and satisfaction in my profession.

So that's how a mostly agnostic actor who plays a pastor on TV ended up writing a foreword for an actual pastor in a legit religious book. Go figure. If faith can positively influence a sports site and a TV show and a political career, maybe there's more to it than the cynicism and stereotyping we're used to. It'd be nice to think that potentially interesting, multi-layered, and guileless faith options still exist among us in real life and not just in wonderfully counter-cultural dramatic scripts.

INTRODUCTION

Nobody understands God completely. You don't, I don't…it's not possible. If you want to know where this book is coming from, that's as good of a place to start as any.

To claim complete understanding of God or scripture is to assume we have the capacity for that understanding. Our mind would need to be as big as God himself, with perfectly keen vision and boundless wisdom accompanying. I've known some sharp, wise, intelligent people in my life. I've never met one with infinity capacity in any of those areas. God won't fit inside any of our heads, nor can he be contained by any theory we can conjure. To claim otherwise reduces God into a brain-sized idol, suspiciously congruent with the exact dimensions and proclivities of one's own mind. That's not only wrong, it's disastrous, the very definition of evil.

It's ironic that so much of American Christianity has devolved into claiming one's own view is authoritative while claiming someone else's is untrue or anathema. Both are true in a way. Everybody carries part of the picture, but the framework crumbles when a single part masquerades as the whole. Everybody's part is inadequate; we all fall short. Trying to make oneself feel theologically superior at the expense of somebody else is an exercise in futility. You spend all your time and energy beating someone else down only to end up smaller and more alone than you started, having turned the message of salvation into a tiny, brittle idol that nobody else can touch, lest your weakness be revealed.

The only way around this horrible fate is to start every theological conversation as we have here: "I don't get it. Let's try to figure it out together."

At first glance writing a book because you *don't* understand seems backwards. It goes against everything our culture teaches about knowledge. But it's the only real reason to undertake such an endeavor.

In this environment, discussion and examination are crucial. Ironically they're the two aspects of scriptural study we value least. We want to breeze past them to find "the answer", not realizing that answers are as temporary and flimsy as our lives and perceptions whereas the community created while searching for them experiences unguessed power and permanence. We think conversation exists so we can find the answers. Instead answers exist—for a time, at least—that we might be prompted to have the conversation.

Arriving at a final, eternal answer eliminates the need for more discussion. Once we find our answer, we don't want to deal with the subject anymore. How ironic that the very people who claim to be most devoted to God are so often invested in doing away with the need for him! If we're going to remain in a living relationship with God and each other we need to write, read, listen, and debate instead of searching for cheap solutions. When you understand the part of God's truth I can illuminate and I understand yours, both of us can imagine a bigger God than either of us could on our own.

We're fortunate to have books like Genesis, presented in the form of a story. Stories aren't about answers. They're meant to be experienced, enjoyed, wrestled with, and debated. Stories always involve a conversation between at least two people—the author and the reader—and the good ones lasso in many more, creating bonds between readers. Rulebooks and answer lists require no particular effort. Stories demand attention, discernment, and imagination.

Modern Biblical scholarship has given us access to more facets of scripture than we've ever had before. The words of the Bible are spread farther today than at any time in history. The greatest hurdle between people and joyful study of scripture is not a lack of precision, intellect, or access, but a lack of imagination. Anthony Burgess' appeal to free will in "A Clockwork Orange" is misguided in a theological light, but like his totalitarian state we who know scripture best often endow it with "the appearance of an organism lovely with colour and juice but is in fact only a clockwork toy to be wound up." We pull it off our shelves and wind it up to spit out the theses and Bible Study sessions and sermons we're comfortable with. We don't want people squeezing the juice out willy-nilly, lest it spatter on our clean clothes or the lovely church carpet.

The chief purpose of this book is to read Genesis as a story…to follow where it leads instead of forcing it where we need it to go in order to prove a point or solve a problem. The main by-product of the journey is meant to be *imagination*. ..the creative power that sprung forth in Eden flowering among us as we read and talk. Not everything we imagine will be equally accurate or valid. We just admitted that no single person can contain the truth. But one person imagining gives tacit permission for those gathered around to imagine as well.

That's what we're doing here: following the story and imagining together. Everything I'm going to share with you is true. But it's part of the truth, not the whole. Some portions may weigh heavier with you than others. Some may seem spurious now but take on great importance later. Some may be meant for another reader who's not you. That's the frustration and joy of this kind of undertaking. You work and study, read and analyze, only to find that for all the work you've put in you're still not at the finish line. At some point you realize that you'll never actually reach that finish line this side of heaven. The best you can hope for is to run the race well, come to understand your purpose and place in the story better, and hope that you might be able to do some good and help others along the way. Oh…and you might have a little fun along the way, seeing the world differently in the process.

So welcome in! You'll quickly find that your background and convictions are less important than your willingness to engage. Mainstream Christians, "spiritual but not religious" folks, atheists…everybody has a voice here. You belong if you've ever opened the Bible and said, "I wonder what that means? Why do people believe this?" Even if the Bible speaks truth, neither the ears that hear nor the minds that process it are pure. The curious and learned, skeptic and true believer stand on equal ground, at least to start with. That's what scripture does to us when we allow it to function properly. It levels us down, then builds us up in a new way that we couldn't have managed on our own.

Let's sit down and talk for a while about wanderers and kings, angels and mystics, and why nudists may be closer to God than any of us. You may agree or disagree with anything printed here. I'll try not to be offended too much as long as you find the stories interesting and offer your two cents as well.

A Note on Editing

Since this is my first writing project of this type, I had the worst editor in the universe: myself. It is absolutely impossible for anyone to catch all their own errors, or to read one's own words as printed on the page without folding in what was intended while writing them. I ask you to view this effort in that light and forgive me typographical and other errors. I'll attempt to correct any I missed in later editions.

1 THE FOUNDATION

In The Beginning

1 In the beginning God created the heavens and the earth.

In the beginning…

The Bible begins in a way no other text can. No date, time, historical reference, geology, genealogy, or cosmology can set a boundary around those three words, "In the beginning…" It was not *a* beginning, it was *the* beginning of *everything*.

In the beginning…

We can't even say, "Before this there was nothing." There was no *before*. My brain short circuits trying to make sense of that concept.

In the beginning…

One being alone existed outside the confines of time and space: God. We don't know how. We cannot construct a "how" without knowing "where" and "when"…neither of which were present until the universe actually began. In the first words of scripture we find out God is different than any of us, incomprehensible, unapproachable. No matter how far we travel, we'll still end up inside creation. We cannot reach outside it, back past that first beginning to see God as he *really* is.

The only God we know is the God *after* the beginning…God in relationship to us and our universe. According to scripture, our story has always been God's story too. We have never been separate.

The beginning came when the unapproachable approached…creating, talking with, and sustaining us. Whatever God is, he chose to be with us. That's what we know.

Almost 8 years ago as I type this my son made me a father. I have a daughter as well. They so fill my life that I can barely remember what I did before they arrived. I know I existed before them. I have pictures to prove it! But whatever my identity was before they arrived hardly matters. I'm known as "Dad" now. That's what I want to be. That is my identity.

Maybe that's what God felt like, making us. God may be something else—something infinitely greater than we can comprehend--but he's chosen to identify himself as our Father, our Maker. Re-defining like that only happens when you love someone more than can be imagined, like a dad loves his children. Scratch beneath the surface of scripture even a little and you see that this is, above all, a profound love story.

In the beginning God created the universe, making the "what" we run around in and the "when" in which we do it. Though we could not come to him (did not even exist without him) he came to us, fashioned us, touched us. In these words we find all of the futility of humankind and all the care God has for us despite it. When we were powerless—before we even existed—God came, God blessed, and God created. He brought into being not just a time and place, but a relationship between himself and his people. The universe and our relationship with him were meant to be one and the same.

Something Out of Nothing

² Now the earth was formless and empty, darkness was over the surface of the deep, and the Spirit of God was hovering over the waters.

The world at this time is described as "formless and empty". Matter, the stuff that comprises our reality, requires shape and substance. The chair I'm sitting on is made up of several rectangles joined together, made out of material strong enough to support my weight. Change the shape or the substance enough and it probably won't be useful as a chair anymore. Take away its shape and substance entirely and it won't be anything. Something with no shape and no substance doesn't exist.

Take away all shape and substance everywhere and you're left with nothing, a void. In the beginning the world was "formless and empty" nothingness…no shape to define, no substance to rely upon. God created the world out of nothing.

The problem with trying to describe "nothing" is that you can't. The closest scripture comes is saying, "darkness was over the surface of the deep".

There was nothing to see. Everything was dark emptiness…a huge ocean of nothing. The only difference between that nothing and the "something" which would follow was the Spirit of God "hovering over the waters".

God creating the world from nothing has deep implications. In his famous television series "Cosmos" astronomer Carl Sagan suggested that we're all made out of star stuff. He said that the basic atoms that make up our bodies came from the fiery furnace of ancient stars, the first denizens of our universe. On a basic, physical level we're all connected, not only with each other but with everything we see.

Creation out of nothing suggests a similar unity on a spiritual level. Without God's Spirit, only formless void remains. Everything I interact with is made up of physical matter plus God's Spirit from which it sprang. According to scripture, the things in my life aren't just made of star stuff, but God Stuff too.

This puts a whole new spin on how I interact with the world. If I think I own a car, I may do whatever I wish with the car. I can drive fast or slow, to good places or nefarious. Either way, it's my car. If the car also belongs to someone else, I have a responsibility to the co-owner. If I'm honorable, I won't do anything with the car that would betray their intent for it, nor make them ashamed that they shared it with me.

Now think not just of co-owning a car, but your house, your hands, the world, the air you breathe, the water you drink, your very life. Everything in the world owes God its existence. God didn't just create the world, he sustains it every day. If God withdraws his Spirit for one millisecond from creation, creation becomes nothing, the empty void it started as.

If my hands are made of God Stuff, gifted to me, I feel an obligation to use them for good purposes. I'm not free to say, "They're mine, I'll do whatever I please with them anytime I want." I'm not doing those things with my hands, but with God's hands too.

In Hebrew (the language of the Old Testament) and Greek (the language of the New), the word for spirit is the same as the word for breath. "Inspiration" is only a couple letters away from "respiration". Every breath echoes the moment of creation. Every time you breathe it's a sign of God's

Spirit moving again. Breathe in, breathe out. You have just marked a new beginning, a new creation reflecting the very first one. God's story is being told through you continually, even while you're asleep!

The Spirit moves through some of us louder than others as we sleep, much to the chagrin of our spouses. But you get the point. Creation isn't just you, it's God and you together continually.

We can take this further. If the people in my life are also made of God Stuff, I am not free to dismiss, neglect, or abuse them. If I do so, even to the least of them, I am also dismissing, neglecting, and abusing God. How I treat others is how I treat him.

Creation out of nothing means that nothing is meaningless. Each interaction—material, relational, whatever—is a holy interaction, a chance to interact with God. He's everywhere!

One of the worst tendencies of modern churches has been to make themselves look important by designating themselves as "holy places" and other places not so holy. "The altar, it's super holy! Only certain people should walk there! The building, it's pretty holy too! Don't run or shout or do normal things. Save those for outside. This is God's House. He lives here!"

The obvious implication is, "God doesn't live out there. Do whatever you wish as long as it doesn't happen in this place or to the people here." We divide the world into holy and ordinary parts. In doing so we miss the whole point of creation itself.

The opening verses of Genesis make clear that feeding your kids boxed macaroni and cheese on a Tuesday night is a holy, Spirit-filled experience. God is even present as you're washing up after. He's in the dishes, in the soap, in the sink, and in you. Every bit of it, from the fluorescent orange powder to the detergent bubbles, is God stuff.

I'm often asked how I know God is real. How do you explain that? Understanding creation from nothing, that soap bottle by my sink sings of God's existence, reminding me that God is present. But for people who don't trust that, it's just melon-scented lye.

No "proof" will bridge the gap between those two views. Most folks claim that seeing is believing. For the person of faith, believing is seeing. Either you'll understand God is everywhere or you'll see God nowhere. There's not much middle ground between. Once you start parsing out where God is and isn't—who God is with and who he's not—you deny the foundation of creation itself.

Trying to prove God is a fool's errand. The moment you succeed in highlighting God in one place/time/person and neglecting his presence everywhere else, you have not proved him, you've told a lie about him and denied him. The only way I've ever been able to show God is to stubbornly trust that he's with *every* person I see, including the one who doesn't believe in him and is asking me for proof. I don't have the proof you seek because I don't think God can be described that way. I will serve, love, and honor you as I would myself, believing God is as much with you as he is with me. That's all the proof I have.

People often want miracles and signs as proof of God's existence. Have you ever heard somebody ask, "Why doesn't God do miracles anymore? And why doesn't he speak to me?" Many preachers and churches are eager to fill that void, claiming particular miracles and messages for themselves. You don't have to flip the television dial very far to find any number of demagogues eager to convince you that God is with them more than anyone else, that their ministry stands alone (or at least tallest) in witness to him.

To those who understand creation from nothing, this makes little sense. I'm not denying that God works through particular people in particular ways. The Bible is full of stories where he did exactly that. But that doesn't mean that he's not working through you too. The same soap bottle that stands testimony to his existence also testifies to the miracle of that existence, and of you being there to witness it. Jacob saw angels ascending and descending a ladder, you see Palmolive.

If you stop a second and think how marvelous it is that *you* are here in this time and place to see that soap, you won't laugh so hard. If you look around the room right now, you'll see hundreds of miracles. If you want to break it down to the atomic or sub-atomic level, you're looking at billions and billions of miracles every second.

The cry of the faithful person sounds like, "My dish soap didn't just vanish from existence! That means God is still here and still at work in my life! What a miracle!"

I'll admit to you right now, understanding and living by this is going to make you look foolish to most folks. Getting unreasonably happy and feeling totally reassured by a bottle of detergent is not something the world understands. Not being able to prove why you're happy beyond, "First it was formless and empty, then not! And it's still not! Yay God!" doesn't help. But dang, it's a really nifty way to live. You no longer need to ask how to see God, instead you wonder how you could *not* see God. You no longer perceive a lack of miracles but an overabundance. You don't wonder what to do with the things in your life, sitting around and waiting for the important moments to come. You start to discover meaning and purpose in each moment. Most of all, you don't just see other random people around you, you see God's miraculous creations. Hate, judgment, violence, and all the nasty things we do to each other become less justifiable and harder to act on. Joy and wonder replace fear and suspicion as relationships become more like they were meant to be. Being enthralled, assured, and excited about things other people see as "common" is one of the neatest rewards of faith.

Creation from nothing fills each day with great joy and great responsibility. Suddenly every moment and every relationship matters. That's a life-changing realization.

Present in the "Now"

Creation from nothing also pins God's presence firmly in the *now*, here, today. I don't want to drift into cheesy metaphysics or self-help, but it turns out all those folks who tell us to "live in the now" may be onto something.

People carry around an unspoken assumption that God existed strongly in the past. We're familiar with the God of Biblical times who showed up with visions and voices from heaven, earthquakes and fire clouds. The God of soap bottles doesn't feel like God to us.

We carry a corresponding assumption that God will exist in the future, in heaven, after we die. Someday we'll meet with God. Someday we'll know him. He can't possibly be in my ordinary Mac-and-Cheese on Wednesday life.

Missing from all of this is a firm sense of God working in the here and now.

Sometimes this lack gets expressed in cries of loneliness. "Where are you, God? Why don't you speak to me? I need you!" Sometimes it becomes a convenient excuse to declare *de facto* independence. "God has left me to my own devices to see what I make of myself. In his absence I am the master of my own world." Sometimes we even cloak the assumption in theological dress. "God is testing you. He's waiting to find out if your faith is strong enough, if your actions are good enough, if your life is pure enough before he shows up."

In all of these constructs God is absent until your life goes well enough to warrant his attention. How convenient! If God responds based on what you do, appears and disappears in response to your actions, then you're the real center of the universe. He's a bit player in your life.

It's not true, of course. If everything we see, including ourselves, is made of God stuff, we cannot get away from his presence. Where can we run where he is not? What words can we speak to make him come or leave? You might as well tell the sub-atomic particles that make up creation to move at your command. It just ain't happening.

You can see the folly of rebellion against God. We are petulant teenagers, stomping away from our parents when we're wholly dependent on them, retreating into isolation in "our" room that they own and give us.

You can grab a Harley, get a horns-and-pitchfork tattoo, and zoom off to the desert proclaiming you're your own man and you'll do without God just fine. When you turn off your bike you'll find God in the sand, God in the tattoo ink, God in the Harley, and God in you. Whatcha gonna do? He's annoying like that.

We need to cultivate a better understanding of God in the here and now, not just the distant past and heavenly future. We need to resist the temptation to cast him out in favor of our own power in this time and place. We need to stop pretending that he shows up on command…that our being really good (or sometimes really evil) can make him appear or disappear.

God is here, right now. Our job isn't to make him come, but to look for him every day. Walking in faith, our world becomes one giant "Where's Waldo" book…except it's the easiest version ever because Waldo is everywhere. Faith calls us to re-train our eyes, to make each day an exercise in seeing God more clearly in the world around us. Wherever you can't see God, there's a hole in your vision to work on.

Think of all the breath Christians have spent drawing lines between us and them. "We're good folks and they're bad. We don't dance and they do. This rap music is awful and Lawrence Welk is pure. We're believers and they're not. We're godly and they're heathens…or worse (gasp!) *atheists*." Every one of these is a denial of God present in the here and now. We say other people have holes in their vision but we're really proclaiming the massive gap in our own.

An atheist proclaims there's no God. A Christian who looks at an atheist and doesn't see God *also proclaims there's no God*. In our haste to justify ourselves we rip apart the story of creation, kicking God out of his own world, denying his power and presence in others. If we kick God out of one place and time, then his power does not hold over all places and times. He ceases to be God.

How ironic that those who claim to defend God most strongly also end up destroying what they were trying to defend in the process.

As people of faith, our job isn't to justify ourselves, nor to sit in judgment over the world, deciding where God is and isn't. Trusting that he's here right now, we're called to wake up every morning asking the same question, "How do I see God today?" Then we spend our whole day looking, trying to see God in as many places, people, and experiences as possible.

The Light Shines in the Darkness

³ And God said, "Let there be light," and there was light.

Speaking of seeing, how apropos that the first element in all of creation was light! Light creates vision. It bounces off of objects, gets absorbed by others, brings color, depth, and perception to our world. Its primacy in creation was not accidental. The first, most ideal purpose of creation is to perceive God in it.

Not all of us see the same way, of course. Some folks might be listening to these words via audiobook, or having them read to them, or scanning them in Braille. The physical light in the story is meaningful, but the metaphorical purpose is as important as the physical vision. Some folks with 20/20 eyesight can't see God a bit. A few times in scripture blind men recognize God when nobody else can.

Think how much light informs us about the rest of creation even today. Big Bang theorists talk about all the matter in the universe compressed to an infinitesimally small point, then exploding in a cascade of light. We measure astronomical distances, the age of far-off heavenly bodies, and their momentum towards or away from us by light.

Light was the beginning of all things for us. If you believe the visions some have described after dying, light is also the end. Light is revelatory.

You know that moment when you're on vacation and you spy Mt. Rushmore or a shooting star or the city skyline for the first time and say, "Look at that!!!"? Our life is meant to be a never-ending chain of those experiences. That's the kind of joy and wonder we were made for. That's why light came first.

And It Was Good...

[4] God saw that the light was good, and he separated the light from the darkness. . [5] God called the light "day," and the darkness he called "night." And there was evening, and there was morning—the first day.

At the end of the first day of creation we get an affirmation that will be repeated several times over in this chapter: "And God saw that it was good".

"Good" is a tricky word here. It doesn't mean good as opposed to evil. As yet no evil existed. "Good" means being right, whole, in line with its purpose, and complete. A thing is "good" when it's what it is supposed to be. Another way to say this is "God made everything holy."

Back in the Garden of Eden "holy" and "at peace, complete, and in tune with its purpose" were one and the same. Nowadays, though, we've glommed so many definitions onto the concept of "holy" that it's almost become a dirty word, as in "Holier than thou." That has little to do with being at peace, in tune with one's environment, and being a seamless a part of life-giving creation. Our common definition of holy (and therefore "good") is pretty much the opposite, in fact.

One of the first things we do with holy stuff is set it apart. "That place is holy, so only the minister walks there. That thing is holy, don't touch it! That person is holy, don't act like yourself around them."

Living in a world of sin gives some justification for this. We need a place apart to remind us that our lives can, and should, be different than they end up being when we walk aimlessly through the world. But we've taken it too far. In the name of protecting our "holy things" and setting them apart, we've created a rift between holiness and our daily lives. That separation did not exist in the Garden. Everything about daily life was good and holy. Our greatest work as people of faith *should* be merging daily life and holiness together.

Instead we do the opposite. We put our holy things on pedestals, separating them from our daily lives. This works out conveniently for us in several ways:

1. We limit holy things to certain spots so that as we get closer to those spots we can pretend like we're better than people who are farther away. "Sure, everybody's a sinner *but* I'm here in church today so I'm less of a sinner than *them*."

2. Reserving holiness to a particular place allows us to leave it behind when convenient. We visit church on a Sunday, see the holy stuff, act holy while we're there, then go on with our week without any particular sense of responsibility to the holiness we just observed. After all there are no statues or pastors in our living room. This is just ordinary old dinner and that's just my husband eating it and belching. Ain't nothing holy about any of that. I don't really have to worry about holiness until I drag the family back to church next week. Now what's on TV?

3. What we put up on a pedestal we also have the power to tear down. This happens to celebrities, heroes, and politicians in our culture. It also happens to ministers, saints, and anybody else we deem holy. We desire to rule over holiness instead of serve under it. If we lift up a fallible person and invest him with power, we become even more powerful by extension when we remove him from the pedestal later. Whether the occasion is malfeasance, annoyance, or just getting tired of them, you'll eventually find yourself tearing down all the holy people you lift to lofty heights.

In each of these three cases we're saying, "Holy, Holy, Holy" as if we're talking about God and goodness, but all the time we're talking about us and our prerogatives. Is it any wonder that people hate hearing Christians talk sometimes?

In a fallen world our definition of "good" becomes paper thin, self-serving, and counterproductive. We need to return to the creation definition of holiness, the "in tune with the world, serving life, and at peace" version. Words like "holy" and "good" shouldn't be reserved to ministers and churches; they belong to all of us, everywhere. We may not ever reach the point of melding goodness and our daily lives perfectly as happened in the Garden of Eden, but we should at least know what "good" really means. We need a definition of holiness that grounds us in creation as God meant it to be, not possessive and judgmental but life-giving, ever-present, and full of energy.

6 And God said, "Let there be a vault between the waters to separate water from water." 7 So God made the vault and separated the water under the vault from the water above it. And it was so. 8 God called the vault "sky." And there was evening, and there was morning—the second day.

9 And God said, "Let the water under the sky be gathered to one place, and let dry ground appear." And it was so. 10 God called the dry ground "land," and the gathered waters he called "seas." And God saw that it was good.

11 Then God said, "Let the land produce vegetation: seed-bearing plants and trees on the land that bear fruit with seed in it, according to their various kinds." And it was so. 12 The land produced vegetation: plants bearing seed according to their kinds and trees bearing fruit with seed in it according to their kinds. And God saw that it was good. [13] And there was evening, and there was morning—the third day.

[14] And God said, "Let there be lights in the vault of the sky to separate the day from the night, and let them serve as signs to mark sacred times, and days and years, [15] and let them be lights in the vault of the sky to give light on the earth." And it was so. [16] God made two great lights—the greater light to govern the day and the lesser light to govern the night. He also made the stars. [17] God set them in the vault of the sky to give light on the earth, [18] to govern the day and the night, and to separate light from darkness. And God saw that it was good. [19] And there was evening, and there was morning—the fourth day.

[20] And God said, "Let the water teem with living creatures, and let birds fly above the earth across the vault of the sky." [21] So God created the great creatures of the sea and every living thing with which the water teems and that moves about in it, according to their kinds, and every winged bird according to its kind. And God saw that it was good. [22] God blessed them and said, "Be fruitful and increase in number and fill the water in the seas, and let the birds increase on the earth." [23] And there was evening, and there was morning—the fifth day.

[24] And God said, "Let the land produce living creatures according to their kinds: the livestock, the creatures that move along the ground, and the wild animals, each according to its kind." And it was so. [25] God made the wild animals according to their kinds, the livestock according to their kinds, and all the creatures that move along the ground according to their kinds. And God saw that it was good.

Creation Mythology

Here's the story familiar to Sunday School alumni, those shanghaied into Vacation Bible School, and most who have debated the merits of teaching Darwin (or subsequent theories) in public school classrooms. Days 2 through 5.5 see the arrival of sky, land, plants, heavenly bodies, fish, birds, and all the animals. Life bursts out everywhere.

You'd think these verses would bring near-universal joy. Not only are they teeming with energy, the whole story is just kind of cool! The cinematic grandeur alone is worth the price of admission.

Unfortunately we've found just as many ways to fight about these passages as celebrate them. "What's a day? What about dinosaurs? Is the story real? Does this explanation preclude all others? Can scientists, evolutionists, or just normal folks who have questions about this story still be considered faithful?"

These questions aren't wrong. Questioning brings curiosity and curiosity is near the heart of faith. I would suggest, however, that the decades of argument spent in "science versus creation" should be regarded as…if not a *waste*, at least somewhat beside the point. We'll never get definitive answers, but we should at least focus on better questions than we usually ask.

This story is part of what I consider Creation Mythology. In our culture "myth" has become equated with "lie". We've seen them busted on TV on a weekly basis. But myth also has an older, stronger definition.

Myths explain complex ideas in universal terms. They're not an attempt at lying. They're an attempt at telling the truth in a way that people can understand. The story in which the truth is contained may not match up exactly with a hearer's knowledge of their world, but that does not invalidate the truth the story conveys. If the truth came straight on the hearer likely wouldn't understand it. Myth helps us absorb truths we couldn't otherwise.

As a homely example, let's consider Aesop's famous fable, "The Fox and the Grapes". A fox finds a bunch of grapes desirable. He tries to reach them multiple times but they remain beyond his grasp. Finally, disgusted, he walks away uttering the phrase, "I bet they were sour anyway."

This story reveals a deep truth about human nature. It's played out in bars every weekend as rejected guys walk away from former objects of desire. Aesop's truth echoes out every time someone says, "I bet rich people aren't really happy with all their money," or, "I'm glad I'm not a shallow idiot like that celebrity." But if Aesop just wrote down, "You people are bitter and foolish, willing to tear down everything you can't possess to make yourselves feel better," everybody would have said, "Up yours, Aesop!" and burned his books on the spot. Foxes and grapes bring the truth home in a way we couldn't otherwise accept. That's the power of a myth.

But you have to ask the right questions of the story in order to understand its meaning. If you ask, "Was that a gray fox or a Tibetan sand fox?" you've missed the point. The better someone answers that question the more you go astray. In order to process the truth of the myth, you have to understand what's central and what's peripheral. The kind of fox, its vertical leap, the type of grape, the relative maturity of grapes at time of jump…none of these really matter. If Aesop heard you debating them he'd write another fable about you, likely "The Dingbat and His Idiot Friend Miss the Point".

The creation story is not exactly analogous to Aesop's Fables because the world exists and something actually happened to make it. Nor am I suggesting God is made up to prove a point like Aesop's fox was. I am saying that the truth of creation is complex enough that it requires some level of myth to explain rightly.

Even now, with the benefit of advanced sciences at our disposal, we're still learning more about creation every day. Even when we understand the workings of the universe, we have a hard time explaining them in a way normal folks can understand. These stories have been around for thousands of years. How would we explain these things to people back then?

Let's pretend the Big Bang theory accurately describes the beginning of the universe (and also assume for the sake of argument that God was behind it). How would you communicate this in a way billions of humans-- sweeping across history from nomadic shepherd days to Mars Missions and beyond—could understand? Could you use physics, chemistry, cosmology? Could you even do that today in a way more than one in a million people could get? Or would you say, "And God said, 'Let there be light'"?

"On the first day, God made light. And it was good.

"On the second day God made the sky, separating everything under the dome from the great ocean above. And it was good.

"Things came in order. Each thing proceeded from the next, in the exact way needed for life to emerge. And it was good. It worked well."

Shepherds, physicists, and Sunday School students can all pick up on this. It's complete. Just about everything we recognize as part of our world is in there. We immediately understand what's being talked about on each day.

The details are enough to establish each subject but not so much that the central truths get obscured.

If Genesis were meant to contain a literal, scientific description of the creation of the universe, the ancients would have written it in a great tome and locked it away until a generation came along with the capacity to understand it. It would remain locked away today, waiting for folks who were smart enough to hear the story.

That is not the way the Bible works. It never has been. The Genesis story belonged to the ancient nomads just as much as it belongs to scientists, modern apartment-dwellers, to you and me, and to our progeny forevermore. The story *had* to be written this way in order to make the book, and the God whose story it tells, present in all times and places.

Not About Days

In order to achieve that end, Genesis regards some details as central and timeless, others peripheral. Fortunately it's pretty clear about which are which. The Bible works like this. It answers some questions completely, remains mute on others, and sometimes leaves you with more questions than you came with. This can be frustrating, but it also helps us learn to ask more faithful questions. Sometimes the things we assume are important end up being trivial because our perception is out of whack.

Many of the popular arguments surrounding the creation story boil down to the definition of a day. Was the world created in 7 days or did it take millions of years?

Was it a gray fox or a Tibetan sand fox?

The Bible is not going to let you make that determination definitively. The creation story already tells you that.

We measure a day by the rotation of the earth. In 24 hours, give or take, we will turn around completely and the earth's position will be pretty close to the same place it was yesterday relative to the stars, especially the sun. That's how we mark the day.

Except if you read the story, the sun and stars didn't show up until Day 4 of creation. God created "day" and "night" on the first day, but even if they were meant to be measured periodically, no sun existed to limit that "day" to 24 hours.

Is the Bible being mean, leaving you hanging, inviting you to argue forever over an impossible question?

No. The Bible is telling you that the exact measure of a day isn't one of the questions it's prepared to answer. We don't need to understand whether God created the world in seven, 24-hour days or asymmetrical days that spanned billions of years which seemed like about a week to the God beyond time. Could a nomad count to a billion? I'm not sure they'd even invented zero yet.

Some things help us understand the central truths of the story. The exact length of a day in creation isn't one of them. God made the world, he ordered it in a way favorable for life, he nurtured and cared for that life…these lie at the heart of creation no matter how long it took to make.

We are certainly free to speculate on such things. It makes for great discussion. But when we start using our definition of "day" as a litmus test, the dividing line between faithful and unfaithful, we have inflated the importance of a matter beyond its bounds.

I cannot speak for everyone on the faith end of things, but for myself, I'd like to apologize to scientists, educators, and intellectually curious folks who have heard people say their life's pursuits were wrong-headed, evil, or unfaithful based on these scriptures. That's not what this story was meant for. It's ironic that a chapter that repeats so often, "it was good" has been used to create so much mistrust and misunderstanding.

But that's exactly what happens when we take something that's supposed to be peripheral and hang our entire worldview on it. What was meant to be good turns to evil; what was meant to unite us tears us apart; the power of love gets channeled into hate. However many solar-based days God took to create the world, he didn't intend it for that.

A Step to the Side: Is the Bible Literally True?

We need to depart from the text for a moment to answer a question that will be plaguing some readers. Using terms like "creation mythology" forces us to address whether the Bible is literally true. Devout atheists and devout Christians both will read "Myth" and be tempted to say, "Aha! He's saying it's NOT really true. Atheists will do so in triumph, Christians in horror. If we don't address it, neither will find reason to read further.

Ask me if the Bible is true and I will give an enthusiastic, "Yes!" It's the truest thing I've ever read. That doesn't mean I understand or agree with it. My agreeing with everything in it would be a sure sign that it's *not* true. Then it would just be the Book of Me. I know darn well that I'm flawed, so any book proclaiming to be true had better knock me on my teakettle every once in a while. I trust that God is God precisely *because* I disagree with him and occasionally don't understand him.

The Bible is true the same way an arrow shot is. It flies straight. It hits the center. It pierces. It does all these things far better than I do...which pretty much disqualifies me from sitting in judgment over it as if I were the barometer of all truth. I dare not say it's untrue, lest I become my own god.

But "literal" is a cheap, narrow way to describe a truth as vast as scripture. It's an attempt to add validity to a Truth that needs no such validation.

Envision a parent sharing something wise, knowledgeable, and good with their children. But afterwards one of the older kids turns to the others and says, "That's right, and you *better listen*! It's *so true* and I'll tell you exactly how it's true!" We don't need that childish coda to comprehend the message. The kid is trying to focus our attention on him instead of what the parent said, to gain power on the back of the parent's words. This is exactly what I hear when someone insists, "It's literally true and that's IT!"

DictionaryReference.com defines "literal" this way:

> In accordance with, involving, or being the primary or strict meaning of the word or words; Not figurative or metaphorical.

The "strict meaning of the words" clause creates a problem for us. By the time you read something in Genesis it's been through at least two languages, Hebrew and English. Chances are it made a trip through, or at least was influenced by, Latin or Greek as well. Each of these languages is distinct. Each word therein carries its own cadence and freight, often with multiple meanings depending on tense, voice, and context. It's hard enough to arrive at a primary or strict meaning for a word in a single language, let alone a word that's been tossed through 3 or 4.

Factor in a gap of a few thousand years between the first publication and the one you're holding and the problem becomes worse. Are you confident that you can determine a single, plain and strict definition for a word that was penned in a completely different time in a completely different culture using a completely different language…a word that evolved through more years of oral history before that? Are you that conversant with the mind and language of 7000 year old nomads from the Middle East? Making a claim to literalism in this sense would take far more knowledge than we possess. Even if we could do so, scripture would only belong in the hands of an elite few with special linguistic knowledge. If you're holding a Bible and you're not such a linguist, you're testifying that you don't really agree with this definition of literalism.

The Bible itself testifies against the, second definition of literal, "Not figurative or metaphorical". When Jesus spoke of the Kingdom of Heaven being like a mustard seed, faith moving mountains, or a farmer sowing seed along a rocky path, he wasn't talking agriculture and tectonic plates. Nobody made better use of figurative metaphors than Christ did through his parables.

The Bible isn't *all* metaphor. When Paul traveled to Ephesus, for instance, he actually entered that city. Some parts of scripture read as history, some poetry, some metaphor, and so on. Trying to translate inherently non-literal forms into strictly literal terms doesn't aid or defend scripture, it breaks scripture and robs us of the chance to understand it.

If your spouse says, "Shall I compare thee to a summer's day? Thou art more lovely and more temperate…" and you run off to cross-reference weather charts and germination periods at your latitude, you're missing something.

Even when they're crystal clear, literal terms often fail miserably at getting to the meaning of a passage. Consider John 11:35, which says, "Jesus wept." It's the shortest verse in the Bible. The literal meaning here is quite clear. Saline-infused drops of water trickled down Jesus' face, originating from his orbital sockets. But how much understanding does that bring you?

Pretend the person you love most in the world is sitting in your living room crying. You walk in the room and say, "Ahhh…saline drops. I see you are experiencing emotion, likely either great distress or great joy. I now understand everything I need to know about this situation. Good day!" Literally, that's true. You have correctly interpreted the situation. Practically speaking, you're one dumb donkey.

You wouldn't make that kind of "literal is completely accurate and wholly sufficient" argument in any relationship in your life. If you tried, we'd probably diagnose it as some kind of social disorder. The Bible is a relationship…our relationship with God. So how can we say, "Everything is literal and that's the only measure of truth here"?

If you take it seriously, the Bible will not let you interpret itself that way. It will appear to contradict itself. It will act confusing. You're going to have to wind yourself into a crazy, convoluted theological pretzel in order to get a simplistic, literal consistency. In the end, you'll be left holding a brittle, imitation of scripture, a finite construction of something eternal and infinitely complex.

Even though scripture is pure, the reading eye and hearing ear aren't. When told the truth we can't handle the truth, nor interpret it 100% correctly. This isn't a problem as long as we're aware of our own shortcomings…as long as we continue to be taught by scripture instead of pretending we already understand it.

Claiming any passage of scripture tells a single truth that is to be interpreted in a single way diminishes God and puts us in his place. "My version is the only version" will not work if you're claiming to serve a greater power instead of mastering it.

There are times when saying a certain passage is literally, historically true has value. Jesus existing, getting crucified, and rising from the dead is pretty important to the Christian faith. Take away the literal truth of that and we have nothing. But there are also times when the truth in scripture can't be understood in purely literal terms. "Not literal" does not mean "untrue". Exploring the metaphorical complexities of scripture doesn't reduce the word, it opens it.

In this matter and in many others of faith, we need to stop equating narrower and more stubborn with stronger. Having your jaw set for your own interpretation is not faithful, but selfish and demeaning. The Bible describes it as, "hardening your heart". It's not a good thing.

"And God Said…"

Did you notice that God created the universe by speaking? "God said…and it was so." God's Word made everything we see, everything we are. It's the foundation of his relationship with us.

In a theme that will be repeated throughout scripture, God touches us in ways common to all humanity. We all engage in some form of communication. Everything you know was first spoken to you somehow. Words may take different form—spoken, written, signed--but everybody has them. You can't be human without communicating and being communicated with.

God comes to us through the very foundation of our being. The poorest shepherd and richest mogul are united by their access to, and need for, language. God is yours, mine, everybody's. If we communicate at all, we have access to him…to the very power he used to create the universe.

Not every word is godly, to be sure, but every word reflects the basic pattern of those First Words. God spoke and the universe sprang into being. We speak and new things spring into being around us as well.

Earlier we talked about creation from nothing putting great responsibility on us, to use the things around us well. God creating through speech puts a similar responsibility on the way we communicate. Words create. Words can destroy. Words are meant to reflect God.

If you were walking around with a couple pounds of dynamite strapped to an active fuse, you'd be careful and aware of each step. Words carry exactly that kind of power.

People of faith mistakenly claim more *privilege* or *access* for their words. "Because I believe, everybody should listen to me, regard my words as good, and follow me." This is mistaken. Faith brings more *responsibility* for one's words, along with the burden of knowing that each word is meant to be a life-bringing reflection of God.

Too many faithful people are eager to elbow others out of the way for the chance to speak. If we understood the importance of what we say, we'd be afraid to speak, lest we fall short of the ideal and misuse our power.

Take a moment to review your words over the last week…not just ones spoken from pulpits and high places, but words to your family, children, co-workers and strangers. For most of us even a cursory examination reveals the need for serious penance. Every one of us takes the gift of voice, meant to bring life to the world, and bends it for our own use. We cannot speak without our selfish prerogatives and stilted viewpoints getting in the way.

I often wonder if God views us the way you'd view a vast herd of five-year-olds running around with advanced weaponry, careless and heedless of its intended power and use. Can you imagine the horror of viewing that scene?

God's Word Still at Work

God created the universe with his Word. When we read scripture we are hearing God's Word. This shows how the Bible functions in our lives. Every time we hear scripture we are created anew! Reading the Bible is a continuation of the very first moments of creation. God comes to us and remakes us. He has not stopped speaking. Creation is not a static, historical event that concluded thousands or millions of years ago. Creation is an ongoing, living relationship between God's Word—still active in the world--and us. It's happening right now.

God's creation is constantly in motion, being made new and right again every time it goes wrong. We never come to the end of our brokenness but creation doesn't stop either. Each time we have done wrong—every time we break something--we hear words that make us right again…not because we understand them fully but because God re-creates us fully. We do not pass into the next moment as the same person we were in the last, nor does the world around us. For every fall there is a renewal. Each day is a new opportunity.

Consider how regimented our lives have become. We spend our lives trying to dampen the new possibilities inherent in each day. We create to-do lists, ordering our lives by tasks and times. We manage rather than experience life, order rather than create.

What we do with our daily tasks, we also do with God's Word. We segment it, seek to narrow it down and define it. We read the Bible and want to know what it means. And by "what it means" we mean, "Give us a simple definition that we can carry in our pocket, pull out when convenient, and never have to think about again." We try to freeze the Word, confine it to our time and culture, and resist any of its attempts to re-create us, even though re-creating us is the only way out of our sins and shortcomings. We are so blind we'd rather have the sins we know than the new life God brings to us. We'd rather tell God to hush than let him save us.

Christians should not hold the Bible sacred because it gives them the right answers. None of us are capable of seeing right, let alone understanding it. We hold the Bible sacred because God comes to us and changes us through these words despite our intentions otherwise.

Consider everything you hate about Christianity. I'm guessing that most of it boils down to a cadre of people claiming that they have the rulebook and God loves them more than you because they follow it. They spend all their time getting you to follow their rules, which amounts to thinking and acting like them. Scripture becomes a tool for some people to control others for their own advantage. Thinking they already understand, they avoid the need to be re-created. Claiming to live under scripture, they put themselves above it and lose its most important function. Proclaiming their firm allegiance to God, they end up denying their deep need for him.

Scripture will not let us sit above it, making what we want out of it to advantage ourselves. It cannot be reduced to a moral code, political outlook, or list of instructions. Scripture changes and re-forms us! All of us are beneath it. All of us come to it needing to be made new.

In scripture God speaks and the world is created again. It's God's great, "Yes, I still care!" echoing through the halls of time. Its words began in the First Moment of Everything and will not be silent until it reaches its final crescendo at the end of all things. (After which all will be made new again one, final time, then peace and joy forevermore.)

If we are not being re-created by scripture, we rob the Bible of its power and purpose, its vibrancy and life. God spoke and all things were made. God speaks and all things are made new. That includes us.

Dignity for All

Being spoken to by God also gives humanity a special sort of dignity. Communication requires relationship. Words spoken into a vacuum, heard and noted by no-one, don't end up mattering. Speaker and listener work together to give words meaning. Both are intrinsic to the process.

It's no accident that the now-classic cut-off, "Talk to the hand!" is used to dismiss those with whom we're in conflict. It denies the power of another person's words. It's shorthand for, "You don't exist." It's quick, it's effective, and it hurts.

The inverse is also true. Speaking to someone means you think they matter. God speaks to us. Our relationship with him is real, powerful, important. By extension we become real, powerful, and important too. That changes the way we look at ourselves and each other.

When I meet someone, I try to remind myself that God is speaking with, to, around, and through this person. I may not know them, agree with them, or even like them, but I may not rob them of their God-given dignity. Instead my job is to listen, to try and hear what God is saying.

I never ask *whether* God is speaking through a person I meet, I ask *what* God is speaking through them. In this way I get to know new people, but also get to know God better through new people. Every person was created to be a gift to the world. My job is neither to deny nor vet that claim, but to trust it and act accordingly.

This throws the horror of sin into shocking relief. When I sin against my neighbor, I'm breaking into the conversation between them and God, trying to drown out his voice with my own self-interested one. God gives them a gift, I try to slap it away or turn it to my use. When we read about Adam and Eve biting the fruit later on, you're going to see yourself in the role of Adam or Eve. I bet you never knew you were the serpent too. That's what we become every time we sin against our neighbor.

Doing this to a person God thinks important enough to speak to makes the offense worse. It doesn't matter if that person would claim to be in conversation with God or not; to me their relationship is inherent in creation itself. They are God stuff, God is talking to them, and I am harming that relationship. The smallest sin I commit against another is an offense committed against God and everything that he has made. The entire weight of sinfulness is inherent in each and every sin.

Why Creation Exists

We claimed above that each part of scripture is good at answering certain questions but doesn't bother with others so much. What are the central questions that the creation mythology proposes to answer?

We've already dispensed with "How God did all this" and "How long it really took", and that's appropriate. Genesis isn't interested in describing molecules and epochs. It tells us that God created with his voice, that things were created in a certain order, and that everything was created for goodness. That's all we get about the "how". Everything "how-related" beyond those powerful, basic assertions is open to discussion.

But Genesis has far more to say about the "why" and "for whom" of creation.

[26] *Then God said, "Let us make mankind in our image, in our likeness, so that they may rule over the fish in the sea and the birds in the sky, over the livestock and all the wild animals, and over all the creatures that move along the ground."*

[27] *So God created mankind in his own image,*
 in the image of God he created them;
 male and female he created them.

On the sixth day the creation mythology reveals its heart. God created the world for us. All the care, detail, and power he put into the process pointed to a single purpose…that we might experience something good.

Why do we like gifts? Why do sweethearts look to each other in expectation on Valentine's Day and children to their parents and Santa at Christmas? It's not so much the stuff we get, it's the idea that somebody cares about us. Gifts are meaningful because someone went to the trouble to remember us, went out of their way to make something happen for us out of the ordinary.

Creation is the ultimate, "Thought of you, went out of my way for no purpose but to show I love you" moment. God made us to experience goodness and created the entire universe around us that we might do so.

Think of the staggering implications here. We spend our whole lives looking for validation. Am I pretty? Am I smart? Am I respected? Am I loved? Think of all the things we do—productive and destructive—to receive those assurances from the world around us. The deep irony here is that the very *existence* of the world answers those questions for us.

Somebody cares about you, means good for you, created you to be loved, created you to have purpose, created you to be a part of something very, very good.

Evangelism Revised

The affirmation inherent in creation reveals the abject horror of traditional Christian evangelism techniques. The stereotype of the "evangelist" is a church person knocking on your door, asking if you'd go to heaven if you died tonight, and telling you all the things that are wrong with you. If you amend your life correctly then God will gift you. That message is exactly backwards.

In the original Greek, evangelism translates as "good news". Yet church folks have drawn power from spreading the opposite, bringing people bad news, making them doubt that God loves them.

Much of the lack of faith in God nowadays doesn't translate to disbelief in God as much as disbelief in the people who claim to bring God's message. As they're standing there trying to convince you of all your faults, playing on your fears so you'll join them, the porch they're standing on and the tree that's waving behind them and the sun that's shining on us all stand in testimony that we *are* loved and that we'd have no purpose for being here if we weren't.

Think of how we treat each other. Think of how we reduce people to objects and roles. "That's my barber and that's my annoying co-worker and ugh…that's my mom calling." People aren't perfect. Some probably deserve rolling of eyes, if not a curt dismissal. But if we saw people as God sees them, as people who are loved and for whom the whole world was made as a gift, we'd not only understand them better we'd find more peace and joy than we could ever imagine.

Sin has corrupted our lives and our vision, but we dare not forget the basic purpose for which we were made. Everyone from the 13-year-old girl standing in front of the mirror wondering if she's pretty to the young mother wondering if this is all there is to life to the octogenarian grandma who asks if there's any purpose left for her gets the same answer. The boy who wonders if he'll ever be loved and the young man who feels like his parents betrayed him and the 50-year-old who's afraid that he didn't make enough money and never found his purpose in life all get the same answer too. "You are loved. I am here. All this is for you. I will bend heaven and earth to let you know that, just as I did in the beginning."

What an amazing message that is to share! Once you've heard it, it's hard to hear anything different. Once you understand it you see people in a whole new way. Life is sprouting everywhere, even in this world clouded by darkness. There's no substitute for this kind of vision, this kind of purpose, this definition of enduring, powerful goodness. It forever changes the way we see and talk about God. Judgment and fear are banished, replaced by hope, joy, and trust.

Made In God's Image

Genesis 1:26-27 contains one of the most beautiful affirmations in scripture: that God made humankind in his image. We could write a whole new book on the theological insight that's been poured into this simple phrase. Some have settled on the physical sense of "in his image", guessing that God's form looks just like ours. Others have posited the existence of a soul, god-like and given to humans as opposed to other forms of life. Humans have an intelligence that no other animal on the planet can match. Humans were given a particular mission in creation that nobody else has in the same way. All these things have been cited as God's image alive in us.

I have no answer to end that debate…nor should it end. One of our primary purposes should be unpacking all the ways that God's image is reflected in our lives. The day that conversation stops is the day we lose sight of our calling.

But I am going to suggest a facet of God's image that's under-represented in these discussions. It stems from the coda to the phrase, "in the image of God he created them, *male and female* he created them".

The importance of "male and female" has nothing to do with gender roles. Those didn't even exist yet beyond the strictly biological. All we know about "male" and "female" at the beginning of creation is that the two were created together to be in relationship with each other, the better to bring goodness into the world.

This is what "image of God" means: that we're meant to be in relationship with each other, meant to create goodness together. Creation isn't an, "I am and you're not" deal, rather, "We are, and we are meant to be together". Our existence is bound up in each other and in the things we do together.

No doubt you're familiar with the Trinitarian doctrine espoused by many churches, the Father, Son, and Holy Spirit? Thousands of books would not suffice to describe that doctrine, but a simple way of looking at things may aid us here. When churches say, "Three persons, One God" they're describing a being who was in relationship with himself before anything else existed. Father, Son, and Holy Spirit are neither wholly distinct nor just different names for the same thing. God is so marvelous that he can hold a conversation, generate love, and be in deep, inseparable relationship with himself. God's very being, his very name, means "togetherness".

Togetherness is the gift God gave to us who are made "in his image". Envision God alone, having an amazing, loving, life-filled relationship in his own being, then deciding, "Why not pull more people into this goodness and make it bigger?" And there we were. We were made to be in relationship with each other and with God…engaged with both, dependent on both, sharing goodness with both.

This floors me as much as anything in scripture. I get pretty excited when somebody invites me to be their Facebook friend. It blows me away that we were created to participate in the greatest social network ever, the perfect, ultimate, loving and life-giving community that existed before time and will endure forever. Our creation was an invitation to be a part of God as our Creator shared his being with us.

Wow.

I feel constrained to add a note that we'll expand on more later. Being created male and female implies certain things about biology and the continuance of life…things that hold true to this day. You're reading this because a male and female engaged in their own creation story.

But nowhere in the story does it say that our *only* roles are biological. Childless people are still made in God's image. Asexual people are still participating in creation. Nor does it say that male-female is the only configuration of "togetherness" that matters or will ever exist. Male-male and female-female and various shades and points along the spectrum…these still describe people together. And they are still God's children.

People try to narrow down "image of God" to a particular act among a particular gender configuration. That's stuffing an impossibly big God with a breathtakingly revolutionary gift for us (Existence! Conversation! Relationship! Mission! Dependence! Creation of Life!) into a small box. Speaking against what they perceive as sin, they commit a much greater offense by robbing creation of its purpose and its first affirmation to humankind. Attempting to purify the world, they replace togetherness with division. This was not intended. God's image is too vast and powerful for that.

²⁸ *God blessed them and said to them, "Be fruitful and increase in number; fill the earth and subdue it. Rule over the fish in the sea and the birds in the sky and over every living creature that moves on the ground."*

Created to Rule

God gave a couple of interesting instructions to his newly-created children. Both raise eyebrows today, for different reasons.

One instruction was to rule, or have dominion over, the other living beings in creation: fish, birds, animals. The intent was clear. Human beings had the capacity and privilege to affect the lives of others, to order things as they saw fit.

This command quickly turns problematic for anyone who understands human shortcomings and Baron Acton's admonition that power corrupts and absolute power corrupts absolutely. Keep in mind that God's instruction was given in a world without sin, spoken to ears that had not been introduced to the concept of evil. When Adam and Eve received this command, "have dominion over" and "do good for/take care of" would have meant the exact same thing.

In a world corrupted by sin, God's command becomes impossible to fulfill the way it was originally intended. The idea is still there, "Do good for the things around you," but our capacity to fulfill it is inadequate. We're forced to ask, "Good for whom?" Because the world is broken "good" for one becomes ill for another. Dominion is characterized by power and the ability to enforce it rather than the capacity to do right.

This is why we get arguments between those who want salmon to spawn freely, those who want to fish salmon, and those who want to dam the river (and damn the salmon) in order to generate hydroelectric power. Who's correct? All of them in a way, but none of them are completely. Every good comes at a cost, every dream carries its own shadow, and all dominion disadvantages somebody.

You can see what sin has done to our world. God gives us a command and we cannot fulfill it. "Rule" and "have dominion" have become corrupted by self-interest and bent vision. The better we're able to exercise them, the more we're able to enforce our will, the more people we disadvantage as we institutionalize the shortcomings in our approach. We retain the power to rule but the ability to generate pure goodness from it, as was intended, is lost to us.

Since we cannot live in a world where "have dominion over" and "do perfect good" are interchangeable, the wise would regard Genesis 1:28 as a sign of how far we've fallen rather than permission to do whatever they want to creation or the creatures in it.

This hits me hard as a church pastor. I have leadership responsibilities. I have the capacity to guide, and even rule, in ways that nobody else in that community does. The only way I dare take up those responsibilities is to understand that my dominion is as faulty as anyone else's, and therefore I *shouldn't* get my own way all the time. The decisions I *don't* make are as critical to the health of our faith community as the decisions I do.

Sometimes I'll intentionally follow ideas and projects I don't agree with just to make sure I'm not ruling from a place of self-interest and weakness. I sing hymns I don't like, help out with programs I would have done differently, and follow people that don't have the same education or experience as I. When forced to choose between dominion and love, I choose love…knowing that's far closer to the "do good" that was intended by this command than my dominion would be.

Like many, I wince when I hear God's command to Adam and Eve. I wish it were phrased differently. I've experienced evil cause by people who jump in with both feet, using "dominion" as an excuse to harm others. Despite my wincing, the command remains. Like it or not, we are given power to affect the world. Each one of us has the capacity to change our environment: physical, social, economic, and otherwise. We cannot abdicate that power, nor can we employ it correctly. We're called upon to examine daily the strengths and weaknesses in the dominion we exercise, be intentional about who it's benefiting or harming, and try the best we can to make love, goodness, and compassion the fruits of our power.

Be Fruitful and Multiply

God's other command to Adam and Eve was to be fruitful and multiply. In this God bestows a gift as powerful as dominion: the capacity to co-create. What God has done, Adam and Eve can now do…on a slightly smaller scale and in different manner, but just as powerful nonetheless. Creation was not meant to be static. It was eternal but not unchanging. The new, the different, discovery and surprise were all built into it.

This shows how generous God was. He didn't just give his children a place and a time, but an entire process to engage in and to grow through. They were able to create as they went. God gave them ability like his own…another aspect of being made "in his image".

Most of us who have created children understand the awe-inspiring power inherent in this gift. Can you remember the first moment you saw your child and realized how the world had changed? Tears and wonder are the usual response. That's exactly how we're supposed to feel when we read this creation story…like we can't believe God really did this and gave us the power to do it too.

The capacity to change creation—its "eternal but not unchanging" nature, even in its perfect form—serves as a correction to those who would claim that the only powerful things in the world are those that do not change. Too many people of faith seek security in walls, in rituals, in songs and practices and social circles that never move. Too often the price of admission to those faith communities is conformation, becoming exactly like the people who are already there. To borrow from the author of Ecclesiastes, this is vanity and wind.

Walls and rituals and predictable circles can be good and powerful. They're necessary in a world awash in sin. But they do not bring safety, let alone faith. God's creation grows! The more rigidly we hold to a particular time and place, the less safety they provide and the less faith they grow. Instead of preparing the way for God and his New Creation our conventions take the place of both. We use the things of God's creation to deny the purpose and power of God's creation.

Change was built into our world from the start. Anyone who makes change an enemy also makes God's work an enemy.

Change must have purpose, direction, and serve goodness, but it's usually better to make a mistake changing than to make no mistakes by staying still. The first way you could go right or wrong. The second way guarantees you're wrong. Imagine if Adam and Eve heard God say, "Be fruitful and multiply" and replied, "No thanks!" (Or more accurately, "OK, but only if every bit of multiplication results in an exact clone of myself.") That wouldn't have worked even when the world was perfect, let alone in a fallen world.

We need to accept God's gift of co-creation joyously and delight in all its permutations, not just new children but new songs, new insights, new discoveries about God and each other. That's why we were put here.

Naturally we also deal with the biological, carnal aspect of God's command. Unless they were supposed to engage in some kind of single-celled binary fission process the Bible doesn't mention, God was essentially telling Adam and Eve to have sex. It's patently obvious, but I'm straining to think of any text on Genesis I've read that acknowledges it as explicitly and joyfully as any other command. This shows you how weird we are.

At one point in theological history the concept of original sin (the sin we all carry inherently) and sex were bound together. The idea was, anybody conceived by sex was corrupted, carrying the taint of their parents' "naughty act" into their own lives and passing it on to their children. At one point the Catholic church felt constrained to declare that Mary, the mother of Jesus, was not conceived by human parents but by God so that no corruption could pass into her and thus none from her to Jesus. Sex was the big goblin, the dirty secret, the source of sin.

But God says, "Be fruitful and increase in number; fill the earth..." God's not only telling them to have sex, he's telling them to have *lots* of sex. Like bunnies. Creation was unstained before that proclamation and presumably creation would have remained unstained after it. Sex is neither the root of sin nor something to be ashamed of, stuffed in the closet and not discussed by "good" people.

Like everything else in creation, sexuality was corrupted at the fall of humanity. It can be used for evil and harm. So can fingernails, red rubber balls, cantaloupe rinds, jet planes, and shish-kabob spears. If we reacted with shame and silence to everything that could be misused we'd have nothing but shame and silence.

Reforming our theology of sexuality is not the purpose of this book, but I couldn't let this passage go by without mentioning this. We don't talk about sex. If we do, it's mostly in terms of judgment. We've botched this horribly. We're paying the price for our foolishness as we watch generations of people trying to negotiate an increasingly complex sexual landscape without feeling like they can turn to others for grounding or advice, including and especially God's people. "Good people don't talk about this" is a *horrible* response to God's command and God's gifts. It'll take generations to undo the harm that's been done by ignoring the presence of sex in the Garden of Eden, if we ever manage it.

Don't even get me *started* on the people who condemn other people's sexuality based on their reading of scripture, who describe the world as fallen to cultural impulses without ever examining the cultural influences that shape their own views of sexuality. Why are we comfortable getting up in front of others and pointed fingers in God's name when we wouldn't be comfortable getting up in front of others and detailing/celebrating our sex life? "Good people don't talk about sex except to condemn what others are doing" is an even worse mantra than "Good people don't talk about sex at all". We should spend our energy fixing how we've addressed sex poorly before we start complaining about how others are talking about it.

[29] Then God said, "I give you every seed-bearing plant on the face of the whole earth and every tree that has fruit with seed in it. They will be yours for food. [30] And to all the beasts of the earth and all the birds in the sky and all the creatures that move along the ground—everything that has the breath of life in it—I give every green plant for food." And it was so.

[31] God saw all that he had made, and it was very good. And there was evening, and there was morning—the sixth day.

Every Green Plant For Food

God's last gift in his opening speech to Adam and Eve concerns their sustenance. He gives them the entire garden to eat from, holding nothing back that is good or delightful to them.

I suppose one could make a vegetarian argument out of this statement. That was certainly true in the Garden of Eden and I assume it'll be true again when the world is restored in heaven. (Personally I'll be hanging out on chocolate ice cream beach right by Lake Cream Soda.) But we're not capable of living now as we did in the Garden. Humanity's fall necessitated the death of some creatures for others to survive. Still, we'll give vegetarians high marks for being closer to the ideals of paradise than the rest of us.

The more universal point here is that God gave his children everything for the sake of goodness, health, and continuing life. Think again of how we use the gifts of creation…food first but also other things.

As you can probably tell from the above paragraph, I don't always eat healthy. My tastes are bent to things that are not good for me. One of my seminary professors used to say, "If you want evidence of sin, head to a buffet. You know the broccoli is good for you but you always end up getting the Chinese Chicken instead." Amen, sister.

Our standards of goodness are mixed up. When we say "good" we usually mean pleasurable, efficient, getting us towards the goal we have set, or giving us more power. Chinese Chicken, raises, our favorite types of music, and the new process that cuts 15 minutes off of our work time with the same amount of effort are "good".

Those definitions aren't sufficient. We are given gifts for purposes of health, to sustain creation, to propagate goodness for communities, not just goodness for self. Everything we encounter is meant to be life-giving.

How much different would our actions be if we asked, "Am I using this for the purpose it was intended or just the purpose that seems good and convenient to me?" Often those intersect. Sometimes they do not. Nobody can decide for another. We all have to answer for ourselves. But how can we answer when we don't even remember to ask the question?

I understand that I don't use food, or my computer, or my car, or my hands and voice, or my job, or my house, or my life for the purposes God intended. I try, but doing so completely is beyond my power. Admitting this not only makes me more careful, but more faithful. Ladling up Chinese Chicken in the buffet helps me empathize with and tolerate weaknesses in others…not that I encourage them or call them good, but I understand we all have them. How can I point my finger at others in condemnation when the nutrition labels in my cupboard show I'm just as godless as I accuse them of being?

Understanding this also helps me empathize with God, insofar as that is possible anyway. How would it feel to give a marvelous gift to your children only to see it misused? I imagine giving a Ken Griffey autographed Louisville Slugger bat to my son then watching him whack his sister over the head with it. Wouldn't you want to take the bat back right away?

Yet we still get food every day. We're still allowed to enjoy buffets without lightning falling from the sky upon our heads. God still loves us and claims us as his family. That God can even stand us is a miracle. That he loves us, sustains us, gives us good gifts and continues to feed us is beyond explanation. He's an amazing dad. He's more of a father than I could be in his shoes, and I love my kids more than anybody who's ever lived. But that's the kind of God we have.

2 *Thus the heavens and the earth were completed in all their vast array.*

² By the seventh day God had finished the work he had been doing; so on the seventh day he rested from all his work. ³ Then God blessed the seventh day and made it holy, because on it he rested from all the work of creating that he had done.

The Day of Rest

Built into the fabric of creation, following six days of work, is the day of rest, the Sabbath. This day God set apart as a time for "not work", a border between the completion of old tasks and the undertaking of new.

Note that this day was not apart from creation, as in, "Six days were creation and then the seventh day was not." Rest was in some way intrinsic to creation, a day and a process every bit as valid and important as those undertaken on Days 1-6.

God didn't rest because he needed to. Had more been required more would have been done. But the Bible says God finished, so he stopped. Since God is the author of all goodness—the very definition of goodness—what God does we are also called to do. Just as Adam and Eve received the power to co-create and order, they received the gift and mandate of rest. The explanation for the seventh day that makes most sense is simply, "God rested because he wanted us to do it too."

It's amazing the number of people who don't. Even folks who consider themselves quite faithful will raise objections and questions regarding the concept of rest on the seventh day. Even bringing up the subject conjures visions of a priest trying to teach confirmation and hearing, "Father, what about if you water your pet snail on Sunday because otherwise he would die? Is that work? And if you cook pancakes on a griddle it's work but reheating them in the microwave isn't? Or is it work if you have to enter the time manually but not if you have a one-touch warming system?"

In seminary I was friends with an aspiring Orthodox Rabbi who had read and memorized reams on the subject. She explained to me things like pushing an elevator button on the Sabbath is forbidden work but you can stand in the elevator and convince some poor Gentile to push it for you, because that's not work. I liked this system immediately. Full credit to all the folks who figured these things out. I also got overwhelmed pretty quickly trying to keep it straight.

Be that as it may, the purpose of the Sabbath is not debating what's allowed and what's not. Sabbath is first and foremost an admission that you are not God. For six days we convince ourselves that the detailed labor of our lives is central, that we can't survive without working and that the world can't survive without us. Sabbath is our reality check. We rest for a day to remember who sustains us and the world around us. It's not us, it's God.

Anyone who thinks that life just can't go on without their attention 24/7 has slipped the rails of reality and fallen into the ditch of delusion. Every one of us knows such people: co-dependent, self-important, acting like they're sacrificing for the sake of others but secretly promoting their own primacy. They consider themselves indispensable. Sabbath reminds us that none of us are that.

On the Sabbath day, we turn over ourselves and our environment to God. Like a child learning to walk letting go of the coffee table for *just a moment* before putting the steadying hand back on, we dare to take 24 hours to be free, to trust instead of control.

This puts our labor and our place in the world into perspective. It's not a question of our work being important or not. It's a question of what *ways* our work is important and in what ways it's less so. Doing good for the world, providing daily bread, discovering our calling in life…these are important. Casting our own achievements as the bedrock of the universe is less so.

In failing to honor the Sabbath we deny our own limits, our own mortality, and our dependence on God and each other to keep us going. We become our own gods.

It's ironic that many of the people in my life who honor the day of rest least are pastors. Of all the people who shouldn't be idolatrizing their own achievements, who should be able to trust in God to run the world for a day while they take a break, you'd think ministers would be the first. Sadly, the message that many ministers want to hear is precisely, "You're indispensable. You are God to us." And the Sabbath goes right out the window as each little task takes on world-shaking importance.

In a world full of frailty and weakness, the day of rest turns out to be good for us. Nobody can run full-tilt their entire lives without burning out or going crazy. We need time to do something different.

I try to work out most every day (except Sunday…my exercise day of rest). A trainer explained to me once that working your muscles actually damages them. That's the pain, weakness, or soreness you feel after a good workout. After that the body goes into healing mode, rebuilding your muscles a little bit bigger and stronger than they were before. The actual physical gains happen not during the workout—the damage phase, but during the period of rest afterwards. If you do not rest, you're piling damage upon damage and eventually you'll hurt your body instead of helping it. The same thing happens to our lives when we ignore the Sabbath.

Sabbath is also our chance to reflect on things that are finished and the new beginnings that await us. My mother was a painter, as is one of my dearest friends now. Between watching them and a little bit of the late Bob Ross, I've come to understand that one of the most challenging things about painting is deciding when the work is done. There's always something to fix, one more brush stroke to make. If you listen to this impulse you reach a point where you're not adding to the vision anymore, but obscuring it. At some point you have to put the brush down, wash the easel, and say, "This is finished…as good as I can make it."

This is what God himself said at the last day of creation: *"Thus the heavens and the earth were completed in all their vast array."*

The day of rest allows us to make those determinations, to ask what things from the past are done or have reached their maximum level of value. It allows us to consider new projects, to start with a blank canvass.

Without this crucial step in the process, we end up working on the same project our whole lives. It may look different or wear different faces, but it ends up being a sad rehearsal of the same old pattern. We're not doing ourselves, our work, or the world any good that way. It may bring us a cheap sense of comfort and order, but it can't bring fulfillment.

The Sabbath is based on trust, hope, and faith. *Not* keeping the Sabbath is based on fear: fear that the world can't get along without us, fear that our work isn't as important as we hope it is, fear that our impact won't be strong enough unless we repeat it continually, fear to put down the old and try something new. It's not that much different than being so nervous on a first date that you can't stand moments of silence, so you fill the air with inane chattering that even you don't really believe in and that makes you look foolish. The day of rest is God's way of saying, "Don't be afraid of the silence in our relationship or in your relationship with the world. We love each other. Trust that and be comfortable in it. Rest; renew; heal; and know that I'll be there for you every day whether you work on this, that, or nothing at all."

[4] This is the account of the heavens and the earth when they were created, when the Lord God made the earth and the heavens.

Another Creation Story???

OK, hold up. We just got done with the creation story. We had the six days and flying fish and the fruitful multiplying and the day of rest at the end! Now we're starting over again???

Yup.

Little known fact: there are actually two creation stories at the beginning of Genesis. Actually the Bible is full of new creation stories, from covenants to kingdoms, Noah to Abraham to Job to Jesus. It never ends, really. But there are two explicitly different accounts of the world's origins right at the start of the Bible, smashed up next to each other.

The official explanation for this is that the creation tradition was passed down from two somewhat different groups…alike enough to credit God for it but different enough to emphasize and explain things in diverse ways. When the time came to write down the story, to codify it for future generations, they decided that choosing one over the other wouldn't do. So they included them both.

I suspect this was decided by committee.

Some might consider this a fault. Personally I think it makes the Bible infinitely more interesting and our focus much sharper. These two stories will not fit together seamlessly. In Story One everything got made before humans. In Story Two Adam came first, before anything. Story One has Adam and Eve coming into the picture at the same time. Story Two contains the famous "rib" account of Eve's creation.

Assuming we're not going to take the easy, cheesy way out and choose sides, what does this tell us?

First, different people and different traditions see things different ways. That does not make one right and one wrong. It's a sign of our fallen nature that none of us knows, let alone understands, the whole story. Given that fact, more than one telling is necessary and they *cannot agree*, else we don't learn anything more from the second than we did from the first.

Second, this "God thing" is complex and cannot be summarized in a couple paragraphs, let alone a bumper sticker or billboard quote. Anyone claiming to have the answers—or in some ways even *an* answer that spans all times, places, and people—is over-simplifying to the point of absurdity.

Faith reveals several cruel, cosmic jokes about life. Here's one: we all have to act upon whatever answer we land on as if it's real and true while at the same time admitting that there's no way it can be completely true.

I've faced this personally hundreds of times while visiting patients in hospital beds. Even when that patient is your parishioner, you don't know them well enough to understand exactly what they need to hear. You may know "healthy them" very well, but "hospital sick them" is a side most of us don't get to see. The difficulty multiplies when you don't know them that well, or at all. Ministers are sometimes called upon to walk into hospital rooms of patients whom they've never met, not knowing what faith sustains them or if they disavow faith completely. Is John 3:16 a life-giving affirmation, the Bible verse they were beaten for not knowing in confirmation, or is reading it at all a presumptuous insult because they're of another faith entirely?

As a minister you walk into that hospital room having no idea what to say. But you absolutely, positively cannot walk in and say nothing because that's more awkward than all of the above options combined. So what do you do? You walk in with a firm commitment to doing whatever good you can in that situation without knowing exactly what form that good will take. You act upon the assumption that walking in will do something positive, knowing that you have no assurance that this is so, only that *not* walking in robs you and the patient of any chance to find the good that might have happened had you entered.

Fortunately the practical solution to the dilemma isn't that hard. When I walk in, I do not lead with scripture quotes, pithy affirmations, or prayer. (How do I know which of those would be best, or if any of them would?) Instead I introduce myself, ask if I may sit, and we just talk. I try to be curious. I try to be open. I try to listen as well as I can to the patient's definition of goodness. When they are powerless in that bed, I try to give them at least this bit of power: that I will hear, respect, care, and act accordingly. Then when I feel like I understand them better, I might offer a particular scripture. Or I might offer none at all, sharing God's Spirit through a non-anxious presence and attention focused on them and their needs instead of my own need to be right and foist off my preconceptions upon them.

In order to do this, I'm forced to hear and process life choices and opinions that are different than my own. I'm forced to submit to the definitions of another instead of holding tightly to my own and blocking out theirs.

In the same way Creation Story One has to listen to Creation Story Two and vice versa...and we have to listen to them both if we're to understand God's Word. At some points one may speak to us more than the other, becoming more appropriate or foundational. But that doesn't mean that either is wrong or that either should be cast out. We enter the pages to listen, not to bring our own preconceptions to the story.

The Bible itself forces us to understand this if we're going to have a relationship with God. Right from the start it doesn't let us think any differently. It doesn't present itself as a clear set of instructions that everyone must understand and follow. It doesn't present itself as a single, unified history to which everyone must subscribe. It offers vast opportunity to explore different ideas--different ways of viewing God and the world—insisting that none of those ideas will be completely right but that we have permission to explore anyway as long as we admit our need to listen rather than dictate.

Diversity among the creation stories also reveals their unshakable core, found in commonalities where they both overlap. God made the world for us because he cares about us and we are his children. Whether we were created before or after Azalea bushes doesn't change that fact. In both stories we find that we're meant to be together, that we are given power, that God is amazingly generous, and that goodness—defined by love and giving--is the ultimate purpose of all his work. It's easy to miss those things amid the myriad details of the two stories, or to lift the *how* of creation up to the sacred and immovable level of the *why*.

When the two stories differ as they do, it's impossible to get hung up on the definition of a day or the order of creation. Doing so forces you to deny the scripture found in one story in favor of the other. We are forced to admit that even if we discovered these things, we would not have revealed the heart of the story.

We are absolutely free to come up with answers to these questions. Both Story One and Story Two offer them. Healthy debate and exploration of all these matters is necessary to our faith journey. How else are we to grow? But when we lock those answers in stone and build our faith on them, constructing walls to shut out dissension and further discussion, the house is sure to fall. It's no longer built on faith in God, but in our perceptions and priorities.

Understanding the message the Bible sends us about how it wants to be read has opened up fantastic new horizons in the community of faith I serve. In most churches the pattern of Bible Study is to read from a scripted topical lesson or to have a leader stand in front and lecture on the ins and outs of the scripture passage in question.

We do it a little differently. We are bold. We tackle entire books whole hog. Each of us comes with a Bible, usually with footnotes, some folks with margin notes from other times they've studied that particular book. We start at the beginning of a book and read through in small doses, a paragraph or two. After we've read each small section, my question to the people assembled is the same: *What do YOU notice here?* This is another way of asking, "What is this story saying to you? What facet of God do you perceive?" To be sure, my theological training allows me particular insight. I share that, along with notes from my own studies. But my observations don't come first and sometimes aren't even that central.

At first people were shocked by this. Here I am, The Pastor, asking *them* what's in scripture? After folks got over the seemingly-backwards nature of this way of studying, they started to get into it. All of a sudden each piece of scripture evoked thoughts, questions, and stories aplenty…many of which I'd never associated with that text before. People weren't afraid to ask, to dare, to share their insights. Participants studied hard. Nobody insisted upon being right; nobody was afraid to be wrong. We all learned together.

In the more traditional model, the room contains one expert and several people learning from that expert. In this model I'm surrounded by theologians and we're all learning from each other and from God's Word. The enthusiasm is amazing.

As an added benefit, we've gone more places in the Bible than we ever dared. Sure we started with easily-digested books like Ruth or the Gospel of Mark, but we soon found our appetite widening. We ventured into heretofore uncharted territory like Judges and those pesky Minor Prophets at the end of the Old Testament. Our crowning achievement was a wonderful trip through the Book of Revelation, the most misused and misunderstood book in all of scripture. Even the veterans among us approached that with trepidation. "We can't just read this, can we? We've heard so much about it and it's so confusing!" Instead we found that trusting each other, being willing to hear diverse stories, we found the book delightful! It was like meeting a person you'd heard was an awful bully and finding them intelligent and inspiring.

We never would have enjoyed experiencing the end of the Bible story had we not paid attention to the lesson it taught in the first two chapters. Scripture isn't simple, nor does it always agree with itself, but those are not signs of weakness, but openings for building a deeper relationship with God and truth.

5 Now no shrub had yet appeared on the earth and no plant had yet sprung up, for the Lord God had not sent rain on the earth and there was no one to work the ground, 6 but streams came up from the earth and watered the whole surface of the ground. 7 Then the Lord God formed a man from the dust of the ground and breathed into his nostrils the breath of life, and the man became a living being.

Dust and Spirit

From the outset the creation story in Genesis 2 differs from the story in Chapter 1. In the first story the world was nothing but water, in this one water is nowhere to be found. Neither was there anyone to tend to the ground. Notice humanity's power and agency in this version. Story One had God commanding Adam and Eve to tend to creation. Story Two implies that creation won't exist until they do so. Humankind's power multiplies exponentially in this version of creation.

In this version the first man was created from two ingredients: the dust of the earth and God's breath. This isn't exactly the "formless and void" creation in Chapter 1 but it's close to it. "Dust" isn't organic, nutrient-rich soil. The imagery here is dry, barren, fit only to be covered by pools of water. This is the dust of the desert, hard soil that won't grow anything, another version of nothingness. Yet God's breath turns even dust into life.

The word for breath here is slightly different than the wind blowing over the waters in the first story. God's gift here is usually translated as "soul": life with some combination of wisdom and intellect and awareness. Imagine sparks scattering from embers when you blow on a muted campfire. That moment when the light brightens and flames sparkle everywhere is what happened when God blew on the barren, inorganic dust.

No matter what element preceded our arrival on earth, Story Two tells us once again that we're made out of God Stuff. Without God's breath we're just empty powder. God alone makes us alive.

I have a wonderful cat named Tubby. He's butterscotch-colored, roly-poly, and somewhat slow. But he's the softest, cuddliest cat that ever was. He loves to crawl up into your embrace as you sleep, nestling against you and wrapping his paws around your arm. It's like he's a sweet little teddy bear.

I've snuggled with stuffed animals before too. They're soft, cute, and about Tubby-sized. But it's different. No matter how squishy and pleasant they feel, a living creature has a spirit that an inanimate object lacks. When Tubby snuggles in my arms at night there's a bond, a two-way connection, something you can't describe but you know is there. You've felt this with people and pets in your life too, I'm sure.

That "something extra" is life. But Genesis 2:7 tells us that the only difference between life and un-life is the breath of God. Ergo what you sense in that moment you embrace a living being—the intangible, deeply-felt difference between polyester puppet and live creature—is God's breath...the very presence of God. No need to ask where he is. You have sensed <u>him. He's been among you</u>. Wherever two or more are gathered God is present. We are not God, but God is with us.

Note that God isn't generated by the love you feel for the person or creature you're holding. He's not a creation of any human emotion or agency, even the most noble. But that moment of unguarded, snuggly warmth makes it easy to sense him…to feel life and, by extension, his presence.

God's entire purpose is to show us life, the beauty of that breath-filled connection. The spark-fire moment of creation illuminates us as glorious God-bearers. Yet we so easily define ourselves by other things. I think of every magazine-cover standard of beauty that's been blasted all over creation and marvel at how far off track our definitions are. We've traded real Beauty and real Being for plastic imitations. If only we could see ourselves and each other as we were meant to be…as God sees us.

Four Rivers

[8] Now the Lord God had planted a garden in the east, in Eden; and there he put the man he had formed. [9] The Lord God made all kinds of trees grow out of the ground—trees that were pleasing to the eye and good for food. In the middle of the garden were the tree of life and the tree of the knowledge of good and evil.

[10] A river watering the garden flowed from Eden; from there it was separated into four headwaters. [11] The name of the first is the Pishon; it winds through the entire land of Havilah, where there is gold. [12] (The gold of that land is good; aromatic resin and onyx are also there.) [13] The name of the second river is the Gihon; it winds through the entire land of Cush. [14] The name of the third river is the Tigris; it runs along the east side of Ashur. And the fourth river is the Euphrates.

In these verses we see the Garden of Eden named for the first time. There's no clear consensus on what the name means, with possibilities ranging from steppes to well-watered to pampered and taken care of, depending on the language and context. All of them seem to fit. This was the place where man did not have to worry, where all he needed would be provided. He was complete, whole, provided for. All kinds of trees, pleasing to the eye and good for food, confirm this perception.

The names of the four rivers—two of which we can pinpoint today—anchor the garden as a physical place, not metaphorical or otherworldly. This does not contrast with our discussion of "creation mythology" above. We want things one way or another. We like stories to be completely allegorical with no connection to historical reality or completely historical and "real" with no greater meaning or purpose. The Bible gives us neither. We have a historical story (or as close to it as we can get) whose meaning and purpose cannot be found in historical detail alone. Put another way, ordinary-seeming things in this story turn out to have extraordinary implications. In God's presence normal things become heavenly and wondrous.

This echoes the story of our lives, particularly our lives of faith. God is in the business of revealing our ordinary as magnificent. He does amazing things through ordinary folks. He teaches profound lessons through ordinary moments. Where particular holy places exist their purpose is to remind us that *all the world* is holy. Holiness is not a little fountain that we dip our fingers in, it's an overflowing river of grace that encircles and covers the land, bringing life and meaning to the most mundane-seeming things.

I often tell my parishioners that if you can't sit down to boxed macaroni and cheese and find God there, you're not going to find him anywhere. Either you see holiness or you don't. Once glimpsed, you can't get away from it. Once contained and bounded, it ceases being holy.

Eden was the first evidence of this. Everything there was normal…fruit, trees, grass, rivers…we can touch the Tigris and Euphrates today. They're just water. But in God's presence they became holy and brought life to the land.

These passages also serve as a reminder of our ultimate unity. Genesis is big on describing various tribes that had a common source but eventually diverged and became enemies. It's significant that four rivers which would eventually spread out into four lands claimed by many diverse peoples all had the same source…a source whose purpose was goodness. We are different but the same water sustains us all.

That One Tree Though…

15 The Lord God took the man and put him in the Garden of Eden to work it and take care of it. 16 And the Lord God commanded the man, "You are free to eat from any tree in the garden; 17 but you must not eat from the tree of the knowledge of good and evil, for when you eat from it you will certainly die."

Here we get to one of the most thought-provoking moments in creation. Amid all this goodness, completeness, and joy, God plops down one tree and says, "Can't Touch This".

The ever-present question: "Why did God put that tree in the garden in the first place???"

Some speculate that God put evil in the garden in the form of this tree. Some paint it as a test, God seeing if Adam and Eve could leave the evil thing alone. I've heard the less-faith-inclined argue that including the tree proves evil came from God, thus invalidating the scriptures and our ideal of him.

This Tree of the Knowledge of Good and Evil was not evil. God didn't plant anything evil in the garden. We like the idea that some things are evil (dancing, gambling, the young generation's music, the internet) and some are good (going to church, saying prayers, knitting). It's a convenient way to look at life. It's also dead wrong.

Evil isn't a separate entity inherent in certain objects and people that you can get contaminated by. Evil is the misuse of things that were intended for good…taking God's life-giving and graceful gifts, using them to generate hurt or untruth or mistrust. What an object *is* doesn't make it good or evil, how it's *used* does.

Dancing was once decried as the devil's work, a gateway to sin. For most folks it wasn't. And even for the folks that did indulge in a little naughtiness after the barn dance…well…they're now your grandma and grandpa, right? So it couldn't have been all evil. Neither was it all good. It was just dancing, a simple act, complex in its implications, not easily categorized.

Music that used to be attributed to Satan now graces the Superbowl halftime show because, unlike "today's music" it's safe enough to show to entire families. Songs born out of the drug culture are routinely played at high school football games while mom and dad sing along to them. Were they bad? Are they good? Probably both, depending on what you do with them.

My hands can be used for amazing things, like typing this book. My hands can also be used for awful things, and I've done some of those too. Some of the words we feel most justified uttering are also profoundly damaging to our marriages. Sometimes admitting our shame heals our relationships like nothing else can. So are our hands and lips good, or evil?

Granted, some things lend themselves more readily to harm than others. Weapons, drugs, visual images…we have to examine them more closely than our average bowl of Froot Loops. But even then we're not going to find inherent evil or good. The occasional bowl of Froot Loops: probably OK. Our eighth bowl of Froot Loops today: probably not.

Good and evil aren't determined by *what* but by *how* and *for whom*. The effects, or fruits, of an action show whether it's good or it's evil, not the mechanics of the action itself. The Tree of the Knowledge of Good and Evil wasn't evil. What Adam and Eve ended up doing with it was.

But why did God even give them the option? Why was that tree there? I'm not sure there's a firm answer to this, but I have my thoughts.

In both creation stories, God is remarkably generous. In the first story he makes Adam and Eve in his own image, gives them the whole world, puts everything under their care, and even gives them the power to co-create and grow the world. Already in the second story God has given humankind life, his own breath, and every tree full of goodness and pleasure. He's about to give Adam incredible power to name everything around him…another aspect of co-creation which we'll discuss in a minute.

In both stories we see that everything God is, God has also made humans into. The power to make, name, create, rule over, walk freely, love, eat, enjoy…they have it all. They are like gods. He has made them in his image.

But here's the thing. With God having given everything to humankind, was there any difference between God and humans? Was there any reason for

Adam and Eve to remember him, to account a relationship with him valuable, to distinguish God as somehow special?

It's not so much that God was big on honor. This isn't like your grandma refusing to send the $10 Christmas check because you didn't write a thank-you note last year. God doesn't operate like that. But when Adam and Eve walked like gods, created like gods, wielded power like gods, it would have been an incredibly short step to, "We ARE gods!" At that point the relationship with the true God—the very foundation of their creation—goes right out the window.

This wasn't about hierarchy and prerogatives. Those would only become important once sin had arrived. It was about good for humankind. It was about Adam and Eve staying in harmony with love and having clarity of purpose. It was about remaining whole, at peace, in right relationship with the world and its Maker. In short, it was about all the things that you and I struggle to find every day and can't quite get a grasp on.

To preserve all this, God created one tree. The Bible doesn't say it was a good tree. The Bible doesn't say it was beyond comparison, outshining all others. The Tree of Life was right there with it, plus a thousand other trees with good stuff to eat. This one tree sat there as a reminder. Humans in the garden had boundless power, infinite joy, eternal life, and total goodness, but they weren't gods. God is God.

That should have been a good thing. It didn't turn out that way. But that wasn't the tree's fault, nor was it really God's. Being like God wasn't enough. We humans couldn't stand not BEING God. Grasping at that last perceived step towards godhood, we ended up losing our ability to perceive, trust in, and act on the very things that made us like God in the first place.

This is the great, cosmic joke. We tried to become like God not realizing that in every way that mattered, we already were. In the trying, lost or perverted everything we were freely given, becoming so unlike God that he had to come and rescue us lest we drown in our utter helplessness. In that great, cosmic joke, we were the punch line.

Not Meant to Be Alone

[18] The Lord God said, "It is not good for the man to be alone. I will make a helper suitable for him."

[19] Now the Lord God had formed out of the ground all the wild animals and all the birds in the sky. He brought them to the man to see what he would name them; and whatever the man called each living creature, that was its name. [20] So the man gave names to all the livestock, the birds in the sky and all the wild animals.

But for Adam no suitable helper was found. [21] So the Lord God caused the man to fall into a deep sleep; and while he was sleeping, he took one of the man's rib and then closed up the place with flesh. [22] Then the Lord God made a woman from the rib he had taken out of the man, and he brought her to the man.

[23] The man said,

*"This is now bone of my bones
   and flesh of my flesh;
she shall be called 'woman,'
   for she was taken out of man."*

[24] That is why a man leaves his father and mother and is united to his wife, and they become one flesh.

The story of Eve's creation receives special attention in the Chapter 2 story. Instead of appearing at the same time as Adam, she is created from his rib. But the means of her creation shouldn't outshine the reason for it.

In Genesis 2:18 God says it isn't good for man to be alone…the first "not good" thing mentioned in the Bible. As we've said before, humankind was created to be in relationship. The garden was not good, perfect, or complete with just one person existing in isolation. At least two were required for goodness to blossom.

Genesis tells us that our relationship with each other is our relationship with God, or at least an indispensable extension of it. We were not meant to be alone. We were meant to congregate, to learn and grow, to love and prosper together. Whatever "good" is, it's bound up in our relationship with other people…as funny, fanciful, or frustrating as they may seem.

The worst times in our lives invariably come when we feel isolated. Depression makes us feel alone. Adolescence can too. Losing a loved one, being diagnosed with cancer, divorce…all of these things make us feel removed from the rest of humanity. We've lost connection with our normal environment; we feel like nobody understands us anymore. Being alone is just about the worst feeling in the world.

There's nothing wrong with being introverted or with heading off to the mountains for a week of isolation if that's your thing. Nobody says we have to be surrounded constantly. I treasure "alone time". But think how empty the world would be without anybody to come back to. How could I type the words you're reading right now without anybody to read them?

In that sense, you're creating this book as much as I am. It's neither mine as the author nor yours as the reader, it's ours together. If either party disappears, the book does not exist anymore. Whatever goes on in our minds, reality happens in the space between us. We need each other. That's the way God made us.

How counter-cultural this is! The world defines power as the ability to get whatever you want. Once you have it, you isolate yourself enough to not be disturbed while you're enjoying it. This is the big dream, to win the lottery and retire to a fenced mansion by a secluded beach with a private yacht. Through the eyes of faith, that's not power but horror, a denial of the purpose for which we were made.

As a pastor I've sat with many people on their deathbeds and heard them reflect on life. To this day I have not met one that said, "I'm glad I had that Mercedes" or "My house was so big!" The only things that matter in the end are the relationships you've created and the goodness you've shared through them. Those who have fostered good relationships tend to face their own passing in peace, understanding that reality doesn't end with them. Those without good relationships lose everything they treasure as death approaches, making it a scary experience.

Wisdom comes from learning which things in life are solid and which are transient and doomed to fail. Build our lives on things that will disappear is folly. We want to hold onto the enduring. Sooner or later we find that means holding onto each other. The quicker we figure that out, the more meaningful our lives become. It is not good to be alone.

A Helper

Eve's purpose went beyond just existing so Adam wouldn't be alone. She was created to be a helper. Over the years we've defined that word poorly, disadvantaging Eve and all womankind in the process.

We're used to thinking of "helper" in economic terms. We pair the idea of "helper" with the idea of "boss" then draw a line between the two. Bosses make decisions, helpers follow and assist. Bosses have knowledge, helpers only need to know what the boss says. Bosses get greater rewards for their superior position. Helpers get by on much less.

When we read Eve is a "helper" we naturally cast Adam in the role of "boss". This is wrong.

The Hebrew word used to describe Eve's role here usually describe what God does for us. "Helper" is a fine translation but the idea of subservience is misplaced. The word actually holds connotations of strength and power. It implies rescue, one person saving another.

If we're going to put one person below another based on these passages, Adam would properly take the lower spot. He needs help. He can't exist or find goodness like this. Eve is powerful; her arrival makes things right.

Men are not exalted or placed over women in this passage. Eve was the strong, authoritative person in the equation. If anything, Adam is painted as the bumbling fool who can't get along without her.

But these passages weren't meant to create a gender imbalance either way. Our culture needs to establish those roles; these verses don't.

Read properly, Genesis 18-24 tells us that our worth does not come from being lesser than or greater than. Our worth comes from working alongside each other for a greater purpose. Adam could not be Adam without Eve and vice-versa.

This was not particular to them, nor is it meant to represent only a pair-bonded relationship between a husband and wife. In Hebrew "Adam" also translates as "mankind" and Eve as "womankind". We all need each other. We save each other from isolation first, then from powerlessness. We grant each other power for the good of all and help each other use it well. That's what being human is supposed to mean.

It's impossible for any two people to be completely equal in our fallen world, let alone for all of us to be. Trying to measure who's ahead will eventually drive you crazy. But we shouldn't lose sight of the original ideal of creation, that none of us is powerful on our own and that all of us have something to bring to the table.

Eve was not a hired hand. Adam was not her boss. We are meant to be united, one flesh.

What He Would Name Them

Verses 19 and 20 tell us that the Lord "brought the animals to the man to see what he would name them; and whatever the man called each living creature, that was its name." Adam got to name each creature, a power more important than it seems on the surface.

We seldom stop to think how much freight a name carries, how it defines us. When a new bride and groom call each other "husband" and "wife" for the first time, lives change. When a child first calls their parent "mama" or "daddy", relationships get cemented. A few syllables bestow a whole new identity and nothing is the same afterwards.

Think of the pride you felt at your high school graduation when your full name was printed on a diploma. Think back even further as your mom yelled your full name up the stairs, indicating that you were in major trouble. How much meaning was poured into those names?

Those with the power to name hold the power to define. Naming brings acceptance or rejection, praise or reprobation. What we are called *matters*. We're free to adopt some things about the name we're given and reject others, but those who name us still hold great sway over our lives.

Throughout scripture God changes many people's names. In Genesis we're going to hear about Abram becoming Abraham, Sarai becoming Sarah, and Jacob becoming Israel. Jesus calls Simon, Peter. On the road to Damascus Saul becomes Paul. Each of these indicates transformation, a moment where destiny alters. Naming changes the world.

Here, in the beginning, it's not God bestowing and changing names, but Adam. If he calls something "cow", it's a cow. If he calls it, "annoying four-footed stinky-beast", that's what it is.

Again we see that God did not withhold a single creative power from Adam in the garden. The world would be defined through Adam's eyes and Adam's voice as much as God's.

We also receive a reminder about how powerful our voices can be, even today. Have you ever seen advice column letters from girls who couldn't get over their dads calling them fat when they were teenagers? Celebrities go astray when everyone around them speaks only what they want to hear, naming them the center of the universe. Entire cultures get persecuted or wiped out because of what they are named, because they are defined as less than human by people in power.

Our voices have the power to bring about great goodness as well. Naming each other as equals, as friends, as integral…welcoming and supporting each other…these things matter.

We need to be aware of the power inherent in naming and use it well.

Naked and Not Ashamed

25 Adam and his wife were both naked, and they felt no shame.

Verse 25 gives us a wonderful little tagline to the second creation story. Adam and Eve stood naked in the garden and were not ashamed.

Consider all the purposes clothes fill in our lives. They protect us from weather. They hide parts of us that we'd rather not share with each other. They help us differentiate between people of different classes, economic status, and organizational affiliation. Clothes don't just reveal the inner self, they quantify it for easy judgment in the social jungle.

None of these things were necessary in the garden. Adam and Eve had no need for protection from weather, thorns, insect bites, or anything else. They were perfectly safe, perfectly taken care of.

Neither did they have anything to hide. Not the least bit of shame intruded on paradise. There was no reason to hide anything—internal or external--from anyone. Everyone knew, loved, accepted, and blended with each other. Judgment and shame were foreign concepts. True selves shone through and received acceptance.

Nor was their need for distinction, stratification, one-upping each other. Each human was perfectly happy with who they were and who other people were. "Haves" and "Have Nots" didn't exist. Everybody had everything.

Nakedness paints as good of a picture of perfect humanity as can be imagined. One sentence says it all. Adam and Eve had no clothes and nobody cared.

Do you want to know how far the world has fallen? Imagine God's people trying to follow this standard today. The horror of Naked Church would confirm instantly that we're not in the garden anymore.

That's humor, of course, but there's a grain of truth to it too. Nowadays when we try to reach for something beautiful and life-affirming—to make things like they were in Eden--we end up with shame and revulsion. We just can't get there. Adopting the outer nakedness wouldn't bring the inner purity, rather the opposite. Now you understand the pain of living in a fallen world. Even when we do things right, they end up wrong.

That said, Adam and Eve's nudity should remind us that there's nothing inherently sinful about the human form. Church folks have obsessed about this for years, as has society at large. You can show people blowing each other's brains out, assaulting each other, and calling each other every name in the book on TV or movies, but throw in a little skin and all of a sudden it's not child-appropriate. "Murder, She Wrote" is wholesome for all. "Naked, She Walked" is rated R or NC-17.

Personally, I'd rather have my children see a little nudity on TV than have them learn that ultimate power comes from your ability to insult another person, exploit their weaknesses, or shoot them with a gun. I'm not a prude about any of this stuff, but on the scale of harmless to damaging, we're rating things all backwards.

Just like everything else in creation, nudity isn't bad or good in itself. The use to which it's put determines its sanctity or peril. The world doesn't want to see Christians unclothed everywhere, but it could probably do with a little more memory of "naked and not ashamed" and a little less culturally-based embarrassment surrounding this issue.

2 THE FALL

Enter the Serpent

3 Now the serpent was more crafty than any of the wild animals the Lord God had made.

At the start of Chapter 3 a new player takes the stage. We don't know much about him, at least not from this text. Many meanings and identities have been ascribed to the serpent, the most prominent of which is Satan, the deceiver, a fallen angel and enemy of God. The Genesis text itself does not make this clear, neither is it opposed to the designation. For our purposes, let's point out two things:

1. When the Bible speaks of otherworldly beings, it tends to leave them in the realm of the unknowable. Nothing is explained here about how this serpent (or Satan, if you wish) arrived in God's good creation, ended up in that tree, took the form of a snake (if it was a heavenly being), or started to talk (if it was just an animal). It's fairly certain there was a power other than humanity working here, for Adam and Eve were still innocent at this point and wouldn't know how to argue themselves into evil. Beyond that, the story doesn't invite us to dwell on the origin or nature of the snake, but its effects.

This will raise cognitive dissonance for some, but remember that we're talking mythology, not moment-by-moment history here. The story is a way to understand the not-easily-known. Whether the snake is Satan or symbol--evil personified or the whole history of temptation stuffed into snakeskin boots—matters less than the result of following his words.

2. In some ways the lack of explanation speaks truer than a satisfying explanation. We are never in deeper danger of succumbing to evil than when we think we know it. Were we able to point to a single figure in a single moment and say, "All evil is contained right there!" we'd have it pinned down. As we're about to find out, humanity doesn't get to pin down evil, evil pins down humanity.

Asking, "Who is that snake? Where is evil? Where does it come from? How do we recognize it?" may be the most faithful response to this story.

Denied an easy answer, we're forced to question, to search. Seeing evil but unable to limit it, we have to wonder where it is now…just as we would with an actual snake who disappeared somewhere inside our house. The lack of clear explanation is an admonishment against assuming you can, or should, know about evil…let alone become secure in that knowledge.

We do know the snake was crafty, shrewd. The text carries the connotation of "too smart for his own good" as well as "up to no good". We're meant to be suspicious of him the moment he arrives onstage. For good reason, as his next question reveals:

Half the Truth, None of the Benefit

He said to the woman, "Did God really say, 'You must not eat from any tree in the garden'?"

Notice the brilliance of the serpent's opening move. His words aren't an outright lie. He didn't make a statement at all! Instead the serpent takes a kernel of truth and twists it.

God did indeed tell Adam and Eve not to eat of one tree, the Tree of the Knowledge of Good and Evil. The serpent bends that truth then builds on it. He exaggerates, adding a sense of denial and longing. A tree put in place to keep relationships holy now seems like a tree God is keeping for himself because he doesn't want to share with his children.

The serpent suggests, implies, finds the worst possible way to explain an event and introduces the possibility that it just might be true. He invites Adam and Eve to believe in the worst about their environment and the people around them, not the best.

Many faithful folks like to paint evil as clearly identifiable, equal in power and opposed to good. It's not that easy. Evil, even the first evil, was never a wholly separate force. Evil does not muster its own life apart from God. Evil perverts things meant for goodness, using them for selfish, harmful, and crafty purposes instead of their original intention.

Since the original intention of all goodness was to bring eternal life, evil by definition becomes "not life", or, more simply…death. People say they're eating beef instead of cow because it makes the meat easier to eat. ("This burger is made of 100% Ground Cow!" is hardly a tantalizing ad slogan.) Similarly we call death "evil" because it makes it easier to do. Given the choice between living and dying, most of us choose life. Change it to a choice between good and evil and the decision gets harder. Evil might be fun! It might be powerful!

We need to remember that anything that isn't life is death, no matter what the form of death looks like. There's a famous scene in the Christmas Movie "Polar Express" where we see a compass rose extending from Christmas tree at the North Pole. All four directions on that rose read "S" for south. When you're standing at the exact North Pole every step you take will be south.

That's how it was in the garden. The serpent didn't have to invent a new world for Adam and Eve, a dark garden to oppose God's light. All he needed to do was get them to take a single step in any direction away from God. They stood in the exact center of life. Any way they turned the compass rose read "D" for "Death".

This was the serpent's great trick, selling death as life. Many centuries have passed since the first humans fell for it, but the game hasn't changed.

Think of all the evil, all the struggles and broken relationships in your life. How many of them start exactly the way the serpent suggested…looking at another person and explaining their actions in the worst way? Every one of us has family members who have fought for years over issues that started as small misunderstandings. Those small differences got explained poorly, extra baggage got glommed onto them, and suddenly they galvanized into "Truth"…something to fight over. If the parties involved could transport back to the original incident they'd see how small and petty it was, but it's taken on a life of its own now. The issue will never be healed because people don't *want* it to be healed. Their interpretation of the truth is more valuable to them than family, peace, or love itself. It may be wrong but at least it's theirs.

This is no different than Adam and Eve saying, "It may be wrong to bite that fruit, but at least the fruit will be mine then." We've all stood in their place. We've not only heard the serpent's whispers, we've followed them.

The Big "But"

Adam and Eve are not going down without a fight. They correct the serpent's worst-possible explanation:

² The woman said to the serpent, "We may eat fruit from the trees in the garden, ³ but God did say, 'You must not eat fruit from the tree that is in the middle of the garden, and you must not touch it, or you will die.'"

Notice that the first ten words of Eve's statement were sufficient to illuminate the falsehood in the serpent's words. God had not said they couldn't eat of any tree, just that single one. It's not like that tree curtained off half of creation. They could have walked around it to any number of fruit-bearing plants and eaten their fill for all eternity. When Eve says, "We may eat fruit from the trees," she speaks of God's generosity, his bounty, his care for them…all of which were conveniently missing from the serpent's explanation.

Those ten words, remembered and held to, would have saved humanity. Except Eve didn't stop there. Right after those ten words came an 11th: "but".

Relationship counselors will generally tell arguing couples that saying, "But…" is poor form when talking to a partner, especially in the heat of battle. We say things before "but" to make ourselves feel better about the really awful things we're going to say after it. Try this on for size:

"Honey, you know I love you and I'll always want to be married to you, but...

"[…you're a fat, disgusting slob now, your wedding outfit is 8 sizes in your past, and I don't even begin to find you attractive anymore, so lay off the Twinkies, huh?]."

Did I even need to type it? As soon as you saw the "but" you *knew* something like that was coming. Everything before the "but" gets invalidated by what comes after.

Representing all humanity, Eve puts up a valiant struggle against temptation for ten words before throwing in the fatal "but". (That's just one clause! We didn't even make it one whole sentence!) Then the invalidating "but" comes in and we're lost.

What are Adam and Eve going to focus on? Not the thousands of trees with infinite food forever, but the one, single thing that they couldn't have…the one tree they couldn't eat…the one distinction between them and God. It wasn't enough for them to gorge themselves and co-create and live like gods, they wanted to BE God. The sting of what the serpent implied they weren't was stronger than a universe full of evidence testifying what they were.

We should hear in this the cry of every 14-year-old Child of God who looks in a mirror and thinks they're gruesome because they have a few marks on their face, because there's a roll of fat where the magazines say a muscle should show, or because their friends developed a chest faster (or sometimes slower) than they. We should hear every parent who tries to bury their children in Christmas presents and finds that it's not enough to make them feel good. We should perceive the gaping maw of depression that eats up goodness and light for those it afflicts. To this very day what we perceive we *aren't* weighs on us far more than the truth of who we *are*. We remain God's children, now and always; we just can't see it anymore.

If you dig even a little into any sin you care to name, you'll find that they're all echoes of this first one.

When the serpent heard the "but", he knew that the doubt he had introduced had tipped the balance. All Adam and Eve needed was a little nudge.

A Truth vs. The Truth

[4] "You will not certainly die," the serpent said to the woman. [5] "For God knows that when you eat from it your eyes will be opened, and you will be like God, knowing good and evil."

Again evil introduces a half-lie. "You will not certainly die." This was untrue. Temptation takes death and makes it look like life. "Cheat on your spouse, you'll feel better. Unleash your frustration on your child, it's for their own good. Claim credit for the work and get a promotion over your teammates. You'll have so much more money!" God gives us life, abundantly, for free, because he loves us. Evil dresses up death in lipstick and a bad wig and asks us to sell ourselves and all creation to buy it. And we go with evil.

If every bit of war, pestilence, racism, poverty, illness, and disaster the world has ever known didn't stem from this phenomenon, you'd just have to laugh.

In this case the wig and lipstick took the form of an implication. "God left something out. He's holding back from you." Keep in mind that Adam and Eve had so far received life, other lives teeming all around them, the power to create and affect those lives, a completely stable living environment, all the free food they could ever want, and the promise that this would last eternally without a single care, worry, or bad thing happening.

"But God left something out," said the serpent. And that implication was enough to make them toss away everything they had been given.

God hadn't left anything out, of course. There was nothing particularly important about that tree. It was there to remind them that they were not him, that they were still in relationship with somebody besides themselves, that they needed more than just themselves or their own whims to rely on.

The serpent was telling *a* truth—when they ate they'd know good and evil like God did—but the serpent was not telling *the* truth. Knowing good and evil was not going to be beneficial to them in the least. In fact it would ruin everything.

In our age of instant access and ubiquitous social media, the distinction between "a" truth and "the" truth is often lost. We seem to think that any thought or observation that can be demonstrated true in one way or another is inherently valuable. This is not always so.

When I officiate a wedding I generally know a truth or two. This blissful couple will soon struggle with each other. As they discover how different their languages of love are, they'll think the other doesn't understand them. As complacency sets in they'll forget to value one another properly. For certain stretches of their union they're going to rue the fact that they're waking up next to this person. And that's without morning breath worming its way into the equation!

All of those things are technically true. Should I then expound upon them in the wedding sermon? Were I to speak those truths, I would actually tell a profound untruth about the marriage in that moment. I would discourage and offend rather than inspire. When marriages work, all of those inconvenient and harsh truths end up leading to a greater one: life is amazing, struggle builds confidence, and getting through several decades with another person and still being able to say, "I love you" at the end of it all is one of the most rewarding things we'll ever experience short of heaven.

The lack of distinction between "a" truth and "the" truth isn't confined to social media either. News media, "reality" TV, public humor, commercials...all sell stilted versions of truths that may be factual but not important or meaningful.

The serpent operated by building seemingly true implications out of half-truths, using a truth to lead us to a mistaken and meaningless version of the truth. In the garden it was shocking. In our world it's your average Wednesday.

Sin Begins

6 When the woman saw that the fruit of the tree was good for food and pleasing to the eye, and also desirable for gaining wisdom, she took some and ate it. She also gave some to her husband, who was with her, and he ate it.

Sometimes we become so familiar with a story that it doesn't register with us anymore. George Washington was the father of our country. Abraham Lincoln freed the slaves. Peter Parker was bitten by a radioactive spider. We repeat the narrative so often that we mentally skip ahead to the good parts.

If I've done my job correctly, the phrase, "When they saw the fruit was pleasing to the eye, they ate it" should bring the mixture of shock, horror, and incredulity that it was meant to carry.

Adam and Eve bit the fruit.

Those bites were a betrayal of the one person who loved them most, infinitely even?

Adam and Eve bit the fruit.

Those bites said to God, "Not only do I not trust you, I want to supplant you…to get you out of the way so I can take whatever I want. You are nothing to me…"?

Adam and Eve bit the fruit.

Those bites named the giver and Creator of the universe selfish. Those bites named the source of love inadequate. Those bites said, "I'd rather have a dead dummy dressed up in a wig and bad lipstick than have a relationship with YOU."

The fruit isn't so pleasing to the eye now, is it? Yet we continue to snack on it today. Every single time you have sinned, you've repeated Adam and Eve's mistake. Every time you've done something unloving or failed to do what is loving because something else seemed more important, you've thought that fruit looked good. Every time you've chased power and acclaim on the world's terms, getting for yourself and your loved ones at the expense of others and believing you'd be happier because of it, you've tasted the juice of that fruit dribbling down your chin.

Many faithful folks have tried to cast this act as one of disobedience. God didn't care that we *obey*, at least not for the sake of obedience itself…or even for his own sake. Obedience centers the focus on God's power. Because God had given *us* such enormous power, he wanted us to care about something besides ourselves! He wanted us to love each other and him and all of creation, to serve each other and the world, to live forever making each day glorious as we shared paradise. God wanted our lives to tell the truth about how much he loves us and how amazing this relationship is.

But caring about others and loving life more than ourselves was the one thing we couldn't manage. We'd rather break the world and deny God than spend one day not getting the prerogatives we think we're entitled to.

You cannot miss the irony here. We insisted upon taking what was already given. Somehow taking made it feel more like ours than just receiving it. Imagine giving your child the gift of their dreams, a gift beyond measure: pony, sports car, their own tropical island…you name it. Then they turn to you and say, "Get the heck out. I'm taking this. It's mine now." How amazingly, blindingly stupid and selfish.

Welcome to humanity.

This is what we do every time we try to take what God has already given. It happens every time we fear we're not good or young or pretty or famous or powerful enough. It happens every time we reach out for something to fill the emptiness inside, not understanding that the very act of taking and grabbing for ourselves *creates the emptiness in the first place.*

They say if you're stranded at sea, don't drink the ocean water. It may look wet but the saltiness will end up dehydrating you more than the water nourishes and you'll perish quicker. That's exactly what happens when we grab and take. The more we look to fill ourselves up, the emptier we get.

Shame…

⁷ Then the eyes of both of them were opened, and they realized they were naked; so they sewed fig leaves together and made coverings for themselves.

⁸ Then the man and his wife heard the sound of the Lord God as he was walking in the garden in the cool of the day, and they hid from the Lord God among the trees of the garden. ⁹ But the Lord God called to the man, "Where are you?"

Adam and Eve realized upon eating the fruit that they were naked, so they sewed fig leaves and covered themselves. After two and a half chapters of Genesis, we finally get clothes.

Remember all that clothing represents, though: the need to cover up and hide from each other, the idea that the gaze of another is harmful or lurid, the need to shelter against the environment, separating people by their ability to create and purchase finer or lesser garments. We can already see the world crumbling around Adam and Eve. The first casualty of sin was their perception of each other.

More cracks in creation became clear when God arrived. As they heard God's voice Adam and Eve knew shame, the price of their wrongdoing. They knew what it was to *not* want to see someone, to hope the other person would just go away. The ground once sustained them; now they wished it would cover them up as God walked by.

When God calls, "Where are you?" he's not just asking for a location. The words carry multiple meanings: "Where have you gone? Where is the 'you' I know and love? What happened to our relationship?" There's a profound sense of loss, the kind only felt after a deep betrayal. Maybe you've had the experience of seeing someone physically after they've betrayed you but not being able to see them like you used to, to experience the closeness you once had together. God knew where Adam and Eve were, he just didn't know *who* they were anymore.

…and Blame

10 He answered, "I heard you in the garden, and I was afraid because I was naked; so I hid."

11 And he said, "Who told you that you were naked? Have you eaten from the tree that I commanded you not to eat from?"

12 The man said, "The woman you put here with me—she gave me some fruit from the tree, and I ate it."

13 Then the Lord God said to the woman, "What is this you have done?"

The woman said, "The serpent deceived me, and I ate."

When he hears God's question, Adam comes up with an immediate explanation. "I was afraid because I was naked, so I hid." He's not just talking about his physical nakedness. Bare skin was no great thing. Adam had always walked around unclothed. God had taken his rib even, been inside Adam's own body. He had been as open as a person could possibly be before his Lord. But now instead of bringing joy, that openness hurt, causing him to fear.

Folks who are dating face a problematic question: "How much do I reveal myself and when?" Comedian Chris Rock once said, "You can't get a partner looking like you do, thinking like you do, acting like you do. You have to present your best self to someone. When you're meeting someone new, you're not meeting them, you're meeting their representative." Somehow we know that showing too much of ourselves too soon will drive others away. This is ironic since the point of dating is generally to find someone you feel comfortable being "yourself" with. Though we ache to be open, we also fear it.

Adam and Eve knew that exact struggle in the garden. They had once been completely open with God and it had been OK…amazingly perfect, even. Now they could not. What they longed for also hurt them. Their descendants face the same problem today.

Then God asked if they ate of the tree. He already knew, of course. The signs were all around them. But this was an important lesson for Adam and Eve. With the world collapsing around them, they could no longer achieve perfection. The best God could hope for was for Adam and Eve to tell the truth about their imperfection.

This also remains true today. Sometimes people of faith claim that they're good…or at least better than others. This is a lie. None of us are good. As the Apostle Paul said, "All have sinned and fallen short of the glory of God." We love to stick our "buts" in there. "Sure I sin, but *those* people, they *really* sin!" To God this is like watching children play with sticks of radioactive uranium and hearing some of them say, "At least we only have one stick! Those kids have five! Yell at them, not us!"

God knows we're not capable of perfection. As was true with Adam and Eve, telling the truth about our shortcomings is the best we can do in a fallen world.

When we fail to admit our imperfection, we deny God and our relationship with him. That's just grabbing the fruit from a different direction. "I don't need you, God. I've got this. I can be holy on my own. Go bother with someone else." Once again we try to become our own gods right in the face of the real one.

Why do churches bother with confession? It's not about the sin itself. Confession is our admission that we're not God, the closest we can come to correcting our fruit-biting inclinations.

Even in this, we are imperfect. Adam himself couldn't tell the truth about the situation…at least not in a way that mattered. His response when questioned by God was, "It wasn't my fault, she did it first!" Then Eve came up with, "The serpent tricked me!"

Adam and Eve had each come up with a truth, but their truths didn't illuminate anything except how deeply sin was already working in the world. Before this the relationship between the couple had been innocent, purely loving. Now blame and resentment had entered the picture. You've heard the phrase, "You always get hurt by those you love the most." This was the beginning of it. Adam couldn't wait to throw Eve under the bus. Eve couldn't do anything but dodge and blame someone else in turn.

Incredibly, some people try to use this passage to justify the assertion that men are superior to women using Adam's excuse: Eve bit the fruit first. "She did it first!" brings no absolution for Adam or remission of his guilt. That claim didn't justify Adam, it revealed the sin at work inside him. That Adam even thought to blame someone showed everything that was *wrong* with the world now, not the way things were *supposed* to be. Those words contained every hurt in every broken relationship through the ages wrapped up into one, awful sentence. This was certainly not a pattern to emulate, let alone an endorsement of patriarchy and male superiority. Eve bit the fruit first but Adam was the first to hurt another by casting the finger of blame. If that's superior, then superior isn't much.

Curses Fall

14 So the Lord God said to the serpent, "Because you have done this,

"Cursed are you above all livestock
and all wild animals!
You will crawl on your belly
and you will eat dust
all the days of your life.
15 And I will put enmity

between you and the woman,
* and between your offspring and hers;*
he will crush your head,
* and you will strike his heel."*

After hearing Adam and Eve's blame game unfold and watching creation crumble around them, God responded with three speeches: one each to the serpent, to Eve, and to Adam.

With the serpent, God spared no feelings. He cursed the snake to be the lowest creature in creation. The snake would find no favor with the Creator of goodness. "Eating dust all the days of your life" means being immersed in the things of death, walking in a land futile and dry, without nurture.

God also points out clearly the enmity between the serpent and humanity, between the snake's offspring and Eve's. Whatever else our lives may be, they're meant to be a fight against evil. We were created to be people of goodness and life. Sin did not end or change that purpose, it just threw the need into sharper relief.

Though the original authors of Genesis could not foresee and did not intend it, for Christians the "he" referenced in verse 15 is the Christ, the promised one, who would come to win victory over sin when we could not. In his very first statement about sin, God promised that good would prevail. Evil "strikes our heels". It does us harm, rendering us unable to walk the path we ought to. But the promised offspring crushes evil's head…not a strike that lames, but kills. God would not, and will not ever, let evil have the last word.

This is hard to understand in a world that hurts so much. We see evidence of our brokenness in the news each day. The more we gain access to each other's lives, the more sin we see.

We've all experienced the devastating effects of illness. We watch natural disasters ravage entire countries. We see people march for justice that never seems to come fully. The best-intended of us invariably go astray. I have. You do too. This is exactly why we don't get the last word, why at the end we are forced to surrender control to One who has the power to save us and make this better.

What Is God's Will?

This passage also points out something important about God's will…an often-misunderstood topic.

When we use the phrase, "It was God's will," we're usually talking about something tragic. You lost your child? "It was God's will. He needed another angel." An earthquake devastates a town? "It was God's will. He must be trying to teach them something."

God *clearly states* his will right here, in the first moment sin entered into the world. We'll have to live with the world's brokenness until all things are made new again, but God WILL NOT let evil have the last word. Whatever evil gets to say or do in the meantime, the final pronouncement will be God's and God will pronounce GOOD for us. Evil will be conquered. Lost children will be restored to their parents. Earthquake victims will get a glorious home. We will live forever in a world where evil has been vanquished, not a trace of it left.

THAT is God's will. That's how we should speak of it. Instead of offering platitudes perhaps we should say, "This won't last forever, and while it does last I'll walk right by your side." Or better yet, perhaps we should leave the speeches to God and show his will through our love, bringing as much goodness as we can to people in difficult circumstances.

Our Turn

¹⁶ *To the woman he said,*

"I will make your pains in childbearing very severe;
 with painful labor you will give birth to children.
Your desire will be for your husband,
 and he will rule over you."

¹⁷ *To Adam he said, "Because you listened to your wife and ate fruit from the tree about which I commanded you, 'You must not eat from it,'*

"Cursed is the ground because of you;
 through painful toil you will eat food from it
 all the days of your life.

*18 It will produce thorns and thistles for you,
  and you will eat the plants of the field.
19 By the sweat of your brow
  you will eat your food
until you return to the ground,
  since from it you were taken;
for dust you are
  and to dust you will return."*

After addressing the serpent, God turned his attention to Eve. He described the agony she would feel in her body bearing children…how every moment of life-giving creation would be accompanied by pain from now on. This was the mark of the damage sin had done: the greater and more profound the creative moment, the greater the suffering that would accompany it.

God also detailed the way sin had broken human relations, informing Eve of the power imbalance that would plague even the best of relationships between men and women.

It's important to note that God was not prescribing the way things *should* be here, but describing the way things were *going* to be now that sin had insinuated itself into human life. Like earlier verses, Genesis 3:16 has been used to justify men taking power over women, ordaining it as right according to scripture. God wasn't saying, "You just broke the whole world! Look how wonderful this is going to be! Go ahead and dominate that girl!" God was simply telling the truth about the pain that broken, twisted relationships would cause.

Every person who's ever used these verses to justify a man taking power over woman should also be campaigning for farmers to plant thorns and thistles instead of crops. That's what God said would happen to Adam. If God was prescribing the way things should be in these passages, we should all sow brambles among the corn and wheat.

God did tell Adam the ground itself was cursed. Sin bent the fabric of the world. What was meant to give life now gave emptiness and death. Adam would have to fight with the ground for sustenance instead of enjoying it freely. Whatever control and power he thought he was achieving by grabbing at that fruit, he lost a thousandfold in the aftermath. Sin could not better the world, only twist and destroy it. Sin does not bring power, it robs humankind of it.

And then came the final truth, the final announcement. Adam and Eve were only dust. Absent love, absent the gift of their creation, absent God, they were just glorified powder. What started as dust would return to dust, that this truth would resound through all the universe.

God does what he can here: speak truth in the face of our lies. When we cannot turn away from our sin, nor undo it, we see the horror it causes. As we witness sin's effects we experience the same loss our Creator experienced when we betrayed him. Once again, we see God making us just like he is. This time it's not such a happy thing.

We may indulge in sin, but we cannot mistake its price, nor confuse it with true goodness. That is the point. Those who cast these verses as "punishment", as if God is vindictive, are missing that point. The only way to know the truth of sin is to experience its truth. Genesis 3: 16-19 is simple truth-telling, no more and no less. What we have created, we will live with.

Moving On

20 Adam named his wife Eve, because she would become the mother of all the living.

21 The Lord God made garments of skin for Adam and his wife and clothed them. 22 And the Lord God said, "The man has now become like one of us, knowing good and evil. He must not be allowed to reach out his hand and take also from the tree of life and eat, and live forever." 23 So the Lord God banished him from the Garden of Eden to work the ground from which he had been taken. 24 After he drove the man out, he placed on the east side of the Garden of Eden cherubim and a flaming sword flashing back and forth to guard the way to the tree of life.

And then we move on. Life in a broken world would look far different, but it would endure. This is affirmed in the first verse after God's great announcement of truth. "Eve would become the mother of all the living."

As we've discussed, naming carries power. The name "Eve" comes from the root for "living". Immediately after a pronouncement full of dust and death comes an affirmation of life, created by the same two people who brought sin into the world. The miracle of redemption is on display for all to see.

God aided Adam and Eve as well. He made clothes for them. That they needed clothes at all was a tragedy. Fashioning them would show just how much the world had changed. Animals had to die, giving up their skins so the humans might live. Goodness now came with a cost, the demand of sin: for every life, a death, goodness for one bringing suffering to another. But God stayed with his children anyway. When they could not walk in perfection with him, he walked in an imperfect world with them.

This point is critical. Many people say, "If God exists, let alone cares about the world, why doesn't he just wipe out evil?" God had that option at this juncture. He could have looked at what Adam and Eve had done, realized that his formerly-good creation was spoiled, and simply wiped it out and started all over again. We never would have known. Some other humans would be living eternally in paradise right now with Boris and Petunia as their progenitors. If God valued a perfect world above anything, he could have had it.

Why didn't God do this? Only one reason makes sense. He loved Adam and Eve still. He was willing to do whatever was necessary to keep them as his children…not just random, interchangeable created beings, but *them*, his *children*.

Loving Adam and Eve (and all of us who would come after) would mean putting up with millennia of rejection, injustice, warfare, sickness, misery, assault, agony, loneliness, mental illness, and everything else sin would bring. God would walk through all of it, keeping his promise to save his children rather than wiping them off the face of the earth.

But let's say God decided to answer our challenge and wipe out all sin. Who would be left behind? Neither Adam nor Eve nor their world would have survived. Nor would any of us. The greatest saints among us know how short they have fallen. As 1 John says, "If we claim we are without sin we deceive ourselves and the truth is not in us."

When we wish God would reveal himself by wiping away sin, we are asking him to go back on the promise he made to Adam and Eve. Instead of being saved, all of us would have to die and the entire universe be remade. Today, as then, God's answer remains the same. "I will not. I will stick with you. As much as it hurts and as much as you'll hurt because of sin, I won't leave you or unmake you."

It's easy to wish that God would smite somebody else we consider evil. His refusal to do so seems to perpetuate wickedness in the world. But that refusal is also an ongoing affirmation of love for us all. God would rather suffer with us than have a perfect world without us.

Even so, God will not let imperfection last forever. That would not be mercy, but cruelty. Imagine racism forever, poverty and starvation forever, cancer forever, or even not being able to have the relationship with your family you want because you can never quite bridge that gap…forever. We fear death when we're young and the world seems full of endless promise. By the time we hit our late nineties most of us have seen the promise of the world mingle hopelessly with its pain. By that time we're usually prepared, if not ready, to go…tired of life the way it is and eager for life the way it's supposed to be.

This is the practical purpose of death, that our suffering will not last forever and that sin will not have the last word. God shut off the garden and the tree of life from Adam and Eve not as punishment, but to keep them from an eternal prison sentence. There need not be an end to love; there must be an end to sin. They cannot be coupled forever. Against that horror the angels guard.

What does this mean? Someday everything imperfect, selfish, and temporary about us will have an end. Our reign of terror and control over our own lives will pass. Only love and goodness will endure. The more enmeshed in the illusion of a self-interested world we are, the more horrible and power-robbing this sounds. The more we realize our inability to make things right, the more of a blessing it becomes.

God walks with us through this life, but not to glorify this life nor the way we broke it. God walks with us for a greater purpose, to take us beyond ourselves into the life we were always meant to have, of which the good things of this existence are just an echo and in which the bad things of this life will be forgotten like a dream.

So, you see, God does answer our prayer in the end, just not in the way we expect. Our evil will have its last day and we too will be cleansed. Then we'll be restored to the perfect life we were meant for but can never reach this side of the grave.

3 LIFE AFTER EDEN

Two Brothers

Adam made love to his wife Eve, and she became pregnant and gave birth to Cain. She said, "With the help of the Lord I have brought forth a man."² Later she gave birth to his brother Abel.

Now Abel kept flocks, and Cain worked the soil. ³ In the course of time Cain brought some of the fruits of the soil as an offering to the Lord. ⁴ And Abel also brought an offering—fat portions from some of the firstborn of his flock. The Lord looked with favor on Abel and his offering, ⁵ but on Cain and his offering he did not look with favor. So Cain was very angry, and his face was downcast.

⁶ Then the Lord said to Cain, "Why are you angry? Why is your face downcast?⁷ If you do what is right, will you not be accepted? But if you do not do what is right, sin is crouching at your door; it desires to have you, but you must rule over it."

⁸ Now Cain said to his brother Abel, "Let's go out to the field." While they were in the field, Cain attacked his brother Abel and killed him.

The first event in Adam and Eve's life was a blessed one. A son was born and soon after, another. Even after the Fall life bloomed. And yet in true form, the first two blessed events in all human history combined to make the first tragedy.

The trouble started when Cain (a farmer) and Abel (a herdsman) brought sacrifices to the Lord. Some see this as an allegory for the struggle between sedentary agriculturists versus nomadic shepherds early in human history. It may be, but whomever was involved—two humans or entire tribes--trouble brewed quickly.

Cain and Abel's difficulty centered around the concept of sacrifice. It was supposed to be a gesture of remembrance, giving up oneself, penance and thanksgiving mingled. Instead it turned inward and became a matter of pride.

Cain offered the Lord his fine vegetables, Abel lambs from his flock. God accepted Abel's sacrifice and not Cain's. In some ways this seems like a jerk-ish move. And maybe it is. If the goal was to maintain peace between the brothers, looking with favor on both sacrifices would have been the politically correct move.

As we've heard many times, life isn't fair. Not everything is equally acceptable. This is true in our relationships with each other as well as our relationship with God. If those relationships are going to be good, we need to listen to the other and value their words.

Who knows why God accepted one sacrifice over the other? Maybe lambs are inherently holier than cabbages. Or maybe Cain offered Brussels Sprouts, which nobody likes. Perhaps Abel's sacrifice of a lamb's life foretold the Paschal Lamb who would one day give himself on the cross, showing that the only possible atonement for sin is death.

This is exactly what sacrifices meant for years. "I know I deserve to be on this altar, God. If justice prevailed you'd be calling me into account, ending my sinful existence on this altar to cleanse the world of my sin. But I'd like to live today so I hope you'll be happy with this ox instead. It's a real nice ox!"

And God would say, "Yes. I accept your ox. Thanks for remembering the truth. I'll use it to feed the guys taking care of the temple."

But even if we can't agree why God favored Abel's sacrifice over Cain, it hardly matters. The point is, the other person in any relationship has the right to their preferences and opinions. When you're in a relationship with them, and especially when you're trying to honor them through gift-giving, you have to take those preferences into account.

(Hear that, all you husbands out there? No vacuum cleaners for your anniversary unless your wife asks for it! The Bible says so!)

Many times after I ask my son to do something, he will pause and try to figure out why I'm asking before he does it. I am trying to train him to do what his dad asks and *then* figure out why. Not only do things work smoother that way, he has a better chance of understanding me by following me than by refusing to follow until he understands why. There's nothing wrong with him asking, or even debating me, as long as he does what I ask first.

Since God is the ultimate Dad, this usually works with him too. Too often we think we can understand before we follow when understanding only comes *through* following. When we do this, we end up like Cain: just not getting it.

God was trying to teach both Cain and Abel about having a relationship with him, about following him. Abel had the easier task; his sacrifice was accepted. Cain had a harder lesson to learn. God wanted to show him something different than he already believed. Instead of being humbled, caring about the relationship, and taking time to learn about the person he was interacting with, Cain did what many of us do in this situation: he got angry.

God warned Cain about his behavior (in the very first recorded utterance of, "You mad, bro?") God assured Cain that he didn't have to be angry. If he took a second and bothered to think of somebody besides himself, this situation was easily resolvable. Goodness was right there if he could just see past his pride. If not, sin would rule him.

God pleaded with Cain to listen. God pleads the same thing to us when we have disagreements with him or, more commonly, with each other. Arguing has become institutionalized in America now. Radio hosts shamelessly spout a single point of view, looking for controversies to fuel anger and boost ratings. "Newscasts" consist of 2-3 opposing "experts" on the same screen talking past each other. Reality TV is nothing but argument, the worst and most intolerant slices of life with normalcy edited out. Self-centeredness isn't just second nature to us, it's become the national language, the basis upon which we're expected to make our corporate decisions.

If you can't understand why Cain couldn't just get over it and listen to God, keep in mind that you don't either. You're not fighting over lambs and veggies, but things you consider important. And yes, there are plenty of critically important things to fight for in this life, but most of the stuff we fight about is pretty silly.

Cain decided to take the stubborn route. Rather than discover something new about God, change his understanding of the world, and get over his wounded pride, he invited his brother out to a field and took care of the issue by killing him.

This seems like a shocking overreaction. Look in the mirror again. How many of us think we've "won" when an election goes our way, when an annoying person at work gets their comeuppance, or when our spouse finally gives in to us? Did we really win? Did we learn anything about other people and the world that broadened our horizons, or did somebody get whacked for our perceived benefit?

Cast Out Again

9 Then the Lord said to Cain, "Where is your brother Abel?"

"I don't know," he replied. "Am I my brother's keeper?"

10 The Lord said, "What have you done? Listen! Your brother's blood cries out to me from the ground. 11 Now you are under a curse and driven from the ground, which opened its mouth to receive your brother's blood from your hand. 12 When you work the ground, it will no longer yield its crops for you. You will be a restless wanderer on the earth."

13 Cain said to the Lord, "My punishment is more than I can bear. 14 Today you are driving me from the land, and I will be hidden from your presence; I will be a restless wanderer on the earth, and whoever finds me will kill me."

15 But the Lord said to him, "Not so; anyone who kills Cain will suffer vengeance seven times over." Then the Lord put a mark on Cain so that no one who found him would kill him. 16 So Cain went out from the Lord's presence and lived in the land of Nod, east of Eden.

Much as he had with Cain's parents hiding in the garden, God addresses this matter with a question. He knows what has happened, but he wants the truth to be visible. "Where is your brother Abel?" holds all the anguish of the parallel, "Where are you?" in the last chapter. We hear God mourning a deep and personal relationship, the agony of the entire world breaking distilled down to a single moment, the loss of a beloved life.

Cain's response is no more adequate than his father's had been earlier. When we hear, "Am I my brother's keeper?" we're supposed to respond indignantly ("Better than your brother's MURDERER!") and with correction ("Yes, you should have been!") We were created to keep and care for each other, especially in families. Cain not only betrayed his brother, but his entire purpose for living.

God responds with another statement of truth and another curse. "Your brother's blood cries out to me from the ground." This indicates that God realizes what has happened, but the juxtaposition of Abel's blood with the earlier blood of sacrifice is also interesting. In his sacrifice, Abel offered his own blood, represented by his lamb and the work and/or wealth he had invested in it. This was acceptable. Cain spilled someone else's blood as a sacrifice to his own pride. This was horrible.

We are tempted often to make other people pay for our shortcomings. One of the hidden truths they teach you in seminary is to beware the preacher who creates an enemy out of certain people or issues and rails against them obsessively. You can bet that the preacher is afflicted by the very issue he's speaking against. Whether his assessment of sin is right or wrong doesn't matter. He *feels* sinful but instead of owning up to it himself, he tries to make other people pay for his guilt. He murders them in the field with his words.

The most devout communities of faith and the strongest family bloodlines are filled with passive aggressive behavior, backbiting, held grudges, and a hundred other practices that amount to forcing other people to atone for your guilt. We fail to take care of each other just the same as Cain failed Abel. We don't hit them with a rock. Instead we kill them by whispering behind their back and turning the rest of the family against them.

If we're not being our brother's (and sister's) keeper we're murdering them…through neglect if nothing else. And we're doing it for the same reason that Cain did. We're unwilling to see past ourselves and credit the incredible importance of others in our life. We don't want to learn about our place in the world, we just want what we want.

God responds to Cain's violation with an appropriate curse. "You think this is how you get ahead? It won't work anymore. Whatever means you had to advance yourself are taken from you." The proud farmer would no longer coax yield from the soil. Instead he would become a wanderer, forced to feel what it's like to be the "other" for the rest of his days.

When Cain objects that people will kill him during his nomadic wanderings, God assures him that he will bear a mark to prevent it. Not so easily would Cain get out of his lesson.

But the very presence of other people in the story raises a question. Weren't there just four people, now three, on the whole earth? Who was going to kill him?

We could bend over backwards trying to reconcile that issue. We could cite again the possibility of "nomads vs. settled agrarians" and the translation of "Adam and Eve" as "mankind and womankind". We could argue that the Story One people were operating from a different background than the Story Two people. Whatever answer you come up with is probably not as important as the thrust of the tale. Selfishness leads to disaster, care for others and the willingness to evolve with them lie at the heart of our relationship with God. Without them even our best sacrifices are futile and only lead to disaster.

Sons Become Peoples

17 Cain made love to his wife, and she became pregnant and gave birth to Enoch. Cain was then building a city, and he named it after his son Enoch. 18 To Enoch was born Irad, and Irad was the father of Mehujael, and Mehujael was the father of Methushael, and Methushael was the father of Lamech.

19 Lamech married two women, one named Adah and the other Zillah. 20 Adah gave birth to Jabal; he was the father of those who live in tents and raise livestock. 21 His brother's name was Jubal; he was the father of all who play stringed instruments and pipes. 22 Zillah also had a son, Tubal-Cain, who forged all kinds of tools out of bronze and iron. Tubal-Cain's sister was Naamah.

23 Lamech said to his wives,

"Adah and Zillah, listen to me;
  wives of Lamech, hear my words.
I have killed a man for wounding me,
  a young man for injuring me.
24 If Cain is avenged seven times,
  then Lamech seventy-seven times."

25 Adam made love to his wife again, and she gave birth to a son and named him Seth, saying, "God has granted me another child in place of Abel, since Cain killed him." 26 Seth also had a son, and he named him Enosh.

At that time people began to call on the name of the Lord.

Genesis 4 ends with the expansion of humankind through divergent lines. Cain and his people prospered in one location. They'd end up as city dwellers, livestock herders, musicians, and blacksmiths. But the people never escaped their roots in sin and fear, as one of Cain's descendants became a murderer and had to call upon his ancestor's protection eleven times over to feel safe. Neither venue-changing nor worldly success can disguise our shortcomings.

Adam and Eve had another son who also began a lineage. This is the earliest example of divergent family members siring separate tribes, a theme which will continue throughout Genesis and which would come to explain the enmity between peoples for centuries to come. They all traced back to a single forefather, yet they despised each other the worse for being related…another example of how sin warps our world.

Genealogy

This is the book of the generations of Adam. When God created man, he made him in the likeness of God. 2 Male and female he created them, and he blessed them and named them Man when they were created. 3 When Adam had lived a hundred and thirty years, he became the father of a son in his own likeness, after his image, and named him Seth. 4 The days of Adam after he became the father of Seth were eight hundred years; and he had other sons and daughters. 5 Thus all the days that Adam lived were nine hundred and thirty years; and he died.

6 When Seth had lived a hundred and five years, he became the father of Enosh. 7 Seth lived after the birth of Enosh eight hundred and seven years, and had other sons and daughters. 8 Thus all the days of Seth were nine hundred and twelve years; and he died.

9 When Enosh had lived ninety years, he became the father of Kenan. 10 Enosh lived after the birth of Kenan eight hundred and fifteen years, and had other sons and daughters. 11 Thus all the days of Enosh were nine hundred and five years; and he died.

12 When Kenan had lived seventy years, he became the father of Ma-hal′alel. *13* Kenan lived after the birth of Ma-hal′alel eight hundred and forty years, and had other sons and daughters. *14* Thus all the days of Kenan were nine hundred and ten years; and he died.

15 When Ma-hal′alel had lived sixty-five years, he became the father of Jared. *16* Ma-hal′alel lived after the birth of Jared eight hundred and thirty years, and had other sons and daughters. *17* Thus all the days of Ma-hal′alel were eight hundred and ninety-five years; and he died.

18 When Jared had lived a hundred and sixty-two years he became the father of Enoch. *19* Jared lived after the birth of Enoch eight hundred years, and had other sons and daughters. *20* Thus all the days of Jared were nine hundred and sixty-two years; and he died.

21 When Enoch had lived sixty-five years, he became the father of Methu′selah. *22* Enoch walked with God after the birth of Methu′selah three hundred years, and had other sons and daughters. *23* Thus all the days of Enoch were three hundred and sixty-five years. *24* Enoch walked with God; and he was not, for God took him.

25 When Methu′selah had lived a hundred and eighty-seven years, he became the father of Lamech. *26* Methu′selah lived after the birth of Lamech seven hundred and eighty-two years, and had other sons and daughters. *27* Thus all the days of Methu′selah were nine hundred and sixty-nine years; and he died.

28 When Lamech had lived a hundred and eighty-two years, he became the father of a son, *29* and called his name Noah, saying, "Out of the ground which the Lord has cursed this one shall bring us relief from our work and from the toil of our hands." *30* Lamech lived after the birth of Noah five hundred and ninety-five years, and had other sons and daughters. *31* Thus all the days of Lamech were seven hundred and seventy-seven years; and he died.

32 After Noah was five hundred years old, Noah became the father of Shem, Ham, and Japheth.

The fifth chapter of Genesis details the line of Adam through his third son, Seth. Plenty of Biblical scholars could make hay out of this field but for most folks, genealogies are less than inspiring. We'll simply note a couple things before moving on.

First, presenting a genealogy implies continuity. Old Testament authors were careful to preserve the sanctity of their lineage. In precise and human way, they showed how the inheritance of God's promise passed from generation to generation. One might almost view this like the passing of the Olympic torch between runners before the games begin.

In addition to the usual motivations of cultural and filial pride that such lists display, the authors want to make sure we know that God's flame never went out, even in the darkest times. This continued right up until the time of Jesus. Two of the four gospels begin with a genealogy much like this one, connecting Jesus to the Genesis folks we're reading about.

Second, you'll notice that these early folks lived a long time. Much gets made of numbers in the Bible…sometimes too much. In this case the specific numbers take a back seat to the sheer weight of centuries. Long life has traditionally been seen as a sign of favor from God. In that way we can see these earliest people as specially connected, not far removed from a life that was originally intended to last forever.

Many fantasy authors draw inspiration from the idea of a past civilization that was somehow greater, now lost. They're drawing from the same well as Genesis 5. These men lived impossibly long lives because of their close proximity to God. They were connected to a world that even we, with all our technological marvels, can only guess at in later days. In a culture that likes to manage, control, and understand every phenomenon, it's good to remember that some things are still beyond us.

While an average life span of 600 years or so seems incomprehensible, this was just a shadow of the eternity God really meant for his children. Even our wildest dreams fall short of God's good gifts to us.

Breaking Boundaries

6 When men began to multiply on the face of the ground, and daughters were born to them, ² the sons of God saw that the daughters of men were fair; and they took to wife such of them as they chose. ³ Then the Lord said, "My spirit shall not abide in man forever, for he is flesh, but his days shall be a hundred and twenty years." ⁴ The Nephilim were on the earth in those days, and also afterward, when the sons of God came in to the daughters of men, and they bore children to them. These were the mighty men that were of old, the men of renown.

⁵ The Lord saw that the wickedness of man was great in the earth, and that every imagination of the thoughts of his heart was only evil continually. ⁶ And the Lord was sorry that he had made man on the earth, and it grieved him to his heart. ⁷ So the Lord said, "I will blot out man whom I have created from the face of the ground, man and beast and creeping things and birds of the air, for I am sorry that I have made them." ⁸ But Noah found favor in the eyes of the Lord.

A two-pronged story begins Genesis 6: weird things are happening between heaven and earth and God is not happy about it. Nor is God happy about much else, to be honest.

As we've said, the Bible tends to mention heavenly beings without being entirely clear on their origin or nature. In Genesis 6 "sons of God", or Nephilim, break the boundary between supernatural and natural, coming to earth to live and generate offspring with humans. This is a violation. We are not sure why, only that some barrier was leapt and the result was super beings upon the earth.

Modern humans tend to resist boundaries. Tell us that we can't do something and we'll prove you wrong. There's nothing wrong with a daring spirit; it's led to some of humankind's greatest discoveries. At the same time we also have to admit our need for boundaries sometimes. No organization can operate without them. In every culture some things just aren't right. Boundaries protect us from harmful options and channel us towards more productive ones.

We've all encountered bad boundaries in our lives, those set for selfish or oppressive reasons instead of for the common good. No boundary is wholly sacrosanct or beyond questioning. But it's also OK to admit that some boundaries just shouldn't be broken. Adam and Eve bit the fruit in an attempt to break the boundary that divided them and God. Stepping over that line cost humanity everything. Boundaries between the heaven and earth aren't meant to be transgressed. Even when we have the power to do so, we lack the wisdom to do it well.

This particular boundary breaking generated humans of great power. This sounds like a positive thing, but extra power in human hands did nothing to curb the rising tide of sin. Instead it accelerated it. Wherever people journeyed they took their shortcomings along with them. The only question was how fast sin would spread.

God looked at the earth and saw that human wickedness was growing beyond any reasonable bounds. Sin infected "every imagination" as people contemplated "continual evil". There was no respite. The abundance of evil made God shake his head and rue that he had created us.

This was quite a turn-around from a couple chapters ago when God stuck with Adam and Eve despite their sin. We're reminded that sin does grieve God. Sin is just as hard for God to abide as it would be for us if we were watching our own children hurting each other, bringing death into the world instead of life.

The Old Testament informs us that God has already tried most of the solutions we want him to try when dealing with sin. (None of it worked, which is why a Savior was necessary.) In Genesis 6 God fulfills the fantasy of the righteous when they say, "Why doesn't God just wipe out all evildoers and be done with it?" That's exactly what he resolved to do here: wash the world clean with a flood, blotting out humankind and all their wickedness.

Yet right after God expressed his frustration we find another ray of hope. One man, Noah, found favor in God's eyes.

A Righteous Man

9 These are the generations of Noah. Noah was a righteous man, blameless in his generation; Noah walked with God. 10 And Noah had three sons, Shem, Ham, and Japheth.

What did Noah do in order to find favor? Simple. He walked with God.

This elegant description conveys an important truth. In our effort to define and control concepts like "goodness" and "righteousness", we convert them into abstract qualities. We hold those qualities apart and talk about God and ourselves living up to them. When we say, "God is good" we mean "God resembles this abstract quality of goodness that I envision and that governs his behavior."

Notice how much of this depends on our own perception. What is goodness? Whatever we determine it is personally. And whatever we determine, we expect God to live up to...or rather bow down to. This way of thinking gives us great power. It puts God underneath us.

When the Bible says "God is good" it means that God IS goodness. Goodness equals God. There is no goodness apart from God or outside of him. It's not an abstract quality that we pin somewhere and join God in the climb towards, nor does it come in measurable quantities that we can fit into our pockets to pull out when we want to feel proud of ourselves. God is goodness; God is love; God himself is righteousness. All of those qualities reside in, and stem from, one being: our Creator.

How did Noah find favor? Not by being righteous by some abstract measure. He walked with God. He spent his life in relationship with Goodness itself, talking to it, striving for it, longing to be near it.

We may expect that Noah—and any figure in the Bible, really—had good days and bad days just like we do. Noah was also able to walk alongside the source of goodness through those days, to stay in relationship with True Goodness even when he wasn't feeling good himself. For this he was accounted righteous.

Righteousness, goodness, love...everything good in the world comes through listening to, talking with, and walking alongside God. There's still room for abstract realizations about good qualities. Sometimes we can say with confidence, "Doing that was righteous." But righteousness is not contained in that act, nor limited to that single realization. What we really mean as people of faith is, "We were walking together with God in that act, and he with us."

Note that this also leaves room for others to be righteous, even if they don't think like us. If righteousness is contained in an abstract box, only those who can see the box and agree with its definition are able to work towards it. If righteousness means walking alongside God, well...God is HUGE. We may well be walking alongside God at the same time another person not at all like us is walking alongside him too, just on the other side. We may have different definitions of "righteous" and be called to different actions because of it. But neither the definition nor the action should become our idol. Instead proximity to the Spirit of God—shown through ongoing listening, loving, and care—becomes our measure.

And Noah named his three sons Shem, Ham, and Japheth. See? Even righteous men sometimes make poor decisions.

A Refuge from Violence

¹¹ Now the earth was corrupt in God's sight, and the earth was filled with violence. ¹² And God saw the earth, and behold, it was corrupt; for all flesh had corrupted their way upon the earth. ¹³ And God said to Noah, "I have determined to make an end of all flesh; for the earth is filled with violence through them; behold, I will destroy them with the earth. ¹⁴ Make yourself an ark of gopher wood; make rooms in the ark, and cover it inside and out with pitch. ¹⁵ This is how you are to make it: the length of the ark three hundred cubits, its breadth fifty cubits, and its height thirty cubits. ¹⁶ Make a roof for the ark, and finish it to a cubit above; and set the door of the ark in its side; make it with lower, second, and third decks. ¹⁷ For behold, I will bring a flood of waters upon the earth, to destroy all flesh in which is the breath of life from under heaven; everything that is on the earth shall die. ¹⁸ But I will establish my covenant with you; and you shall come into the ark, you, your sons, your wife, and your sons' wives with you. ¹⁹ And of every living thing of all flesh, you shall bring two of every sort into the ark, to keep them alive with you; they shall be male and female. ²⁰ Of the birds according to their kinds, and of the animals according to their kinds, of every creeping thing of the ground according to its kind, two of every sort shall come in to you, to keep them alive. ²¹ Also take with you every sort of food that is eaten, and store it up; and it shall serve as food for you and for them." ²² Noah did this; he did all that God commanded him.

God then explains to Noah what he is about to do. He is going to make an end of all flesh because the world is "filled with violence".

This is as good a definition of sin as any, a fine description of why God gets upset with us. Violence indicates harm done to another. It carries connotations of injustice and self-interest. A surgeon removing a tumor with a scalpel is invasive and causes pain, but that's not exactly violence.

The tumor itself does violence, as do people hitting each other, berating each other, stealing from each other, and so on.

Another way to look at it is to say the world was full of people looking to promote their self-interest and willing to stop at nothing, including harming others, in order to get their way.

This is a critical corrective to those willing to trample over others to promote their definition of "good". Even if the original concept is good and holy, the violence one does while enforcing it renders those qualities moot. The end does not justify the means. Christians, especially, need to remember this in a world where most public portrayals of the faith involve violent looking (or sounding) protesters trying to make a point about God. Whatever evil they're protesting against probably isn't half as bad as attaching that kind of violence to God's name and calling it holy.

God tells Noah that he's about to meet violence with justice. He's going to send a flood to sweep away the wrongdoers, showing them the inevitable endpoint of sin, stopping their misdeeds forcibly. These violent people have abused and trampled each other and creation. They're going to get a bitter taste of their own medicine.

God also gives Noah a merciful out. He tells Noah to build a boat…a huge one. Noah and his family will ride out the storm. But they'll not be alone. They'll carry two of every animal to repopulate the earth after the flood. Creation is about to be made new again. The wrong will die so righteousness can live.

Noah's family is also to accompany him. God will establish a new covenant with them, following up on the first promise he made to Adam and Eve. This is another sign that this is meant to be a brand new creation.

Let's see if people can do better this time.

Another New Creation Story

7 Then the Lord said to Noah, "Go into the ark, you and all your household, for I have seen that you are righteous before me in this generation. 2 Take with you seven pairs of all clean animals, the male and his mate; and a pair of the animals that are not clean, the male and his mate; 3 and seven pairs of the birds of the air also, male and female, to keep their kind alive upon the face of all the earth. ⁴ For in seven days I will send rain upon the earth forty days and forty nights; and every living thing that I have made I will blot out from the face of the ground." ⁵ And Noah did all that the Lord had commanded him.

Chapter 7 begins with what seems like a basic counting problem. We just heard about two of each animal, now the updated memo says two of some, 14 of others. What's the deal?

Remember we said earlier that the stories in Genesis did not start out as a unified document, but were relayed through different traditions down through the years. This is one of those places where the traditions said two different things, so they included them both.

Notice the distinction this tradition was concerned with: clean and unclean animals. These were dietary and sacrificial terms established by law long after the Great Flood. This version of the story asks us to remember the importance of those edicts, claiming they were critical even back in Noah's time. Creation may be made anew, but the difference between acceptable and unacceptable is clear and unchanging.

So who boarded the ark really, a pair of each animal or a pair of some and seven pairs of others? Does it matter? If it did, we'd probably get a much clearer reading. People of faith are free to disagree on some matters. One pair people and seven pair people can all be faithful. The point of the story was the ark, flood, and a new world. It's a story of cleansing and redemption, not counting chickens and possums.

Hurry Up and Wait

⁶ Noah was six hundred years old when the flood of waters came upon the earth. ⁷ And Noah and his sons and his wife and his sons' wives with him went into the ark, to escape the waters of the flood. ⁸ Of clean animals, and of animals that are not clean, and of birds, and of everything that creeps on the ground, ⁹ two and two, male and female, went into the ark with Noah, as God had commanded Noah. ¹⁰ And after seven days the waters of the flood came upon the earth.

Then 600-year-old Noah spent what was undoubtedly the most uncomfortable week of his life on that boat with all those animals, waiting for the waters to come. Then they did, just as God had said they would.

Next time you think God's word is a long time coming, imagining sitting with ostriches and mole rats for a week while your wife gives you "the look" because you just spent your life savings on a dry-docked ocean liner with neither ocean nor a drop of rain in sight.

The Flood Arrives

11 In the six hundredth year of Noah's life, in the second month, on the seventeenth day of the month, on that day all the fountains of the great deep burst forth, and the windows of the heavens were opened. 12 And rain fell upon the earth forty days and forty nights. 13 On the very same day Noah and his sons, Shem and Ham and Japheth, and Noah's wife and the three wives of his sons with them entered the ark, 14 they and every beast according to its kind, and all the cattle according to their kinds, and every creeping thing that creeps on the earth according to its kind, every bird according to its kind, every bird of every sort. 15 They went into the ark with Noah, two and two of all flesh in which there was the breath of life. 16 And they that entered, male and female of all flesh, went in as God had commanded him; and the Lord shut him in.

17 The flood continued forty days upon the earth; and the waters increased, and bore up the ark, and it rose high above the earth. 18 The waters prevailed and increased greatly upon the earth; and the ark floated on the face of the waters. 19 And the waters prevailed so mightily upon the earth that all the high mountains under the whole heaven were covered; 20 the waters prevailed above the mountains, covering them fifteen cubits deep. 21 And all flesh died that moved upon the earth, birds, cattle, beasts, all swarming creatures that swarm upon the earth, and every man; 22 everything on the dry land in whose nostrils was the breath of life died. 23 He blotted out every living thing that was upon the face of the ground, man and animals and creeping things and birds of the air; they were blotted out from the earth. Only Noah was left, and those that were with him in the ark. 24 And the waters prevailed upon the earth a hundred and fifty days.

I mentioned above that numbers tend to get too much attention in scripture. Even so, the Bible tends to repeat certain numerals. 3, 7, 12, and 40 are all popular. Each has special meanings. 40 can be read simply as, "A whole bunch" or in this case, "a whole long time". 40 days and 40 nights means, "It rained as much as you can possibly imagine". When it finished, water covered the whole earth, drowning everything with the breath of life in its nostrils. The flood became a giant eraser, wiping the earth clean in a single, mighty deluge.

Note here the poetic justice as the "windows of heaven were opened" in Genesis 7:11. Remember the boundaries between heaven and earth being broken as the Nephilim hopped from heaven to earth? You can almost hear God saying, *"This* is what it looks like when boundaries are broken! You really don't want this to happen."

As the rain ceased, the small remnant in the ark were all that remained of humanity and God's promise to Adam and Eve. Creation would begin again with Noah's family and their raft full of animals. The erasing wasn't the end, rather the prelude to something new, another try.

God Remembers Noah

8 But God remembered Noah and all the beasts and all the cattle that were with him in the ark. And God made a wind blow over the earth, and the waters subsided; 2 the fountains of the deep and the windows of the heavens were closed, the rain from the heavens was restrained, 3 and the waters receded from the earth continually. At the end of a hundred and fifty days the waters had abated; 4 and in the seventh month, on the seventeenth day of the month, the ark came to rest upon the mountains of Ar'arat. 5 And the waters continued to abate until the tenth month; in the tenth month, on the first day of the month, the tops of the mountains were seen.

The first words of Chapter 8 are precious. "But God remembered Noah…" This is the flip side of "Noah walked with God." Theirs was a deep and intimate relationship. All the waters of the flood could not wash it away. God would not forget his companion, nor humanity.

All of us have moments when we feel like God has abandoned us. Usually they come when our world gets washed away. Nothing will make you feel better in those moments. Like Noah, all you can do is hold on and hope. God has not abandoned you; he remembers you. The deepest, most tragic flood is a prelude to something new. You may have to wait a while to see it, but no evil can overcome God's promise to restore you and the world.

GARDEN TO DESERT

Because he remembered Noah, God made a wind blow over the earth, hearkening back to the wind that blew over the face of the deep at the beginning of all things. The new creation was underway.

In Genesis 8:2 the boundaries between heaven and earth were set once again, this time to stay. Note the wording, "the rain from the heavens was restrained". The implication is that not everything otherworldly is friendly to us. God serves as our atmosphere, protecting us from forces (Primeval? Natural? Supernatural?) that we could not endure without him.

We don't give God nearly enough credit for this. Without God's sheltering hand, chaos and emptiness would overwhelm us just as surely as the sun's rays would fry us were the ozone not over our heads. The world went bad when the boundary between heaven and earth got jumped by the Nephilim. The world went *really* bad when that boundary disappeared entirely. God shelters his people, making order out of chaos. We need this in order to survive.

With order restored to Noah's world, the waters began to recede to their normal levels. For 150 days the ark floated on nothing but ocean. Afterwards the keel hit bottom…on the top of a mountain. That's how far reaching these waters were. Three months later actual mountaintops appeared.

The Waters Recede

6 At the end of forty days Noah opened the window of the ark which he had made, 7 and sent forth a raven; and it went to and fro until the waters were dried up from the earth. 8 Then he sent forth a dove from him, to see if the waters had subsided from the face of the ground; 9 but the dove found no place to set her foot, and she returned to him to the ark, for the waters were still on the face of the whole earth. So he put forth his hand and took her and brought her into the ark with him. 10 He waited another seven days, and again he sent forth the dove out of the ark; 11 and the dove came back to him in the evening, and lo, in her mouth a freshly plucked olive leaf; so Noah knew that the waters had subsided from the earth. 12 Then he waited another seven days, and sent forth the dove; and she did not return to him anymore.

40 days later (there's 40 again) Noah did as most of us do in such situations, sending out a test raven equipped with the latest sonar to take a sounding

of the ocean depth. But "Ra(ven)dar 1.0" had a glitch and the bird simply flew around until it could land, never returning to drop its data back at the ark. (NASA engineers will commiserate, no doubt.) This leads us to the important Biblical lesson, "Never trust a Raven".

Having learned from his first experiment, Noah upgraded his hardware to a dove. Three times he sent out the bird. The first time it returned without any sighting. The second time it came back with an olive leaf, a sign that the waters had reached tree level, at least. Seven days later Noah released the dove and it disappeared. That's when Noah knew it had found a place to land and he could release the ark's captives.

God's New Promise

[13] By the first day of the first month of Noah's six hundred and first year, the water had dried up from the earth. Noah then removed the covering from the ark and saw that the surface of the ground was dry. [14] By the twenty-seventh day of the second month the earth was completely dry.

[15] Then God said to Noah, [16] "Come out of the ark, you and your wife and your sons and their wives. [17] Bring out every kind of living creature that is with you—the birds, the animals, and all the creatures that move along the ground—so they can multiply on the earth and be fruitful and increase in number on it."

[18] So Noah came out, together with his sons and his wife and his sons' wives. [19] All the animals and all the creatures that move along the ground and all the birds—everything that moves on land—came out of the ark, one kind after another.

Noah and his family emerging from the ark can be compared to newborns emerging from the birth canal. Another new creation was at hand. God gave similar instruction to this batch animals as he had the first. "Be fruitful and multiply. Grow this thing." The new world was off to a solid start.

[20] Then Noah built an altar to the Lord and, taking some of all the clean animals and clean birds, he sacrificed burnt offerings on it. [21] The Lord smelled the pleasing aroma and said in his heart: "Never again will I curse the ground because of humans, even though every inclination of the human heart is evil from childhood. And never again will I destroy all living creatures, as I have done.

²² "As long as the earth endures,
seedtime and harvest,
cold and heat,
summer and winter,
day and night
will never cease."

Having just seen a first-hand (and half-year-long) demonstration of God's power, Noah offered a proper sacrifice to him immediately upon landing. This pleased God.

Then Genesis gives us a rare glimpse into God's mind as he vows never to try anything like this again. Even knowing that humans will do evil—that his cleaning wouldn't last forever—God still promises to take care of them, keeping times and seasons ordered for their benefit.

The experiment "Wipe All Obvious Evil Off of the Earth" did not end up supporting its original hypothesis. Evil wasn't gone. Sin had traveled right along with the humans, bobbing up and down above the water in that ark. No subsection of humanity—even one comprised of the best humans walking closest to God—is able to leave it behind. Since "every inclination of the human heart is evil from childhood", smiting evil not be effective short of ending all creation and starting over.

New Blessings and Commands

9 Then God blessed Noah and his sons, saying to them, "Be fruitful and increase in number and fill the earth. ² The fear and dread of you will fall on all the beasts of the earth, and on all the birds in the sky, on every creature that moves along the ground, and on all the fish in the sea; they are given into your hands. ³ Everything that lives and moves about will be food for you. Just as I gave you the green plants, I now give you everything.

⁴ "But you must not eat meat that has its lifeblood still in it. ⁵ And for your lifeblood I will surely demand an accounting. I will demand an accounting from every animal. And from each human being, too, I will demand an accounting for the life of another human being.

⁶ "Whoever sheds human blood,
 by humans shall their blood be shed;
for in the image of God
 has God made mankind.

⁷ As for you, be fruitful and increase in number; multiply on the earth and increase upon it."

Every time God creates the world a covenant accompanies the new creation. Covenants are descriptions of the way things should be and promises from God that he will do what is necessary to make things right.

The covenant in Genesis 9 begins with the same instruction God gives to all living beings: be fruitful and multiply. Create life and fill the earth.

Noah and his sons also get their version of the gift God once gave to Adam. Everything in creation would be given into their hands. Note the subtle change in Genesis 9:2 though. Adam was given dominion that he might name and order things well, becoming like a shepherd. But Noah's family live in a fallen world, not the Garden come again. Their dominion is held in force by the fear and dread their charges feel towards them. Appropriately so, for all of those charges are now branded as edible…a direct departure from the fruit-and-veggie diet in Eden. As it turns out Noah and company didn't just preserve ecological diversity in the ark, they stored their lunch there.

But God gives an admonition not to eat meat with its lifeblood still in it, a prelude to prohibiting shedding each other's blood. Life is to be respected. Living beings reflect God. We are God's children. The violence that preceded the flood is branded wrong, unacceptable. Those who practice it will fall to it. There was no need for this kind of proclamation in idyllic Eden. In a world broken by sin, justice must accompany mercy.

Then God urges humankind to create more life once again. They are to be people of life, not of death. They are meant to enrich and grow into the world, not impoverish it. God says the same thing to us today. Whether or not we bear children is immaterial. Our words and actions either create life or destroy it. God charges us to be life-bringers.

Even More Promises

⁸ Then God said to Noah and to his sons with him: ⁹ "I now establish my covenant with you and with your descendants after you ¹⁰ and with every living creature that was with you—the birds, the livestock and all the wild animals, all those that came out of the ark with you—every living creature on earth. ¹¹ I establish my covenant with you: Never again will all life be destroyed by the waters of a flood; never again will there be a flood to destroy the earth."

¹² And God said, "This is the sign of the covenant I am making between me and you and every living creature with you, a covenant for all generations to come: ¹³ I have set my rainbow in the clouds, and it will be the sign of the covenant between me and the earth. ¹⁴ Whenever I bring clouds over the earth and the rainbow appears in the clouds, ¹⁵ I will remember my covenant between me and you and all living creatures of every kind. Never again will the waters become a flood to destroy all life. ¹⁶ Whenever the rainbow appears in the clouds, I will see it and remember the everlasting covenant between God and all living creatures of every kind on the earth."

¹⁷ So God said to Noah, "This is the sign of the covenant I have established between me and all life on the earth."

The thought that flitted through God's head in Genesis 8:21 is spoken explicitly in Genesis 9:11. God promises all living beings that he will never again flood the earth and destroy it. He has the power and he has reason, but he voluntarily withholds his hand because he cares more about people than about either power or reason. This is the way God operates.

Many churches attempt to follow God by gaining power and justifying their reasoning over and against the people they were meant to serve and bring life to. These churches may claim they're following God. They're not following the one we see here.

You can smell a church that values power over people almost immediately. When a newcomer enters they're full of questions and don'ts. "Who are you? Who are you related to? Don't sit there, that's reserved. Don't touch the knives in the kitchen drawer, they're laid out just so. Don't question or, God forbid, try to change how we do things. Do you know how much better we are than those around us?" Few churches are quite that crass about it, but you don't have to scratch down far to find their core belief in themselves. Churches can get pretty big convincing people that they're joining a powerful, exclusive club of the right-minded and well-destined.

Meanwhile here's God, quietly picking up all the people those churches are mowing over and leaving out. He says to them, "I'm your God. Yes…yours. Those cranky people missed the point entirely." When we use our power to diminish a person, God will lift up that person and favor them. This is true even if the power we use is supposedly the power of faith.

Our purpose is not to wipe out evil folks from our midst. Our purpose is to thank God that he's not wiping *us* out again. We remember and honor his mercy to us by showing it to the people around us.

To seal his promise, God sets the rainbow in the clouds, a sky-marker to remind him (and us) when rain appears that it won't overwhelm everything. (This was thousands of years before, "Siri? Remind me not to destroy all life on earth today.") When we see the rainbow we receive reassurance. God will not break his promise.

Notice too that God is thinking big here, establishing this covenant with all living creatures on earth. Noah and his sons may be at the top of the food chain, but they're not the only beings God cares about. Humans equate "ones on top" with "ones that matter". In ideal world, those on top use their power to bless those underneath, making everybody matter. That's what God does.

The Ham Goes Bad

[18] *The sons of Noah who came out of the ark were Shem, Ham and Japheth. (Ham was the father of Canaan.)* [19] *These were the three sons of Noah, and from them came the people who were scattered over the whole earth.*

[20] *Noah, a man of the soil, proceeded to plant a vineyard.* [21] *When he drank some of its wine, he became drunk and lay uncovered inside his tent.* [22] *Ham, the father of Canaan, saw his father naked and told his two brothers outside.* [23] *But Shem and Japheth took a garment and laid it across their shoulders; then they walked in backward and covered their father's naked body. Their faces were turned the other way so that they would not see their father naked.*

²⁴ *When Noah awoke from his wine and found out what his youngest son had done to him,* ²⁵ *he said,*

"Cursed be Canaan!
 The lowest of slaves
 will he be to his brothers."

²⁶ *He also said,*

"Praise be to the Lord, the God of Shem!
 May Canaan be the slave of Shem.
²⁷ *May God extend Japheth's territory;*
 may Japheth live in the tents of Shem,
 and may Canaan be the slave of Japheth."

²⁸ *After the flood Noah lived 350 years.* ²⁹ *Noah lived a total of 950 years, and then he died.*

Noah used his newfound power as Master of the New Creation to plant a vineyard. Then he promptly got drunk and naked. Classy.

One of Noah's sons—the one named after lunchmeat—saw his father's predicament. Not only did he not help, he ogled his elder then told his two brothers about it as if it were juicy gossip. (Perhaps as revenge for the whole naming thing?) The brothers got a blanket and did a backwards shuffle into the tent so as not to shame their father in his distress. Noah appreciated that and promptly invoked a blessing for them and a curse on the son who had shamed him.

It's odd to think of, but some of our greatest blessings come from our handling of evil, or at least awkwardness. When something's wrong, what do you do? Do you observe it as entertainment? (See also: any number of talk shows that claim to "help" people by putting them on display for the amusement of others.) Do you point fingers? Do you scuttle away and spread the news? Or do you quietly, respectfully, and kindly move to address the situation as best as you can, honoring the one in distress as you would want to be honored in similar circumstances, even if their own wrong behavior caused that distress?

A Tower to the Sky

Chapter 10 of Genesis is concerned with the lineage of the elders, drawing it further down through history. You may read it if you care to.

Chapter 11 begins with a curious story about a tower that to this day no two people pronounce the same.

11 Now the whole world had one language and a common speech. ² As people moved eastward, they found a plain in Shinar and settled there.

³ They said to each other, "Come, let's make bricks and bake them thoroughly." They used brick instead of stone, and tar for mortar. ⁴ Then they said, "Come, let us build ourselves a city, with a tower that reaches to the heavens, so that we may make a name for ourselves; otherwise we will be scattered over the face of the whole earth."

⁵ But the Lord came down to see the city and the tower the people were building. ⁶ The Lord said, "If as one people speaking the same language they have begun to do this, then nothing they plan to do will be impossible for them.⁷ Come, let us go down and confuse their language so they will not understand each other."

⁸ So the Lord scattered them from there over all the earth, and they stopped building the city. ⁹ That is why it was called Babel—because there the Lord confused the language of the whole world. From there the Lord scattered them over the face of the whole earth.

Humankind is advancing. People are beginning to develop a sense of architecture and technology. They're getting smart and shrewd, moving beyond the primitive. But to what end? In Genesis 11:4 they design a grand plan to "make a name for themselves" with a tower that "reaches to the heavens".

We find the sins of the ancestors coming around again as these people seek to rival God (Adam and Eve's mistake) by breaking the boundary between heaven and earth (the mistake that prompted the flood). Needing to "make a name for themselves" implies that the name and power God has bestowed upon them as his children isn't enough. They want more and they'll do anything to get it.

One of the complaints about modern society is that we have better tools than ever before, but lack the wisdom to use them for goodness. Turns out that's an age-old condition.

In Genesis 11:6 God claims that if humanity is left unchecked, they'll be able to accomplish everything they plan. Once upon a time when I read this verse, I thought God seemed petty or mean, like he wanted to hold humanity back because he was afraid of them. Now I understand that he's afraid *for* them.

The "plans" of humanity God is referring to aren't technologically-inspired, Star Trek utopian dreams. God is referencing our sin, selfishness, and propensity for breaking the world. If your child found a really ingenious way of doing something awful, you'd stop him from doing that awful thing even if his methodology was impressive. That's the situation God found himself in. He said, "If humanity is allowed to control the world unchecked, they're going to destroy it and each other. So let's make that control a little harder."

God's solution was fascinating and simple: he "confused" their language so one builder couldn't understand another. Builder #1 would say, "Please may I have some bricks?" while Builder #2 heard, "Sir, your igloo is full of pudding." Tower construction was about to hit a major setback.

As languages diverged, so did people. The initial fear in 11:4 "being scattered over the face of the earth" became reality in 11:9. This happens to us too. In trying to avoid an eventuality we fear, we cause it to happen. This is especially true when we try to seize power, forcing the world into our way instead of questioning what our way should be in faithful service to God. In this case the ancient peoples dispersed across the land, each harboring their own language. They couldn't accomplish their goals anymore. They didn't even know how to talk to each other.

4 STORIES OF ABRAHAM

The latter part of Genesis 11 describes the generations between Noah's son Shem and the next significant figure in our story, Abraham. It recounts 8 generations following Shem, ending with Terah, Abraham's father. The most notable thing about this list is the diminished lifespan of these later elders. The list lingers in the 100-400 year range for each patriarch, still significant but far short of the 700-900 year lifespans that were common earlier. The connection with Eden and eternal life was failing.

Genesis 11: 27-32 introduces us to Abram—not yet known as Abraham--the son of Terah, who lived with his father in the town of Ur. Abram married a wife, Sarai, but she was unable to conceive and they had no children. Midway through his life Terah scooped up Abram and Sarai, plus Abram's nephew Lot, and left Ur for the land of Canaan. Ur was a great city near Babylon, Canaan a stretch of coastland on the Mediterranean. The party only made it halfway, traveling up the Euphrates River and stopping at the town of Harran. They settled there until Terah died, which is where our story picks up.

Receiving a Call

12 The Lord had said to Abram, "Go from your country, your people and your father's household to the land I will show you.

The pivotal moment in Abram's life started with a call from God. People often say of ministers and missionaries, "They have a call". This is accurate as far as it goes, but the description reduces faith to a possession carried by a select few. A call is not something you have, it's something you engage in. And we're all called in one way or another. You have a call…a purpose for which you were placed on the earth.

We're used to thinking of calls in terms of "want to" or "don't want to". We run potential calls through a battery of questions. Will this be easy or hard? Is it what I expected or different? Will it be advantageous to me or will it require me to sacrifice too much? All of these miss the point. Calls are not choices between good and bad, beneficial or not. They're the difference between meaning and emptiness, doing something that endures and something that is quickly forgotten.

Abram could have refused to budge, remaining comfortably in Harran. But then he never would have become "Abraham" and we never would have heard of him. He'd just be some dead dude…we wouldn't even know his name. Abram may have seen his call as a choice between staying or going, but it was really a choice between meaning something incredible to the world and not meaning much.

That's true of our calls as well. Whatever brings meaning into this world because you do it, whatever you accomplish that will outlast you, that's your call. Your call may be a profession. You might live out your call through your family. Calls can come through a particular talent or getting thrust into odd situations you don't know how to deal with. You may find multiple calls at once. Sometimes your call changes as you go through life. However you realize your call, when you pursue it faithfully, serving God and others as you do so, it gives your life enduring meaning that it wouldn't have had otherwise.

When you think of things this way, the call question looks different. No longer is it, "Do I have a call or not?" Nor is it, "Should I follow my call or refuse?" Who would opt to *not* have any meaning or purpose? Calls force us to ask more important questions than these. "What is my call and how do I pursue it in the most faithful way possible today? How am I being guided into doing what is needful for those around me?"

For Abram, the answer was fairly clear. God told him. "Get up and go to the land I will show you." From that moment on, Abram's camel came equipped with heavenly GPS.

God's Pledge to Abram and His Descendants

² "I will make you into a great nation,
  and I will bless you;
I will make your name great,
  and you will be a blessing.
³ I will bless those who bless you,
  and whoever curses you I will curse;
and all peoples on earth
  will be blessed through you"

In Genesis 12: 2-3 God detailed the outcome of Abram's call, giving Abram a sneak peek at the meaning his life would have. Abram would be made into a great nation. God would favor him, making his name renown. Abram himself would be a blessing to others, a conduit of God's favor to those around him. Those who favored Abram, God would favor. Those who did not favor him, God would not be pleased with.

As if that wasn't enough, God promised that all people on earth would be blessed through Abram. This later came true, as Abram's descendants carried God's word for years. Had they not done so, we wouldn't have it today. The Book of Genesis and this book *about* Genesis are direct results of God's promise to Abram coming true.

Abram's descendants were also the people from whom Jesus, the Savior, would come. The gospel of Matthew begins by drawing out Jesus' lineage. The name at the top of the list, the patriarch at the root of Jesus' family tree, is Abraham.

The Journey Begins

⁴ So Abram went, as the Lord had told him; and Lot went with him. Abram was seventy-five years old when he set out from Harran. ⁵ He took his wife Sarai, his nephew Lot, all the possessions they had accumulated and the people they had acquired in Harran, and they set out for the land of Canaan, and they arrived there.

GARDEN TO DESERT

⁶Abram traveled through the land as far as the site of the great tree of Moreh at Shechem. At that time the Canaanites were in the land. ⁷ The Lord appeared to Abram and said, "To your offspring I will give this land." So he built an altar there to the Lord, who had appeared to him.

⁸ From there he went on toward the hills east of Bethel and pitched his tent, with Bethel on the west and Ai on the east. There he built an altar to the Lord and called on the name of the Lord.

⁹ Then Abram set out and continued toward the Negev.

Genesis 12:4 says, "Abram went," following God's call just like that. It was a huge journey to describe with just two words. The trip from Ur of the Chaldees to Harran, where Abram resided when God called him, had been 600 miles. The Promised Land lay another 400 miles away, making Abram's journey 1000 miles long. That's a daunting trip even today. Imaging walking it through unfamiliar territory with everything you own trailing behind you on the backs of camels and donkeys. With Abram went his wife, Sarai, and his nephew, Lot.

At a couple significant stops Abram built altars, crediting the Lord for the journey and asking guidance as he traveled. We tend to judge journeys—spiritual and physical--by their destination. If we ended up in a good place, it was a good trip. But destination isn't the only important part of our faith journey. Like Abram, we walk in faith not really knowing what's around the next bend…unable to clearly perceive our destination. We cannot control our ending point, but we can honor the process we go through to get there.

Few people receive their realizations about faith all at once from angels on high trumpeting news. We read scripture day after day, participate in faith communities week after week, and slowly, as we engage in that process, wisdom seeps into us. Each small point of engagement becomes a marking place, our altar to the Lord along our journey echoing the ones Abram built.

These little "altar moments" are important. They remind us that we're connected to God, that we're not traveling alone nor is the journey all our own. They allow us to measure progress, to see the scope of our evolution in faith. Sometimes if we're lucky they also serve as guideposts for those around us. Bethel and Shechem , where Abram built his altars, would become important to his offspring and their descendants.

We can't expect to start a journey at 5 years old, think randomly our whole lives, then show up at 50 in the right place, fully understanding the trip. Life isn't a big leap, it's a series of small steps. The only way to find faith in the big moments is to walk in faith in the hundred little moments we encounter each day.

Trouble in the Promised Land

10 Now there was a famine in the land, and Abram went down to Egypt to live there for a while because the famine was severe.

When Abram reached the Promised Land, he found it wasn't all milk and honey. The entire region was suffering a famine, a catastrophic lack of food.

Famine is a critical problem in any age, but particularly in ancient times. The only sources of food came from local fields. When food was scarce, nobody ate…not people, not livestock, and least of all new visitors with their camels. Abram was unable to stay. Instead he recorded the first instance of a common theme in the Bible: when people got in trouble they headed to Egypt. This powerful nation always seemed to be equipped with whatever earthly goods God's people were missing. But in almost every case trouble arose, as it would here.

Life's road is long but seldom easy. Charlatans would sell you the idea that people of faith get exempted from life's struggles, earning free pass from its difficulties. I've not yet met that person, nor do such people show up in the Bible much. Imagine Abram's frustration after traveling hundreds of miles to a strange land while following God's call, only to find out that the land couldn't support him. Can't you just see Sarai looking over at her husband as they made the turn for Egypt, pleading, "Can't you just pull over and ask for directions?"

And Abram replies, "I did! This was it!!!"

Yet neither Abram nor his family quit. They walked hundreds of more miles to another foreign land, knowing they'd eventually have to retrace every step.

The quality of a life is not determined by the amount of difficulties faced, but by holding on and overcoming them. This is true of all lives, including the lives of the most faithful and blessed of God's children.

A Crafty Scheme

[11] As he was about to enter Egypt, he said to his wife Sarai, "I know what a beautiful woman you are. [12] When the Egyptians see you, they will say, 'This is his wife.' Then they will kill me but will let you live. [13] Say you are my sister, so that I will be treated well for your sake and my life will be spared because of you."

[14] When Abram came to Egypt, the Egyptians saw that Sarai was a very beautiful woman. [15] And when Pharaoh's officials saw her, they praised her to Pharaoh, and she was taken into his palace. [16] He treated Abram well for her sake, and Abram acquired sheep and cattle, male and female donkeys, male and female servants, and camels.

[17] But the Lord inflicted serious diseases on Pharaoh and his household because of Abram's wife Sarai. [18] So Pharaoh summoned Abram. "What have you done to me?" he said. "Why didn't you tell me she was your wife? [19] Why did you say, 'She is my sister,' so that I took her to be my wife? Now then, here is your wife. Take her and go!" [20] Then Pharaoh gave orders about Abram to his men, and they sent him on his way, with his wife and everything he had.

Abram perceived another sort of difficulty in entering Egypt. Other men might desire his wife and figuring the most expedient way to get her would be killing him. To avoid this, he arranged a con with her. He asked her to identify herself as his sister. Then men would approach him with generosity, hoping to win his favor and earn her hand.

As we grow up we learn to protect ourselves: socially, emotionally, sometimes even physically. This is necessary in a world that would eat us alive otherwise. Even so, it's good to remember that the only real security lies in God. Without God sheltering us, all of our schemes come to naught. At best we preserve ourselves for a while, living in fear that others will take away what we hold most precious. Trusting in God's will to save us, nothing can be taken that will not be restored. Our heart rests not on temporary things—be they blessings or troubles—but with eternal peace.

Abram sought to protect himself in Egypt. His plan didn't work. Or rather it worked *too* well. Pharaoh's officials noticed Sarai and took her into the royal palace, presumably to become a royal concubine or wife. As the leading male member of Sarai's family (her "brother"), Abram was rewarded richly more richly than he ever dreamed with livestock and servants…the currency of the time. The only catch was, he just lost his wife.

God was not having this. He sent disease into Pharaoh's household, which would have been taken as a sign of divine disfavor. Somehow Pharaoh and his staff isolated Sarai as the cause of that disfavor. Pharaoh summoned Abram and the jig was up.

Taking another man's wife to be your own was bad form in any country. Heavenly anger falling upon the palace because of it underscored the offense. Pharaoh ordered Abram, Sarai, and everyone associated with them out of the kingdom at once.

A Selfish Choice

13 So Abram went up from Egypt to the Negev, with his wife and everything he had, and Lot went with him. 2 Abram had become very wealthy in livestock and in silver and gold.

3 From the Negev he went from place to place until he came to Bethel, to the place between Bethel and Ai where his tent had been earlier 4 and where he had first built an altar. There Abram called on the name of the Lord.

5 Now Lot, who was moving about with Abram, also had flocks and herds and tents. 6 But the land could not support them while they stayed together, for their possessions were so great that they were not able to stay together. 7 And quarreling arose between Abram's herders and Lot's. The Canaanites and Perizzites were also living in the land at that time.

8 So Abram said to Lot, "Let's not have any quarreling between you and me, or between your herders and mine, for we are close relatives. 9 Is not the whole land before you? Let's part company. If you go to the left, I'll go to the right; if you go to the right, I'll go to the left."

10 Lot looked around and saw that the whole plain of the Jordan toward Zoar was well watered, like the garden of the Lord, like the land of Egypt. (This was before the Lord destroyed Sodom and Gomorrah.) 11 So Lot chose for himself the whole plain of the Jordan and set out toward the east. The two men parted company: 12 Abram lived in the land of Canaan, while Lot lived among the cities of the plain and pitched his tents near Sodom. 13 Now the people of Sodom were wicked and were sinning greatly against the Lord.

14 The Lord said to Abram after Lot had parted from him, "Look around from where you are, to the north and south, to the east and west. 15 All the land that you see I will give to you and your offspring forever. 16 I will make your offspring like the dust of the earth, so that if anyone could count the dust, then your offspring could be counted. 17 Go, walk through the length and breadth of the land, for I am giving it to you."

¹⁸ So Abram went to live near the great trees of Mamre at Hebron, where he pitched his tents. There he built an altar to the Lord.

A little wiser and a lot richer, Abram journeyed from Egypt back to the Promised Land, now free from famine. A family quarrel arose because of the new-found wealth in livestock acquired from Pharaoh. Hemmed in by locals, competing for precious water and crops to feed their abundant animals, the herdsmen of Abram and his nephew Lot began to fight. Civil war was brewing within the family.

Abram solved this in a gracious manner. He took Lot to a place with a view, showed him the entire land, and said, "You call dibs on whatever part you want. I'll go another direction from you."

Lot surveyed the landscape and made his decision. He chose the entire plain of the Jordan river…the biggest source of water and most fertile land possible. The plot also featured a charming city or two for those who liked urban life.

They say the three rules of real estate are "Location, Location, Location". Lot skated away with water, food, and access to civilization, leaving his uncle to make do with less desirable territory.

This was an impudent move on Lot's part. He was the nephew, the younger of the two men. He owed all the wealth trailing behind him to Abram and Sarai. The entire trip was happening because of his uncle, not because of him. Abram was being generous by letting Lot pick first. Lot did not return that generosity. Lot's decision favored himself at the expense of the man he should be favoring above all men.

After Lot left to claim the prime real estate, the Lord comforted Abram, saying, "Look around. Everything you see is going to be yours. You're not going to lose, but gain more than you've ever imagined." God told Abram that he'd have offspring as numerous as the dust of the earth and that there was no way he could out-walk the land that they'd inherit from him.

Abram, in typical fashion, headed to a likely camping spot and built yet another altar to the Lord. God wasn't forgetting him and he wasn't forgetting God. Abram's simple remembrance would end up far more powerful and enriching than the grand schemes Lot was planning.

Not Owing Evil

Genesis 14 begins with several local monarchs fighting. The Kings of Sodom and Gomorrah, the cities right next to Lot's land, ended up losing the battle, getting stuck in tar pits, of all things. Their victorious enemies carried off all their wealth, which included Lot, his family, and all his possessions. (It's only after you've bought the house that you find out how annoying the neighbors are.)

When this was reported to Abram, he gathered the men of his household trained in war—318 in all—and set off to rescue his nephew. Using a sneak attack at night, he managed to rout the enemy and recover the captives and their possessions. After freeing Lot and restoring him, Abram wanted to make good with the other kings, returning their stolen possessions to them. But...

21 The king of Sodom said to Abram, "Give me the people and keep the goods for yourself."

22 But Abram said to the king of Sodom, "With raised hand I have sworn an oath to the Lord, God Most High, Creator of heaven and earth, 23 that I will accept nothing belonging to you, not even a thread or the strap of a sandal, so that you will never be able to say, 'I made Abram rich.' 24 I will accept nothing but what my men have eaten and the share that belongs to the men who went with me—to Aner, Eshkol and Mamre. Let them have their share."

The King of Sodom offered to make Abram even richer than he was already, giving the entire plunder to him. Abram, presaging the fair trade and ethical investment movements of today, refused to take any wealth that came from wicked hands. He refused to let the king or anyone else think that Sodom's wealth had made him rich rather than God. He took a share for the soldiers around him, but refused to take anything for himself…a direct contrast to the actions of his nephew in the last chapter.

The story invites us to reflect on the power of generosity versus the power of greed. Selfishness appears to get one ahead in the short term, but selfish Lot was swept away by a war he had no chance of controlling. Abram rode to Lot's rescue by winning a battle he had no business winning. The fruits of greed withered while the power of righteousness prevailed.

This story also reminds us that everything we do is a witness, whether we intend it to be or not. Abram may have desired that wealth, but he decided giving the correct witness to Sodom and the world was more important than riches.

Few situations in our lives are truly neutral. We either show faith to others through our actions or we show something else. We either bring life to the world or bring death. People see. They know and learn from us. What we do matters.

Abram's Great Reward

15 After this, the word of the Lord came to Abram in a vision:

"Do not be afraid, Abram.
  I am your shield,
  your very great reward."

Chapter 15 contains another dialogue between Abram and the Lord. Fresh off the victory over the local rulers, God tells Abram that he need not worry about worldly powers. God himself would be Abram's shield. God would also be his "very great reward".

We usually regard the positive effects that come from God's blessings (wealth, health, etc.) as the blessings themselves. We consider money or longevity our reward. But God promised *himself* as a reward to Abram. What riches could compare with that? Infinite love, joy, peace, and life would be Abram's. These would become his inheritance, God's gift to all his offspring. This would hold true whether those offspring were as rich as Abram himself or sat on the street penniless.

The things we call blessings come and go. God's self-giving nature lasts forever. We must be careful not to confuse the two.

Children Like the Stars

² But Abram said, "Sovereign Lord, what can you give me since I remain childless and the one who will inherit my estate is Eliezer of Damascus?"³ And Abram said, "You have given me no children; so a servant in my household will be my heir."

⁴ Then the word of the Lord came to him: "This man will not be your heir, but a son who is your own flesh and blood will be your heir." ⁵ He took him outside and said, "Look up at the sky and count the stars—if indeed you can count them." Then he said to him, "So shall your offspring be."

Abram responds to God's declaration with a heartfelt question. In his words we hear the ache of his deepest longing, as yet unfulfilled. Abram had heard the talk about children, but he hadn't seen any yet. He and Sarai remained childless. When Abram died, his head steward would inherent everything he owned.

But God replied that this would not be so. He reiterated his promise of children as numerous as grains of dust, just more poetically this time. "Can you count the stars? That's how many offspring you'll have." Abram's family would be so big he wouldn't even be able to number it.

Sometimes we think God doesn't know what we need or want just because we haven't gotten it yet. He knows. He delights in fulfilling our needs. Filling us up has been God's specialty since the beginning of time.

Sometimes we misidentify our needs. For most of us, "I need more money in order to be happy" isn't precisely true. Getting more money wouldn't fill the emptiness inside us, so it's not surprising that this prayer isn't answered immediately for everyone. Plus basic economics says that if everyone gets more money, the money isn't worth as much anymore, leaving everyone pretty much where they were before.

For other people, like Abram, fulfillment is a matter of timing. We might have the right desire, but we're not in the right place among the right people at the right time to see it come true. This happens all the time with romantic relationships. We seek out partners to fulfill us, often settling for less than we desire, not understanding why we're still not happy. Then finally we figure out that if we walk with integrity and show goodness to the world, we're already full. We don't need a partner to fill us up. Then guess what? Mr. or Ms. Right appears and our dream comes true. We weren't ready before and neither was the world around us. Now we are and it happens.

We shouldn't just sit back and wait for God to do something in our lives. Abram didn't. He asked and he sought. The longings of our heart often lead us to our true calling, which we find by pursuing them. Like Abram, we should walk our path and chase after goodness every day.

But just as fruit comes in due season, so come the tangible signs of God's favor. Patience is a necessary component of faith. Pick the fruit too soon and it's sour. When it's ripe, it's also sweetest.

The True Meaning of Righteousness

6 Abram believed the Lord, and he credited it to him as righteousness.

Genesis 15:6 deserves to be isolated, underlined, and marked in highlighting pen as a verse none of us ever forget. The Apostle Paul didn't. He would later cite it in Romans as one of the quintessential examples of faith in all of scripture.

The key word in this sentence is "believed". Our understanding of faith hinges on it.

We've been taught that belief is a mental process, usually meaning we agree with something. We "believe in" the things we have affinity for: political parties, philosophies, and the like.

Failing that, we sometimes come to believe things that are proven to us. By this we mean we understand the subject and we are intellectually convinced it is true.

In both cases we're talking about believing things that have already been demonstrated. We observe, we rationalize, we credit, therefore we "believe".

The belief being talked about in Abraham's verses is none of those things. Abram may have approved of God's promise, but he hadn't seen it yet. He had plenty of reasons not to believe intellectually. He was old, as was Sarai. They had no children. The longing inside him had become a gnawing doubt, to the point that when God promised to give his own self to Abram, Abram's reply was, "Yeah, but what about this???"

Abram may have believed intellectually that God *could* give him children, but believing that he *would* was a different matter altogether.

The best description of the faith Abram expressed in Genesis 15:6 is TRUST. Abram didn't *know* God was going to do this. He couldn't *prove* it. It hadn't been *demonstrated* to him and he couldn't begin to *understand* how it would happen. *But in the absence of all these things, Abram still trusted that God would do as God said he would.* And this trust was reckoned to Abram as righteousness.

"Belief", the way we define it, happens when we're sure, knowledgeable, and in agreement with a subject. Trust happens precisely when all these things are absent, when we have nothing else left. Belief puts us in control, trust happens when we admit we're out of control.

God doesn't give a crap about our belief. It's faulty anyway. God reckons trust as righteousness. It's the only right thing that people with screwed up beliefs like us can manage.

Speaking of righteousness…we think it depends on doing the right things. But we don't understand the right thing to do. Our vision has been bent by sin. What we call "good" is inevitably imperfect. We're incapable of being perfectly right. That's why we needed God to save us instead of just waltzing back into Eden ourselves.

But God says to Abram here—and by extension to us—that righteousness is different than we thought. Even though we can't be good ourselves, even though we live in a fallen world, we can still trust. *Trust and believe*

I often ask my son to trust me even when he doesn't believe me. He doesn't know that red-hot burner on the stove will hurt him. He's not touched one. He doesn't understand electricity and principles of heat conduction. He doesn't even know how to turn on the stove. But dad says to him, "Don't touch". When he trusts that—even not knowing why—he'll be safe. If he mistrusts, if he think the world runs on the basis of what he perceives and believes, he'll get burned.

Trust equals righteousness. Belief in our ability to make the right choices and control the world equals death.

Abram and Sarai couldn't have a child. They had no idea what to do about it. Everything they tried had failed. All they could do was trust.

What great hope for the lost, the lonely, all who fall short in the world and are powerless to correct it. Bright, shiny people who get everything their way and claim to be "good" actually aren't. They're imperfect like everyone else, but they don't admit it. They "know", but their knowing leaves no need to trust. This is not righteousness, it's illusion. Meanwhile the beggar, the tax collector, the prostitutes and lepers have nothing left to them

GARDEN TO DESERT

but to hope and trust in God. In doing so, they become more righteous than the saints.

Belief is an internal quality. Trust is a relationship. Believe disappears in the face of doubt. The need for trust increases the more precarious the situation is. Whether you believe in and understand God intellectually is a relatively minor thing. (Does your belief cause him to exist or cease to exist?) But God cares very much that you trust in him.

Churches have wasted centuries trying to get people to believe in God when they should have been showing people they can trust in God. They're two different impulses entirely and much of the current negative public perception of churches can be traced to Christian communities following the wrong route.

Teaching people to believe in God entails proving, arguing, dividing, and ultimately rejecting if the proof doesn't work. So many churches operate on the basis of, "We believe, you don't." From this stems all the churchy ugliness that makes most people cringe. Holier-than-thou people look at the new folks with distain, demanding they measure up before they're allowed in God's company. Angry sign-wielders on the corner yell horrible things at folks who are different than they. Preachers use scripture to convince their congregations that they're right and others are wrong, that they're the chosen ones and everyone else is doomed. This is where teaching "belief" leads.

Showing people they can trust takes patience, kindness, learning about others and their situations, speaking in someone else's language, engaging in a world beyond yourself. It means comforting people through difficulties instead of explaining those difficulties away. It means admitting the darkness instead of covering it up with illusions and platitudes. Compassion trumps doctrine, forgiveness trumps fear, God's presence overrides God's supposed absence as our eyes turn upward and outward to find him instead of inward.

Belief cannot win. Executed perfectly it turns into self-righteous conviction that blinds the believer and excludes others. Executed poorly, it breaks apart.

Trust cannot lose. When things go right it grows and is confirmed. When things go wrong it's needed all the more.

Adam and Eve's failure came from seeking to believe instead of trust. They wanted to know more. They wanted proof. They wanted the power to decide themselves. The only thing God asked was to trust him. Lack of trust was the sin that broke the world. Active trust is the closest we get in this life to repairing it.

Abram trusted God and God reckoned that to him as righteousness.

If you want to become a 50% better theologian right this instant, every time you read "belief" or "faith" in scripture, translate them as "trust". You'll understand far more about our relationship with God than you did prior.

Assurance for Abram

⁷ He also said to him, "I am the Lord, who brought you out of Ur of the Chaldeans to give you this land to take possession of it."

⁸ But Abram said, "Sovereign Lord, how can I know that I will gain possession of it?"

⁹ So the Lord said to him, "Bring me a heifer, a goat and a ram, each three years old, along with a dove and a young pigeon."

¹⁰ Abram brought all these to him, cut them in two and arranged the halves opposite each other; the birds, however, he did not cut in half. ¹¹ Then birds of prey came down on the carcasses, but Abram drove them away.

¹² As the sun was setting, Abram fell into a deep sleep, and a thick and dreadful darkness came over him. ¹³ Then the Lord said to him, "Know for certain that for four hundred years your descendants will be strangers in a country not their own and that they will be enslaved and mistreated there. ¹⁴ But I will punish the nation they serve as slaves, and afterward they will come out with great possessions. ¹⁵ You, however, will go to your ancestors in peace and be buried at a good old age. ¹⁶ In the fourth generation your descendants will come back here, for the sin of the Amorites has not yet reached its full measure."

¹⁷ When the sun had set and darkness had fallen, a smoking firepot with a blazing torch appeared and passed between the pieces. ¹⁸ On that day the Lord made a covenant with Abram and said, "To your descendants I give this land, from the Wadi of Egypt to the great river, the Euphrates— ¹⁹ the land of the Kenites, Kenizzites,

Kadmonites, ²⁰ Hittites, Perizzites, Rephaites, ²¹ Amorites, Canaanites, Girgashites and Jebusites."

Here we see Abram needing reassurance. None of us are capable of trusting perfectly. Abram asks the question we all want to ask when we're called upon to trust, "How will I know?"

In the end, there's no satisfactory answer to it. We never do know. Two people getting married never know if they're doing the right thing. You either trust that someone loves you and operate on that basis or you don't. If you do that, you've got a marriage. If not, you don't. Nobody ever knows what having a child will be like either. You just do what you do and trust it'll turn out.

God understands that we need assurance, though. As we trust, we look for signs that we're on the right path. Abram got one here. He makes ritual sacrifice and God comes to him in a vision, assuring Abram of his lineage, predicting Israel's captivity in Egypt, promising him a long and full life.

The fact that Abram needed this vision shows the limits of our belief. We always think, "If God wants something, why doesn't he just show up and tell me? I'd sure listen then! I'd believe!" How many times has God spoken to Abram now? Yet Abram still needs reassuring.

God showed up in the person of Jesus Christ. Did people believe him? Not even his disciples understood him really.

Proof is never enough. We always want more. Trust endures.

Belief only stretches as far as our brains can encompass. Trust reveals the full nature and power of God.

Agreement and assent are glasses of water, full but liable to be tipped over. Trust is the ocean. You can throw a mountain into it. It'll get disturbed—it might even change a little—but it will still dwarf the mountain as its waves will roll onward around it.

Their Own Plan

16 Now Sarai, Abram's wife, had borne him no children. But she had an Egyptian slave named Hagar; 2 so she said to Abram, "The Lord has kept me from having children. Go, sleep with my slave; perhaps I can build a family through her."

Abram agreed to what Sarai said. 3 So after Abram had been living in Canaan ten years, Sarai his wife took her Egyptian slave Hagar and gave her to her husband to be his wife. 4 He slept with Hagar, and she conceived.

When she knew she was pregnant, she began to despise her mistress. 5 Then Sarai said to Abram, "You are responsible for the wrong I am suffering. I put my slave in your arms, and now that she knows she is pregnant, she despises me. May the Lord judge between you and me."

6 "Your slave is in your hands," Abram said. "Do with her whatever you think best." Then Sarai mistreated Hagar; so she fled from her.

Even Abram's and Sarai's trust had limits. It's the human condition. Told that a great nation would spring from them but not seeing the results, they decided to take matters into their own hands.

Carrying on the family line was critically important in ancient days. When a man and wife were unable to conceive, a wife would sometimes offer up one of her servants to her husband in her stead. The resulting child would be considered the heir. This primitive surrogacy kept marriages intact and families growing.

Abram and Sarai decided that this was the route for them. Jumping the gun on God's plan, Abram took Hagar as another wife and they conceived a child. Thinking herself now the favored wife, Hagar began to put on airs. Abram corrected that impression quickly, giving Sarai permission to treat Hagar harshly, reminding her where she came from. With both women arguing and mistreating each other, the camp must not have been a happy place. Knowing that as a slave, she was not going to win this battle, Hagar fled.

Nobody who's seen the International Space Station in orbit or photographs of distant galaxies from the Hubble Telescope can doubt humanity's capacity to conceive marvelous things. We're ingenious. But no plan can outmaneuver sin. Every human design will have flaws…none more so than schemes to fulfill the longing inside that only God can fill.

Abram and Sarai made a sound, sensible move here. It wasn't the move that God designed for them, though. Marrying Hagar was meant to solve problems. Instead it created more, not only for Abram, but for his offspring.

Moving Forward

[7] The angel of the Lord found Hagar near a spring in the desert; it was the spring that is beside the road to Shur. [8] And he said, "Hagar, slave of Sarai, where have you come from, and where are you going?"

"I'm running away from my mistress Sarai," she answered.

[9] Then the angel of the Lord told her, "Go back to your mistress and submit to her." [10] The angel added, "I will increase your descendants so much that they will be too numerous to count."

[11] The angel of the Lord also said to her:

"You are now pregnant
  and you will give birth to a son.
You shall name him Ishmael,
  for the Lord has heard of your misery.
12 He will be a wild donkey of a man;
  his hand will be against everyone
  and everyone's hand against him,
and he will live in hostility
  toward all his brothers."

13 She gave this name to the Lord who spoke to her: "You are the God who sees me," for she said, "I have now seen the One who sees me." 14 That is why the well was called Beer Lahai Roi; it is still there, between Kadesh and Bered.

15 So Hagar bore Abram a son, and Abram gave the name Ishmael to the son she had borne. 16 Abram was eighty-six years old when Hagar bore him Ishmael.

Before Hagar got far, an angel of the Lord appeared to her. We've built up a mythology around angels, but in simplest terms the word means, "Messenger of God". Sometimes Old Testament angels appear to be the shining beings we're used to, other times the "angel" is God himself, or the face of God. I'm not sure the distinction is important for us. All of us become angels when we share God's message through word and deed. We become God's face and voice in the world.

This particular angel had a message for Hagar. "Turn around. We're gonna make this right." Abram and Sarai had taken a detour on the path, but God was going to make it come out ok, rejoining Hagar's branch to the main road.

The angel told Hagar she was to name her son Ishmael. Abram would be the father of a great nation that was not of Ishmael, but God would grant Hagar and Ismael descendants without number too, paralleling Abram's promise. This might cause problems, as Ishmael would be a "wild donkey of a man", brawling and contesting with everybody. By extension his descendants would be too. But God would provide for their destiny anyway.

Here again we see a God determined to redeem our mistakes. He doesn't call the mistakes right, but he turns them around in such a way as to make something come of them. Some of us have been taught that if we do well God will be with us and if we do poorly he won't. He's with us in either case, through our triumphs and our mistakes. He's working for us in every moment.

Once, long ago, one of the young ladies in the youth ministry of my church got pregnant. Part of the church was horrified. Another part wanted to throw her a baby shower. There was conflict, but the baby shower side won. Nobody would encourage teenagers to have children, but once the baby was on the way the focus shifted. God's plan for that place now involved a tiny new member. Both child and mother needed caring for. Following the plan didn't mean pointing fingers, but buying diapers.

Even if we think something is a mistake, our service to God is to make the most good come out of that mistake as possible…to fill the hole that mistake created with love and grace just as God does.

So God spoke to Hagar and assured her that he would watch out for her. She named God as "the one who sees her" and rejoiced that she had seen him as well. Then she returned to Abram and to the camp.

Another Covenant

17 When Abram was ninety-nine years old, the Lord appeared to him and said, "I am God Almighty; walk before me faithfully and be blameless. 2 Then I will make my covenant between me and you and will greatly increase your numbers."

³ Abram fell facedown, and God said to him, ⁴ "As for me, this is my covenant with you: You will be the father of many nations. ⁵ No longer will you be called Abram; your name will be Abraham, for I have made you a father of many nations. ⁶ I will make you very fruitful; I will make nations of you, and kings will come from you. ⁷ I will establish my covenant as an everlasting covenant between me and you and your descendants after you for the generations to come, to be your God and the God of your descendants after you. ⁸ The whole land of Canaan, where you now reside as a foreigner, I will give as an everlasting possession to you and your descendants after you; and I will be their God."

⁹ Then God said to Abraham, "As for you, you must keep my covenant, you and your descendants after you for the generations to come. ¹⁰ This is my covenant with you and your descendants after you, the covenant you are to keep: Every male among you shall be circumcised. ¹¹ You are to undergo circumcision, and it will be the sign of the covenant between me and you. ¹² For the generations to come every male among you who is eight days old must be circumcised, including those born in your household or bought with money from a foreigner—those who are not your offspring. ¹³ Whether born in your household or bought with your money, they must be circumcised. My covenant in your flesh is to be an everlasting covenant. ¹⁴ Any uncircumcised male, who has not been circumcised in the flesh, will be cut off from his people; he has broken my covenant."

In Abram's 99th year, God delivered another message to him. Guess you're never too old to try something new. The rainbow had been the sign of the last covenant God made with humanity. The next sign would be a little more…personal.

God first urged Abram to walk with him and be blameless. He was to remember God in everything he did. Note the active verb "walk" in Genesis 17:1. Trust is a relationship to be lived out. You only get out of bed in the morning because you trust something important is going to happen that day. We're to understand God as the author of importance and dedicate every step we take to him.

Once upon a time people thought church was the place where you showed up to look good. You'd do your time in the pews on Sunday morning and the rest of the week was yours to pursue as you wish. Few people would be so crass as to admit it openly, but functionally that's how they behaved.

We tend to regard church and faith as part of life…something we do for an hour or two alongside all the other things we engage in. God will not fit as "part of our life" though. We have to reduce him terribly in order to make him that small, to the point that what remains is no longer God at all.

People like to compare themselves against each other. "Faith is only 3% of their pie chart and it's 12% of mine! I'm awesome!" Faith shouldn't be part of the pie chart at all. It should be the tray beneath, holding up the whole pie.

Faith is supposed to be a walk, present and central everywhere we go. That doesn't mean we're called to spend 16 hours a day in church. It means what the Spirit shows us in church goes with us and informs the rest of our life. Faith changes how we do our daily tasks, aligning them with goodness and grace.

After urging Abram to keep walking with him, God promises again to greatly increase Abram's numbers (the deepest desire of Abram's heart). Abram then fell down on his face (one would assume in awe and gratitude) as God spoke the rest of the covenant.

Through this covenant God changed Abram's name from Abram (honored father) to Abraham (father of multitudes). Abraham's own name would reflect his grand dream, which God was about to make come true for him. The equivalent today might be turning to a 16-year-old boy and saying, "Henceforth you will be known as 'Fleet of Lamborghinis'." Coooool.

Next God said he'd made Abraham a father of many nations. Note the past tense here. To Abraham the fulfillment of the promise remained in the future. To God it was already a done deal. If God says it, you can bank on it. God reiterated Abraham's fruitfulness here too, which didn't just mean having many offspring, but bearing fruit in the world. Fruit delights and nourishes. Abraham would do likewise, feeding the world through his family.

God also promised not just to be Abraham's God, but the God of all his descendants too. You can hear God emphasizing the kids over and over again. God told Abraham the covenant would be everlasting, never to be broken.

Abraham would also receive land, not just borrowed but inhabited. The land would belong to him and his offspring. Small wonder that the Hebrew people would come to regard land and faith as united; both came from God in the same breath.

Then God delivered the outward sign of this covenant for his people. Their males were to be circumcised. All men in the household plus any joining the household would undergo this ritual.

Discussing the meaning and purpose of circumcision belongs properly to those with far greater knowledge and passion for the subject than I. There's no doubt that the chosen people were marked in a place both intimate and central to life, making it hard for them to forget God's covenant with them. Dedicating infants this way set a path before them, marking them as God's before they're even aware of it.

Though Christians would later regard circumcision as optional—an outward sign of inward faith, but not the faith itself—the idea of dedicating, marking, and promising would endure throughout the ages as God's children sought to walk with him. They subtly inhabit almost all parts of the church service to this day, including Christian baptism.

Circumcision also set apart God's people from other nations of the time, those who didn't know God. God's desire to create a distinct and unified people was evident. To the modern reader, this sounds almost like bigotry. We must remember the unique situation of the ancient Hebrews. As yet they weren't even a race, just Abraham, his wife, and a promise. The family would grow in a hostile environment, surrounded by oppressors in Egypt and numerous tribes with rival gods in the Promised Land. Any number of those tribes had customs and rites that would be far easier to follow than God's. All of them would tempt the Israelites to stray. God gave them as clear of a start—as distinct of a separation from idolatry and unfaithful practices--as possible.

On the other hand, we must bear in mind that ultimately the story of the Old Testament is a story of failure, a reminder that we humans can't save ourselves or even recognize the Savior when he comes among us. Abraham and his family represent all humanity…the best of humanity, even. In Genesis God says, "I took the best people I could find and gave them the clearest instructions possible." The final chapter to that story reads, "And they still blew it." That's something for all of us to think about.

How many times do we say to God, "Just give us the list of rules and show us the path you want us to take and we'll do it!"

Bzzzt! No you won't.

Abraham goofed up a time or two. So did all his children, which includes Christians, at least by adoption. God shows us once again that what we *think* will save the world, won't actually do it. That's why we needed him to do it for us.

Notice that all the important parts of these covenants come from God. "I'm going to make you fruitful, build a nation, give you land, change your identity, establish kings from you, and be with you forever. Do you think you could snip yourselves and not forget me?"

"Sure," we say. Then we start snipping ourselves, think that makes us more special than others, regard ourselves as the center of the universe because of it, and promptly forget God. We're lucky he sticks with us.

The Biggest Promise

15 God also said to Abraham, "As for Sarai your wife, you are no longer to call her Sarai; her name will be Sarah. 16 I will bless her and will surely give you a son by her. I will bless her so that she will be the mother of nations; kings of peoples will come from her."

17 Abraham fell facedown; he laughed and said to himself, "Will a son be born to a man a hundred years old? Will Sarah bear a child at the age of ninety?" 18 And Abraham said to God, "If only Ishmael might live under your blessing!"

19 Then God said, "Yes, but your wife Sarah will bear you a son, and you will call him Isaac. I will establish my covenant with him as an everlasting covenant for his descendants after him. 20 And as for Ishmael, I have heard you: I will surely bless him; I will make him fruitful and will greatly increase his numbers. He will be the father of twelve rulers, and I will make him into a great nation. 21 But my covenant I will establish with Isaac, whom Sarah will bear to you by this time next year." 22 When he had finished speaking with Abraham, God went up from him.

Sarai also gets a name change directly from the lips of God. The root "Sar" stems from "chieftain" or "captain". The final form of her name does not differ in meaning significantly from the first. Sarah is regarded as royal, the mother of all her people who will come after.

But even after all this Abraham has trouble trusting. When Sarah is confirmed as the mother of nations—just as Abraham had just been confirmed as the father—Abraham fell to his face laughing. Biologically this was impossible. 50 years ago, maybe…but Sarah conceiving now?

Abraham even begs God to make Ishmael the chosen son, since it's easier to see that happening. Immediately God tells Abraham that the obvious ways are not always his ways. Sarah will bear a son, to be called Isaac. Oddly enough, Isaac means "He laughs". Perhaps this was a little needle poke at Abraham for his incredulous reaction to God's promise.

(Thank God old Abe didn't have indigestion that day or his son may have been named something truly awful!)

God makes clear that Isaac's children will bear the everlasting covenant and be his peoples, but he will not forget Ishmael either, just as Abraham has requested. Ishmael will become the father of twelve rulers, paralleling the twelve tribes of Israel which would be founded by Isaac's grandsons.

Getting Snippy

23 On that very day Abraham took his son Ishmael and all those born in his household or bought with his money, every male in his household, and circumcised them, as God told him. 24 Abraham was ninety-nine years old when he was circumcised, 25 and his son Ishmael was thirteen; 26 Abraham and his son Ishmael were both circumcised on that very day. 27 And every male in Abraham's household, including those born in his household or bought from a foreigner, was circumcised with him.

We see that Abraham started off well, circumcising himself, his son, and all the males of the household that very day…no doubt leading to exclamations of, "Uhhh…God told you *what*???" from all around the camp.

Nobody said following God was going to be easy or make you popular with your friends.

Three Visitors

18 The Lord appeared to Abraham near the great trees of Mamre while he was sitting at the entrance to his tent in the heat of the day. 2 Abraham looked up and saw three men standing nearby. When he saw them, he hurried from the entrance of his tent to meet them and bowed low to the ground.

³ He said, "If I have found favor in your eyes, my lord, do not pass your servant by. ⁴ Let a little water be brought, and then you may all wash your feet and rest under this tree. ⁵ Let me get you something to eat, so you can be refreshed and then go on your way—now that you have come to your servant."

"Very well," they answered, "do as you say."

⁶ So Abraham hurried into the tent to Sarah. "Quick," he said, "get three seahs of the finest flour and knead it and bake some bread."

⁷ Then he ran to the herd and selected a choice, tender calf and gave it to a servant, who hurried to prepare it. ⁸ He then brought some curds and milk and the calf that had been prepared, and set these before them. While they ate, he stood near them under a tree.

The next we see Abraham, he's taking his ease at his tents when the Lord appears to him in the form of three messengers. Abraham saw them and immediately invited them in, gracious and hospitable.

Abraham didn't ask who these fellows were. He didn't question who they were related to. He didn't require them to undergo membership training or subscribe to his point of view before welcoming them fully. Instead he hurried to them, bowed low, and gave them everything he could on first sight, without distinction.

That "everything" included water to wash their feet, shade to rest in, gourmet beef and cottage cheese (Eww!), and bread baked from 36 pounds of the finest flour. He went overboard. He didn't even eat beside them, nor did he sit in their presence. He stood while they enjoyed.

Almost every mythos has its hospitality stories. Most speak of reward for the hospitable host and condemnation for the inhospitable. George R.R. Martin played off of this theme to add drama to the infamous Red Wedding scene in Game of Thrones, for instance. Some cultures even have specific deities to watch over hospitality. You never know when that beggar at your door might turn out to be your god in disguise. This is echoed in Matthew 25, when Jesus said judgement would hinge on how we treat the least of people among us. This is how we treat God himself.

Hospitality is a part of our mission of faith. God shows up in the faces of people all around us. We're not meant to greet those faces with suspicion, but deep generosity. We're not supposed to ask first, to demand and then give. We're meant to greet people with a giving spirit immediately and continuously.

One of the great joys of the parish I serve is that its people have adopted this lesson. We reside in an old farming community now turned into a bedroom town. People face constant temptation to define the church by its past, by an entrenched group of steady members. That seems safest, most convenient, and in some ways most powerful.

Instead we turn ourselves inside out. We make sure you cannot tell the difference between our members and non-members. We let people fiddle around with our church, suggest hymns, guide Sunday School lessons, create and participate in social events. As soon as people walk in the door they're told of grace and of power, both of which flow from their hands as much as ours.

When someone comes to our door in need there are no questions asked…their needs are met. Occasionally we may get "taken" for a tank of gas or a bag of groceries. Usually we allow ourselves to be taken, trying to out-give the slyness and replace it with love. We figure giving away the occasional misplaced meal is a small price to pay for genuinely feeding all comers.

This wars against the instinct to protect and advance ourselves. Those instincts may be smart, may even be useful upon occasion, but they're not God. They're not something to build our daily lives or practices around. Erring on the side of being too gracious, too hospitable, has occasionally been trying, but it has not let us down.

Nor did being hospitable let Abraham down. As it turns out, the visitors also had a matter to discuss with him and his wife.

The Time is Here

⁹ "Where is your wife Sarah?" they asked him.

"There, in the tent," he said.

¹⁰ Then one of them said, "I will surely return to you about this time next year, and Sarah your wife will have a son."

Now Sarah was listening at the entrance to the tent, which was behind him.¹¹ Abraham and Sarah were already very old, and Sarah was past the age of childbearing. ¹² So Sarah laughed to herself as she thought, "After I am worn out and my lord is old, will I now have this pleasure?"

¹³ Then the Lord said to Abraham, "Why did Sarah laugh and say, 'Will I really have a child, now that I am old?' ¹⁴ Is anything too hard for the Lord? I will return to you at the appointed time next year, and Sarah will have a son."

¹⁵ Sarah was afraid, so she lied and said, "I did not laugh."

But he said, "Yes, you did laugh."

These visitors brought the promise that the couple's long-dreamed dream would come true. Just as Abraham had earlier, Sarah laughed when she heard this prediction. But the visitors reiterated that nothing is too hard for the Lord. One of the visitors would return the next year and Sarah would have a son. To me this seems like kind of an odd promise…I'd want some clarification as a husband what exactly he's returning *for*. But Abraham and Sarah understand the implication of divine blessing here rather than anything more nefarious.

The visitor questions why Sarah laughed at the news. Where is her trust in the Lord? Abraham has had enough of these moments, it was probably time for her to have one. Sarah tried to deny that she laughed even when it was clear she did.

Nobody likes to be wrong. People of faith especially don't like their disbelief or failings pointed out. This is silly. I've been wrong a thousand times. (Sharper minds than mine will probably point out a dozen errors in this book already.) I've also failed to trust more times than I can count…failed to believe in God's purpose for me, doubted that there was a purpose, doubted that there was a God, even. If I've done it as a book-writing pastor, you probably have too.

Doesn't it feel better to say that out loud? The world would be a much better place if we would all admit that we're mistaken, disbelieving people instead of pretending like we're correct and believing folk all the time. Nobody can relate to a "perfect" person. Perfection is a lie that nobody achieves. If Abraham and Sarah—the king and queen, father and mother of all God's people—couldn't manage it I don't think you or I can. Communities of faith work much better when they speak honestly and theologically correctly. The first thing we should say together is, "All of us are mistaken. All of us have doubts. Somehow God works through silly people like us anyway. It's OK to admit your mistakes and doubts too. We'll get through them and make something good happen together."

This is part of the reason why every service of worship in our church begins with a confession. We all raise our voices and say that we have fallen short…myself included. We're all on an even playing field: we messed up, we denied, we laughed and thought we knew better than God. If God doesn't forgive us and visit us at the appointed time, all our work will be barren anyway. So we might as well get over ourselves and trust in him.

God says, "Yes, you did laugh."

We reply, "Yes, I did, Lord. Forgive me."

Bad News for Sodom

[16] When the men got up to leave, they looked down toward Sodom, and Abraham walked along with them to see them on their way. [17] Then the Lord said, "Shall I hide from Abraham what I am about to do? [18] Abraham will surely become a great and powerful nation, and all nations on earth will be blessed through him. [19] For I have chosen him, so that he will direct his children and his household after him to keep the way of the Lord by doing what is right and just, so that the Lord will bring about for Abraham what he has promised him."

[20] Then the Lord said, "The outcry against Sodom and Gomorrah is so great and their sin so grievous [21] that I will go down and see if what they have done is as bad as the outcry that has reached me. If not, I will know."

Along with the fantastic proclamation about Isaac came some bad news. The end was drawing nigh for Sodom and Gomorrah. The cities were so wicked that it was time to blot them off the earth, a redoing of the flood motif, just with fire instead of water this time.

Once again we're constrained to mention that this is often something people secretly wish God would do…maybe not smite entire nations but at least segments of them that we consider enemies. Sodom and Gomorrah show what happens when God does just that. Did wickedness cease? Was the world a paradise again or did new evil just grow over the old?

These stories aren't here so you can point and say, "Look at those wicked people, thank God I'm not one of them!" They're here so you can *stop* saying that (because it doesn't work) and start doing something productive to bring goodness into the world instead.

In any case, the children have been bad and God himself is coming down to check in on them. If the wickedness is as bad as he thinks, there's going to be trouble.

Searching for Righteousness

22 The men turned away and went toward Sodom, but Abraham remained standing before the Lord. 23 Then Abraham approached him and said: "Will you sweep away the righteous with the wicked? 24 What if there are fifty righteous people in the city? Will you really sweep it away and not spare the place for the sake of the fifty righteous people in it? 25 Far be it from you to do such a thing—to kill the righteous with the wicked, treating the righteous and the wicked alike. Far be it from you! Will not the Judge of all the earth do right?"

26 The Lord said, "If I find fifty righteous people in the city of Sodom, I will spare the whole place for their sake."

27 Then Abraham spoke up again: "Now that I have been so bold as to speak to the Lord, though I am nothing but dust and ashes, 28 what if the number of the righteous is five less than fifty? Will you destroy the whole city for lack of five people?"

"If I find forty-five there," he said, "I will not destroy it."

29 Once again he spoke to him, "What if only forty are found there?"

He said, "For the sake of forty, I will not do it."

30 Then he said, "May the Lord not be angry, but let me speak. What if only thirty can be found there?"

He answered, "I will not do it if I find thirty there."

31 Abraham said, "Now that I have been so bold as to speak to the Lord, what if only twenty can be found there?"

He said, "For the sake of twenty, I will not destroy it."

32 Then he said, "May the Lord not be angry, but let me speak just once more. What if only ten can be found there?"

He answered, "For the sake of ten, I will not destroy it."

33 When the Lord had finished speaking with Abraham, he left, and Abraham returned home.

When the Lord makes known his intentions for the local cities, Abraham is startled. He knows some of these people. They're neighbors. Besides, Lot and his family live there. Thus ensues one of the most interesting passages in all of scripture. Abraham takes it upon himself to bargain with the Lord.

Though he has a rooting interest in the game because of Lot, Abraham is not bargaining for himself here. Having large, wicked cities nearby may actually be counterproductive for him and his offspring. Instead he's bargaining for the sake of others and for righteousness.

Many of us have tried to negotiate with God. This usually amounts to, "Please save me!" Ironically enough, God has already done that. We just don't see it yet. Abraham is asking something different: "Please save them!" And Abraham's bargaining extends beyond all proper bounds, even to the point of being cheeky. He's not going to let go of the matter.

God agrees with Abraham's reasoning every step of the way, allowing the argument to continue precisely because Abraham isn't arguing for anything selfish, but for the sake of people not his own. Thousands of years later Christ would spend plenty of time trying to get people to do just this to no avail. This was one of Abraham's finest moments.

It also points out that we have permission to argue with God! We may not be right, we may not be able to see the big, eternal picture, but God would rather have us argue with him honestly than praise him dishonestly. He'd rather have us bargain and struggle with him than not engage at all.

Again we're reminded of the well-meant utterances, "Well, it was God's plan" or, "They're in a better place now" at funeral meals. There might be a kernel of truth in there somewhere, but functionally it ends up sounding like, "OK, grieving person, hush up and don't argue with God. He gets to snuff out your loved one if he wants to. So there."

This is not a faithful response to grief. A person who has just lost a loved one is probably struggling with God, maybe arguing with him, not understanding why it had to be *their* loved one that he "needed as another angel". God is OK with that! Why aren't more of his people OK with it?

God is big. God is eternal. He can absorb arguing and shaking fists and lashing out in anger directed towards the heavens. You know what? *He's feeling that same way too.* He feels it every time someone experiences a loss, which is exactly why he shook his own fist at the serpent and said, "Get on the ground! This will not prevail!" Yet we, as God's people, seem to have such a hard time dealing with people who are experiencing those feelings. We want to give them an answer, to protect God from their accusations, to silence those who most need to be heard.

Could it be that we're more concerned that they're arguing with us and our faith than we are that they're arguing with God? We're afraid they might break our fragile shell, expose our own doubts, prove us wrong. So we don't let them argue in front of us. We make them go hide in their dark, empty bedroom if they want to get into a back-and-forth with the Almighty.

And yet here's Abraham, father of our faith, arguing with the Lord in anguish about something that seems inevitable. And God is not only letting him, God's *agreeing* with him.

Abraham starts out the conversation with some simple logic. "Aren't you the God of Righteousness? Then how could you let the righteous perish along with the wicked? That wouldn't be right. Do you want the whole world to think you're a rotten judge?" Then Abraham makes his first foray. If there are 50 righteous people in the cities, will God stay his hand?

God agrees. If 50 righteous people live there, he'll call the whole thing off for their sake.

Then Abraham slides the bar a little lower. How about 45?

God agrees to 45.

Errr…40?

Yes, 40.

Then Abraham starts to really push his luck? 30? 20? Sure…OK. 20.

Ummm…please don't be angry God, but… [insert small voice here] 10?

For the sake of even 10 people, God agrees not to destroy the cities. Abraham's bargaining has gone far better than anyone could imagine! He convinced God with his initial pitch and then got his client to accept 20% of the initial offer. Get that man to a used car lot!

Except ten righteous people could not be found.

The common reaction to this is, "Wow! What wicked cities!" Fair enough, but I'd suggest another. If a census were taken in your town, how many righteous people would be found? I'm not talking about *seeming* righteous, nor looking righteous in comparison to others, but honest-to-goodness, do-not-sin righteous.

Are you righteous? Are any of us? The correct answer is, "No. There aren't any righteous people here." That's why we need God's mercy and forgiveness instead of striding up to the gates of heaven and saying, "Let me in! I've earned it, buddy!"

This isn't a story about the wickedness of two cities, it's the story of how lamentably short we all fall. Were God in the business of nuking bad folks, we'd all need to duck and cover. Hearing about the times he actually did wipe out the unrighteous, we learn to be thankful that he ended up choosing a different way to save us.

Wickedness on Display

19 *The two angels arrived at Sodom in the evening, and Lot was sitting in the gateway of the city. When he saw them, he got up to meet them and bowed down with his face to the ground.* **2** *"My lords," he said, "please turn aside to your servant's house. You can wash your feet and spend the night and then go on your way early in the morning."*

"No," they answered, "we will spend the night in the square."

3 *But he insisted so strongly that they did go with him and entered his house. He prepared a meal for them, baking bread without yeast, and they ate.* **4** *Before they had gone to bed, all the men from every part of the city of Sodom—both young and old—surrounded the house.* **5** *They called to Lot, "Where are the men who came to you tonight? Bring them out to us so that we can have sex with them."*

6 *Lot went outside to meet them and shut the door behind him* **7** *and said, "No, my friends. Don't do this wicked thing.* **8** *Look, I have two daughters who have never slept with a man. Let me bring them out to you, and you can do what you like with them. But don't do anything to these men, for they have come under the protection of my roof."*

9 *"Get out of our way," they replied. "This fellow came here as a foreigner, and now he wants to play the judge! We'll treat you worse than them." They kept bringing pressure on Lot and moved forward to break down the door.*

With destruction imminent, God sent messengers to Lot to warn him to flee the doomed city. Like Abraham had under the trees of Mamre, Lot recognized something special in these visitors and invited them to lodge with him. The angels initially refused, but Lot insisted, and for good reason. Before the night was done, all the men from the city, young and old, surrounded Lot's house and demanded that he send the visitors out for their sexual pleasure. We now begin to see how wicked Sodom is.

Those who attribute this wickedness to the genders of the persons involved (presuming homosexuality as the great sin of the cities) are missing the mark. It's a lamentable interpretation that has gone on far too long.

These passages are about rape and an utter lack of regard for other people. They do not center on homosexuality. When Lot went out to convince the crowd to disperse, he offered his two virgin daughters to them instead. Anyone who thinks that the offense in these verses is men having sex with men should be perfectly OK with this. That would solve the problem, would it not? Then we have good old man-on-woman intercourse and the wickedness would be gone.

But it's not, is it? The story would be just as horrific if the crowd had accepted Lot's daughters in place of the angels and assaulted them. It would be every bit as much of a violation. The people would be just as wicked and the town just as deserving of destruction. Who's trying to rape whom is not the main problem here, but the fact that such a violation is promoted in the city at all.

These passages have as much to do with consensual homosexual intercourse as gang rape has to do with sex in the marriage bed. We can probably find passages in the Bible that lead to a discussion of the topic of homosexuality, but this ain't it. Those who would insist otherwise are pointing fingers at others without absorbing the lesson that this is about them, too.

Nobody Wants to Leave

10 But the men inside reached out and pulled Lot back into the house and shut the door. 11 Then they struck the men who were at the door of the house, young and old, with blindness so that they could not find the door.

12 The two men said to Lot, "Do you have anyone else here—sons-in-law, sons or daughters, or anyone else in the city who belongs to you? Get them out of here, 13 because we are going to destroy this place. The outcry to the Lord against its people is so great that he has sent us to destroy it."

14 So Lot went out and spoke to his sons-in-law, who were pledged to marry his daughters. He said, "Hurry and get out of this place, because the Lord is about to destroy the city!" But his sons-in-law thought he was joking.

After the crowd surges forward, the visitors use a little Angel-Fu, snatching Lot back inside the house and blinding all those outside so they couldn't find their way in. In a sense these men were blind already, so the punishment seems theologically appropriate as well as effective. God's ultimate weapon is to reveal the truth. That's all we need to condemn us.

The angels then urge Lot to find anybody else remotely related to him and get them out, because this city is going down. If we ever doubted the justice in God's decree, that scene at the doorstep proved it.

Lot hurried to speak to his sons-in-law, the men pledged to his daughters. Like Abraham and Sarah, they laughed at God's message. This time it would prove to be a fatal mistake.

Rain of Fire, Pillar of Salt

15 With the coming of dawn, the angels urged Lot, saying, "Hurry! Take your wife and your two daughters who are here, or you will be swept away when the city is punished."

16 When he hesitated, the men grasped his hand and the hands of his wife and of his two daughters and led them safely out of the city, for the Lord was merciful to them. 17 As soon as they had brought them out, one of them said, "Flee for your lives! Don't look back, and don't stop anywhere in the plain! Flee to the mountains or you will be swept away!"

18 But Lot said to them, "No, my lords, please! 19 Your servant has found favor in your eyes, and you have shown great kindness to me in sparing my life. But I can't flee to the mountains; this disaster will overtake me, and I'll die. 20 Look, here is a town near enough to run to, and it is small. Let me flee to it—it is very small, isn't it? Then my life will be spared."

21 He said to him, "Very well, I will grant this request too; I will not overthrow the town you speak of. 22 But flee there quickly, because I cannot do anything until you reach it." (That is why the town was called Zoar.)

23 By the time Lot reached Zoar, the sun had risen over the land. 24 Then the Lord rained down burning sulfur on Sodom and Gomorrah—from the Lord out of the heavens. 25 Thus he overthrew those cities and the entire plain, destroying all those living in the cities—and also the vegetation in the land. 26 But Lot's wife looked back, and she became a pillar of salt.

It's incredible that even after all this, Lot and his family had a hard time leaving Sodom behind. When we're entrenched in wickedness, leaving it is difficult even under the most obvious of circumstances. Sometimes the only hope we have is the one Lot got: that the Lord will take us by the hand and lead us out, unwilling though we are. You can just hear the angels saying, "Come on...COME ON!!!" and tugging on their hands. We hear echoes of baptismal waters closing in on our heads and drowning the old, unwilling self, so that a new life may rise. Even though that new life is glorious, still our minds go, "Noooo...I'd rather hang on to the things of death." We never get over our sin; we're never able to choose our way out of it. God has to burn it out of us before its power will loosen.

Once outside the city, the angels issued a command to flee and not look back. Even now Lot objected. He didn't want to head to the mountains. He claimed the distance was too far. Remember that mountaintops are often where we're said to meet God, while the towns here represented the life of Sodom. Lot's fear played a part in his refusal, but he was also clinging to his life instead of his God.

Lot's choice illustrates our pattern with sin. We want out, but not all the way out. Just far enough not to get us in trouble will do. We leave behind the most obvious vestiges of our wrongdoing but we want to retain the core comforts of it. "Thank God I'm not the self-centered person I was in my 20's...except around my wife and at my job." Or, "I can't quit cold turkey, but I'll try to cut back." We knock off the cigarette habit only to take up cupcake consumption instead. We do this with all our sins, not just the most evident ones.

Even so, God's angels conceded to Lot's request. God was bending over backwards for these people. When Lot and family reached the town, destruction came.

Famously Lot's wife disobeyed the command not to look back and became an overgrown salt lick. Bending only goes so far. At a certain point you're over a line that it's hard to come back from. Push a sin hard enough and it'll break you.

Belief Enough for Two

27 Early the next morning Abraham got up and returned to the place where he had stood before the Lord. 28 He looked down toward Sodom and Gomorrah, toward all the land of the plain, and he saw dense smoke rising from the land, like smoke from a furnace.

29 So when God destroyed the cities of the plain, he remembered Abraham, and he brought Lot out of the catastrophe that overthrew the cities where Lot had lived.

The next morning Abraham ascended the hillside to look over the plain and saw that God's warning had come true. Ten righteous people could not be found. The cities were destroyed. But God had remembered Abraham's sorrow and saved his nephew Lot.

God saving Lot for Abraham's sake brings up an interesting point. Plenty of people come to me and say, "Pastor, my friend/relative doesn't believe in God. How can I convince them?"

Short answer: you can't. But why don't you try believing enough for both of you? I don't mean grabbing their hand and praying for them when they're unwilling or not-so-subtly leaving religious tracts on their coffee table. I'm talking about showing twice the love, twice the forgiveness, listening to them twice as hard…being twice the friend or relative you would have otherwise. Don't assume that what's going on inside their head keeps God from caring about them every bit as much as he cares about you. Abraham believed enough for him and Lot, and at least temporarily, it did Lot some good. Try that approach with the folks in your life and see what happens.

Lot's Destiny

30 Lot and his two daughters left Zoar and settled in the mountains, for he was afraid to stay in Zoar. He and his two daughters lived in a cave. 31 One day the older daughter said to the younger, "Our father is old, and there is no man around here to give us children—as is the custom all over the earth. 32 Let's get our father to drink wine and then sleep with him and preserve our family line through our father."

33 That night they got their father to drink wine, and the older daughter went in and slept with him. He was not aware of it when she lay down or when she got up.

34 The next day the older daughter said to the younger, "Last night I slept with my father. Let's get him to drink wine again tonight, and you go in and sleep with him so we can preserve our family line through our father." 35 So they got their father to drink wine that night also, and the younger daughter went in and slept with him. Again he was not aware of it when she lay down or when she got up.

36 So both of Lot's daughters became pregnant by their father. 37 The older daughter had a son, and she named him Moab; he is the father of the Moabites of today. 38 The younger daughter also had a son, and she named him Ben-Ammi; he is the father of the Ammonites of today.

Lot's eventual destiny was curious. He ended up not being able to stay in the town of Zoar (how often our desires go astray as perceived safety turns out unsafe) and he had to travel to the mountains after all. There the man who had once chosen the prime real estate all for himself ended up living in a cave.

In verses that we don't often hear in church on Sunday morning, Lot's two daughters continued the family line (and their place in it) by getting their father drunk and then conceiving children with him. From Lot's line came the Moabites and Ammonites.

Two things are worth noting here:

1. This is another one of those "distant cousin" stories that explains how everyone in the region was interrelated.

2. The Moabites and Ammonites were often rivals, if not enemies, of the Israelites, so it would be culturally pleasing to describe their origins as two cave-dwelling daughters getting their clueless, idiotic father drunk and perpetuating a form of incest that is taboo in almost every culture. In some ways we have permission to take these "where we came from" stories with a grain of salt, at least understanding who described the history and for what purposes. Some parts of scripture weigh more than others. If any random Moabites or Ammonites are out there reading, God loves you too. Sorry about what we said about your mom.

Revisiting a Gambit

20 Now Abraham moved on from there into the region of the Negev and lived between Kadesh and Shur. For a while he stayed in Gerar, 2 and there Abraham said of his wife Sarah, "She is my sister." Then Abimelek king of Gerar sent for Sarah and took her.

3 But God came to Abimelek in a dream one night and said to him, "You are as good as dead because of the woman you have taken; she is a married woman."

4 Now Abimelek had not gone near her, so he said, "Lord, will you destroy an innocent nation? 5 Did he not say to me, 'She is my sister,' and didn't she also say, 'He is my brother'? I have done this with a clear conscience and clean hands."

6 Then God said to him in the dream, "Yes, I know you did this with a clear conscience, and so I have kept you from sinning against me. That is why I did not let you touch her. 7 Now return the man's wife, for he is a prophet, and he will pray for you and you will live. But if you do not return her, you may be sure that you and all who belong to you will die."

8 Early the next morning Abimelek summoned all his officials, and when he told them all that had happened, they were very much afraid. 9 Then Abimelek called Abraham in and said, "What have you done to us? How have I wronged you that you have brought such great guilt upon me and my kingdom? You have done things to me that should never be done." 10 And Abimelek asked Abraham, "What was your reason for doing this?"

11 Abraham replied, "I said to myself, 'There is surely no fear of God in this place, and they will kill me because of my wife.' 12 Besides, she really is my sister, the daughter of my father though not of my mother; and she became my wife. 13 And when God had me wander from my father's household, I said to her, 'This is how you can show your love to me: Everywhere we go, say of me, "He is my brother."'"

14 Then Abimelek brought sheep and cattle and male and female slaves and gave them to Abraham, and he returned Sarah his wife to him. 15 And Abimelek said, "My land is before you; live wherever you like."

16 To Sarah he said, "I am giving your brother a thousand shekels of silver. This is to cover the offense against you before all who are with you; you are completely vindicated."

17 Then Abraham prayed to God, and God healed Abimelek, his wife and his female slaves so they could have children again, 18 for the Lord had kept all the women in Abimelek's household from conceiving because of Abraham's wife Sarah.

All together now: *"AGAIN, Abraham???"*

But can you blame the guy? He keeps getting rewarded for it.

Genesis 20 is a replay of the "Pharaoh Likes Sarah" story from Genesis 12, just with a different king. You know the deal.

Abraham moves around a little bit, encounters a foreign monarch, and instructs Sarah to say she's his sister. Even at 90 years of age Sarah is such a hottie that the king can't resist. But when Mr. Royal Pants takes her to wife, God curses the joint.

This time when questioned by the king, Abraham explains the whole scheme. The major revelation out of all this is that Sarah is apparently Abraham's half-sister through his father, so the "sister" explanation is not a total lie. (And Lot, you are redeemed…a little.)

Even after hearing the whole convoluted story King Abimelek still loads up Abraham with a virtual fortune of livestock and extra slaves, then invites Abraham to settle anywhere in his land that he likes. I guess God made him an offer he couldn't refuse.

In the middle of all this, Abraham notices that all of this double-marrying might be a *slight* inconvenience to his wife, so he makes up for it by paying 25 pounds of silver…to her brother.

Then Abraham prays to God, tells him he can knock off the divine extortion racket, and God opens up the wombs of all the women around Abimelek again.

The overarching lesson here: If an old dude shows up in your town with a lady he says is his sister and she looks kind of hot, don't touch her. It's a scam.

Isaac Arrives

***21** Now the Lord was gracious to Sarah as he had said, and the Lord did for Sarah what he had promised. **2** Sarah became pregnant and bore a son to Abraham in his old age, at the very time God had promised him. **3** Abraham gave the name Isaac to the son Sarah bore him. **4** When his son Isaac was eight days old, Abraham circumcised him, as God commanded him. **5** Abraham was a hundred years old when his son Isaac was born to him.*

6 Sarah said, "God has brought me laughter, and everyone who hears about this will laugh with me." 7 And she added, "Who would have said to Abraham that Sarah would nurse children? Yet I have borne him a son in his old age."

Having followed the story up until now, you should be throwing your hands in the air and cheering at this point. Finally the promise has come true. Abraham and Sarah have their baby boy.

Abraham keeps his son in the covenant, of course, circumcising him as is proper. He names him Isaac as God commanded, but the laughter inherent in his name doesn't stem from disbelief anymore, but joy. Sarah now has that unbridled, amazed, infectious laughter that releases all the prior sorrow and pain, inviting everyone who experiences it to celebrate along with.

The Cost of a Son

8 The child grew and was weaned, and on the day Isaac was weaned Abraham held a great feast. 9 But Sarah saw that the son whom Hagar the Egyptian had borne to Abraham was mocking, 10 and she said to Abraham, "Get rid of that slave woman and her son, for that woman's son will never share in the inheritance with my son Isaac."

11 The matter distressed Abraham greatly because it concerned his son. 12 But God said to him, "Do not be so distressed about the boy and your slave woman. Listen to whatever Sarah tells you, because it is through Isaac that your offspring will be reckoned. 13 I will make the son of the slave into a nation also, because he is your offspring."

14 Early the next morning Abraham took some food and a skin of water and gave them to Hagar. He set them on her shoulders and then sent her off with the boy. She went on her way and wandered in the Desert of Beersheba.

15 When the water in the skin was gone, she put the boy under one of the bushes. 16 Then she went off and sat down about a bowshot away, for she thought, "I cannot watch the boy die." And as she sat there, she began to sob.

¹⁷ God heard the boy crying, and the angel of God called to Hagar from heaven and said to her, "What is the matter, Hagar? Do not be afraid; God has heard the boy crying as he lies there. ¹⁸ Lift the boy up and take him by the hand, for I will make him into a great nation."

¹⁹ Then God opened her eyes and she saw a well of water. So she went and filled the skin with water and gave the boy a drink.

²⁰ God was with the boy as he grew up. He lived in the desert and became an archer. ²¹ While he was living in the Desert of Paran, his mother got a wife for him from Egypt.

As is usually true in this fallen world, joy came with a cost attached. The arrival of one son meant the departure of another.

Ishmael--Abraham's first son, now supplanted by the infant Isaac—had an understandable reaction to the baby's arrival. He wasn't happy. He showed it passive-aggressively, being a little snot at Isaac's weaning feast. This was enough for Sarah, who had not been fond of Ishmael or his mother for some time. Now that she had her own boy, she wanted them out…partly for personal reasons, also to ensure that the family inheritance fell to her son alone.

Abraham balked at this, but God assured him that he would take care of the boy. Abraham loaded Hagar and Ishmael with food and water, then sent them out into the desert.

Fortunately God also resides in forsaken places. After they had exhausted their supplies, Hagar was so convinced that they were going to perish that she walked away from her son so she wouldn't have to watch him die. But God showed her a well of water and bade her lead her son to it. The desert became his home and his inheritance.

God favors us most when we're at the end of our rope. It's not an accident that he mostly meets his prophets in remote places. When you feel cut off from everything and everyone else, God is still there. Sometimes it takes losing everything to discover what you really had in the first place.

Treaties and Testing

Genesis 21 ends with Abraham making a treaty with local kings, who now recognize God's hand in everything he does. Earlier we claimed that everything we do is a witness. This shows it. Even the foreign rulers with no clue about Abraham's God recognized his power and goodness.

But just as things are finally starting to go good for Abraham…

22 Some time later God tested Abraham. He said to him, "Abraham!"

"Here I am," he replied.

² Then God said, "Take your son, your only son, whom you love—Isaac—and go to the region of Moriah. Sacrifice him there as a burnt offering on a mountain I will show you."

³ Early the next morning Abraham got up and loaded his donkey. He took with him two of his servants and his son Isaac. When he had cut enough wood for the burnt offering, he set out for the place God had told him about. ⁴ On the third day Abraham looked up and saw the place in the distance. ⁵ He said to his servants, "Stay here with the donkey while I and the boy go over there. We will worship and then we will come back to you."

⁶ Abraham took the wood for the burnt offering and placed it on his son Isaac, and he himself carried the fire and the knife. As the two of them went on together, ⁷ Isaac spoke up and said to his father Abraham, "Father?"

"Yes, my son?" Abraham replied.

"The fire and wood are here," Isaac said, "but where is the lamb for the burnt offering?"

⁸ Abraham answered, "God himself will provide the lamb for the burnt offering, my son." And the two of them went on together.

If you felt the joy at the birth of Isaac in the last chapter you should feel the horror here. We should preface this story by saying that child sacrifice was not in God's repertoire. In fact it was a hallmark of other nations around Israel who worshiped idols, a practice that God detested. It's not ok to ask people to hurt their children, God will not ask this of you or anyone else around you. Killing Isaac was not the point of the story.

Genesis 22:1 says the request to sacrifice Isaac was a test for Abraham. He had wanted this boy more than anything in his life. Was he in love with God or in love with the dream he wanted God to fulfill?

We go through this test in daily life in minor ways. Almost every young couple I marry comes equipped with ready-made definitions of what they want a husband or wife to be. In pre-marital counseling they tell me, "I'm marrying him because he's this and that and this other thing." That's true as far as it goes, but that's only part of the story. Along with those lovely husband qualities will come other qualities less lovely, plus surprises neither one of them were anticipating.

Every spouse eventually faces this test: *Am I in love with my husband/wife or am I in love with my idea of what a husband/wife should be?* Do you love your spouse or do you love the marriage ideal you think they're fulfilling. Do they matter, or are they just fulfilling a role in your head?

God was asking this of Abraham in a grand way. "What's the single greatest thing in your life, Abraham? Are you willing to sacrifice it for me? Which matters more to you, me or all the blessings you've gotten?"

I love my children more than I've ever loved anyone in my life. They opened up whole new avenues of love for me. They're the biggest, most important people I've ever encountered…the most precious gift I can imagine. But I will not teach them that I am the center of their universe, nor that they are the center of mine. Instead God gave us as gifts to each other. It looks like we're gathering around each other. Really we're gathering around him. He's the center; he's the source.

I am flawed. I make all kinds of mistakes, parenting and otherwise. I'd like my children to emulate me, but I prefer them to emulate God as much as possible. On the day I die, I will want my children to know that the core of our love isn't passing away with me. It still lives on…not through some version of me, but through the God who gave us that love to begin with. Our love is but a pale copy of his. Through him, that love will be magnified infinitely and last forever.

I am willing to sacrifice my centrality in the lives of my children in order for them to understand the truth. I am willing to say the greatest love I have ever known still comes in second. I am willing to say that God is more important than any particular blessing that he imparts.

Though he must have been grieved to the core at the request, Abraham was willing to say this too. So he and Isaac trekked off into the wilderness together.

On the third day (remember that) he found the spot. As Father and son approached the place of sacrifice, Isaac asked one of the most poignant questions ever posed. "Dad, where's the lamb for sacrifice?"

Abraham replied, "God will provide it." Whether he said it in hope, prophecy, confidence, or just to conceal the truth from his son a little longer, we'll never know. Either way, it turned out to be the greatest leap of trust Abraham ever made.

The True Sacrifice

⁹ When they reached the place God had told him about, Abraham built an altar there and arranged the wood on it. He bound his son Isaac and laid him on the altar, on top of the wood. ¹⁰ Then he reached out his hand and took the knife to slay his son. ¹¹ But the angel of the Lord called out to him from heaven, "Abraham! Abraham!"

"Here I am," he replied.

¹² "Do not lay a hand on the boy," he said. "Do not do anything to him. Now I know that you fear God, because you have not withheld from me your son, your only son."

¹³ Abraham looked up and there in a thicket he saw a ram caught by its horns. He went over and took the ram and sacrificed it as a burnt offering instead of his son. ¹⁴ So Abraham called that place The Lord Will Provide. And to this day it is said, "On the mountain of the Lord it will be provided."

Dutifully, but one must imagine regretfully, Abraham bound his son and laid him on the altar. Then he took out his knife to slay him.

Are you horrified at this scene? You're supposed to be. Hold onto that for a second as we retreat from the personal description to the underlying theology behind it.

By rights, *all* of us deserve to die. Nothing imperfect may live forever. If God were truly just (instead of merciful) he would have snuffed us all out and started over as soon as Adam and Eve bit the fruit. As hard as it is to imagine, had Abraham's knife descended God would not have owed him a debt. Theologically, justice would have been served.

How fortunate we are that God doesn't think this way. He cares about us more than he cares about evening the scales.

Though God had the right and power to call in this sacrificial debt, he didn't do it. Returning to the narrative, you can hear the emotion and urgency in God's call from heaven, actually repeating Abraham's name, "Abraham! Abraham!" That kind of repetition doesn't happen much in scripture. It indicates unparalleled intensity. God really, really wanted Abraham to stop.

"Don't do it!" said the voice. "Now I know you love me, not just yourself and your dreams."

Even so, this might all be seen as a cruel, nearly petulant exercise on God's part—merely a nasty way to test someone--except for what happened next.

In a thicket Abraham and Isaac saw a ram caught by its horns. They went over, grabbed it, made the sacrifice, and went on their way. Who cares, it's just a sheep, right?

Except this sacrificial ram wasn't just a sheep. It prefigured the ultimate sacrificial lamb to come: Jesus, God's own Son. Look at all the parallels: three days, the ram given in substitution for our lives, his head draped in thorns, caught in a moment he couldn't escape lest someone else die instead.

Recall every bit of horror and revulsion you felt as we paused with Abraham's knife poised above Isaac. Remember saying, "Who could do this? Who could ask this of another? How brutal and wrong! This should never happen! No matter what you say it isn't right!" Remember how your heart ached for Abraham , burned with anger towards whomever made him do that?

Now consider this: Abraham's son wasn't actually sacrificed, but God's son was. God did exactly what he stopped Abraham from doing.

And God's Son went to the cross because *we* messed up, to fix the world that we broke. We made him do that. We didn't cry, "No...stop!" when he was sacrificed. We shouted, "Crucify him!" and taunted him as he hung there.

People usually read this story and feel loathing towards the demanding God, empathetic sadness for the humans Abraham and Isaac. If we truly understood God's story, we would feel empathetic sadness towards God and his Son, loathing for the humans who demanded that his Son be die for them.

God gave his own Son precisely so we wouldn't have to give ours...so there would be no Isaacs on the altar...so that our sons and daughters could have eternal life, knowing mercy and forgiveness instead of a demand for sacrifice that could never be fulfilled. He loves us that much.

We caused him to sacrifice his Son, and yet he loves us that much.

As it turned out, this was far less of a test of Abraham than a demonstration of God's amazing grace and mercy. What started out as one of the most horrible stories in the Bible ends up one of its most beautiful and heart-wrenching.

The Promise Restated

15 The angel of the Lord called to Abraham from heaven a second time 16 and said, "I swear by myself, declares the Lord, that because you have done this and have not withheld your son, your only son, 17 I will surely bless you and make your descendants as numerous as the stars in the sky and as the sand on the seashore. Your descendants will take possession of the cities of their enemies, 18 and through your offspring all nations on earth will be blessed, because you have obeyed me."

19 Then Abraham returned to his servants, and they set off together for Beersheba. And Abraham stayed in Beersheba.

Here God reiterates his care for Abraham and the promise he has maintained all along. Abraham has obeyed and thought of God before himself, countering the transgression committed by Adam and Eve when they disobeyed and bit the fruit. It was another good moment after an incredibly hard story.

Restating the promise also assures Abraham (and us) that God is a God of giving, not of taking. He demands far less than he ought, gives far more than we merit.

Sarah Passes

At the end of Chapter 22, Abraham hears news of his relatives from back home who have all had children.

Then time passes and we say goodbye to one of the people we've come to love.

23 *Sarah lived to be a hundred and twenty-seven years old.* ² *She died at Kiriath Arba (that is, Hebron) in the land of Canaan, and Abraham went to mourn for Sarah and to weep over her.*

³ *Then Abraham rose from beside his dead wife and spoke to the Hittites. He said,* ⁴ *"I am a foreigner and stranger among you. Sell me some property for a burial site here so I can bury my dead."*

⁵ *The Hittites replied to Abraham,* ⁶ *"Sir, listen to us. You are a mighty prince among us. Bury your dead in the choicest of our tombs. None of us will refuse you his tomb for burying your dead."*

⁷ *Then Abraham rose and bowed down before the people of the land, the Hittites.* ⁸ *He said to them, "If you are willing to let me bury my dead, then listen to me and intercede with Ephron son of Zohar on my behalf* ⁹ *so he will sell me the cave of Machpelah, which belongs to him and is at the end of his field. Ask him to sell it to me for the full price as a burial site among you."*

¹⁰ *Ephron the Hittite was sitting among his people and he replied to Abraham in the hearing of all the Hittites who had come to the gate of his city.* ¹¹ *"No, my lord," he said. "Listen to me; I give you the field, and I give you the cave that is in it. I give it to you in the presence of my people. Bury your dead."*

¹² *Again Abraham bowed down before the people of the land* ¹³ *and he said to Ephron in their hearing, "Listen to me, if you will. I will pay the price of the field. Accept it from me so I can bury my dead there."*

¹⁴ *Ephron answered Abraham,* ¹⁵ *"Listen to me, my lord; the land is worth four hundred shekels of silver, but what is that between you and me? Bury your dead."*

¹⁶ *Abraham agreed to Ephron's terms and weighed out for him the price he had named in the hearing of the Hittites: four hundred shekels of silver, according to the weight current among the merchants.*

¹⁷ *So Ephron's field in Machpelah near Mamre—both the field and the cave in it, and all the trees within the borders of the field—was deeded* ¹⁸ *to*

Abraham as his property in the presence of all the Hittites who had come to the gate of the city. ¹⁹ Afterward Abraham buried his wife Sarah in the cave in the field of Machpelah near Mamre (which is at Hebron) in the land of Canaan. ²⁰ So the field and the cave in it were deeded to Abraham by the Hittites as a burial site.

After a long life that ultimately saw her fulfill her greatest dream, Sarah passed.

Even after all his years in Canaan and with all his wealth and acclaim, Abraham still termed himself a foreigner in the land. But his conduct had been such to earn the respect of the Hittites, at least, who offered him any tomb at their disposal in which to bury Sarah. He chose one in the field of Ephron, then engaged in a reverse bargaining battle, Ephron trying to give him the land, Abraham trying to pay for it.

It's worth noting that the Hebrew is unclear here. The word could be "give" or it could be "sell", so perhaps the bargaining was actual. Either way, the conduct between two peoples that could have been (and would later become) enemies speaks volumes here. Even people who didn't know God knew Abraham as a Godly man. When you show God's Spirit, people respond.

Match dot-Camel

24 *Abraham was now very old, and the Lord had blessed him in every way.* ² *He said to the senior servant in his household, the one in charge of all that he had, "Put your hand under my thigh.* ³ *I want you to swear by the Lord, the God of heaven and the God of earth, that you will not get a wife for my son from the daughters of the Canaanites, among whom I am living,* ⁴ *but will go to my country and my own relatives and get a wife for my son Isaac."*

⁵ *The servant asked him, "What if the woman is unwilling to come back with me to this land? Shall I then take your son back to the country you came from?"*

⁶ "Make sure that you do not take my son back there," Abraham said. ⁷ "The Lord, the God of heaven, who brought me out of my father's household and my native land and who spoke to me and promised me on oath, saying, 'To your offspring I will give this land'—he will send his angel before you so that you can get a wife for my son from there. ⁸ If the woman is unwilling to come back with you, then you will be released from this oath of mine. Only do not take my son back there." ⁹ So the servant put his hand under the thigh of his master Abraham and swore an oath to him concerning this matter.

Abraham was aging now. One of his few remaining concerns was finding a proper wife for his son. Keep in mind that the local selection was limited to women who, for the most part, neither knew God nor believed in him. Abraham was wary of the influence of local culture on his tiny family in this still-strange land. So he did what he could. He gave a servant the unenviable task of traveling back to his homeland to find a wife for his son among his own family and people.

We all like to dabble in playing matchmaker, maybe arranging for a couple of friends to get together and hoping it goes well. Just imagine that your boss, the guy who controls your entire life, said, "Here's what I want you to do. Get on a camel, ride 400 miles, and find the perfect wife for my only-most-precious son, who by the way will also become your next boss. No, they don't get to meet first. That's your job! Make sure she's a good woman, that he'll like her, and that this marriage will work. Don't screw this up."

It's always amusing to think of how many things could have gone wrong here. Only a complete fool would take this assignment voluntarily. You can bet that the servant was cursing the day he was born every step of that journey.

Kindness Wins Out

¹⁰ Then the servant left, taking with him ten of his master's camels loaded with all kinds of good things from his master. He set out for Aram

Naharaim and made his way to the town of Nahor. ¹¹ *He had the camels kneel down near the well outside the town; it was toward evening, the time the women go out to draw water.*

¹² *Then he prayed, "Lord, God of my master Abraham, make me successful today, and show kindness to my master Abraham.* ¹³ *See, I am standing beside this spring, and the daughters of the townspeople are coming out to draw water.* ¹⁴ *May it be that when I say to a young woman, 'Please let down your jar that I may have a drink,' and she says, 'Drink, and I'll water your camels too'—let her be the one you have chosen for your servant Isaac. By this I will know that you have shown kindness to my master."*

¹⁵ *Before he had finished praying, Rebekah came out with her jar on her shoulder. She was the daughter of Bethuel son of Milkah, who was the wife of Abraham's brother Nahor.* ¹⁶ *The woman was very beautiful, a virgin; no man had ever slept with her. She went down to the spring, filled her jar and came up again.*

¹⁷ *The servant hurried to meet her and said, "Please give me a little water from your jar."*

¹⁸ *"Drink, my lord," she said, and quickly lowered the jar to her hands and gave him a drink.*

¹⁹ *After she had given him a drink, she said, "I'll draw water for your camels too, until they have had enough to drink."* ²⁰ *So she quickly emptied her jar into the trough, ran back to the well to draw more water, and drew enough for all his camels.* ²¹ *Without saying a word, the man watched her closely to learn whether or not the Lord had made his journey successful.*

Still cursing inwardly, Abraham's servant loaded up a mini-caravan with all kind of goodies then set off on his journey. He arrived without incident and parked the camels by the town well.

In ancient times the town well was a gathering place, sort of a primitive singles bar if you will. Young women often came to draw water for their families. But water was a town's most precious resource. Locals could be forgiven for not wanting to share it, or their young women, with strangers.

Abraham's servant, knowing all this, prayed that God show kindness to Abraham. Then he proposed a test. He'd ask girls for a drink. He asked God to lead him to the right girl by making her not only give him a drink, but water his camels too.

That servant was pretty wise. It was a good test. I often tell young folks that kindness and generosity are underrated qualities when looking for a romantic partner. I suggest they watch to see how a person responds to the wait staff at a restaurant, checkers in a store, strangers on the street, and the like. Anybody can put on a front and be nice to you. You want to be with people for whom kindness is a habit. It'll keep you together and sane longer than any other trait will.

Before the servant had even finished praying an eligible, beautiful, amazing young woman came walking up to the well. The servant made a beeline for her and blurted out, "Excuse me? Could you spare some water?" Sure enough, she gave him a drink and watered his camels as well.

"Easiest…job…ever" thought the servant. "I'm glad I got it!"

As it turned out, the girl's name was Rebekah and was some kind of cousin to Isaac, which is just what they were looking for.

Rebekah was also engaging in a practice that holds people of faith in good stead. She had a task to finish, drawing water for her family. But she didn't just see the well and the task in front of her, she also saw the people around her as important. The stranger she met wasn't an annoyance, but an opportunity.

Take the Rebekah Test yourself. Which of these are you more likely to think?

1. "That's the grocery clerk, why the heck is she so SLOW???"

2. "That's a human being who happens to be checking out my groceries right now. She's doing it slowly, but she's still a human being."

The first sees people in terms of tasks, the second tasks in terms of people. Your response to the checker will differ radically depending on which view you take.

If you're like most of us, you usually take Option 1. You see the register, the bags, the cart and the food far more clearly than you see the person standing behind that counter. We spend our lives dehumanizing others as everybody around us becomes a tool for our own purposes.

Life is not made up of to-do lists. The guiding symbol of our lives is supposed to be the cross, not the check mark. We miss what God has in store for us because we're so busy controlling our day, our environment, and the people around us.

Rebekah would have been completely justified in saying, "My task is to draw water. This stranger is impeding my task. I must dispose of him." Instead she looked at that servant, saw a person, and acted accordingly. She poured faithfulness and love into the world and God poured ten times as much right back at her.

Rebekah's Family

[22] When the camels had finished drinking, the man took out a gold nose ring weighing a beka and two gold bracelets weighing ten shekels. [23] Then he asked, "Whose daughter are you? Please tell me, is there room in your father's house for us to spend the night?"

[24] She answered him, "I am the daughter of Bethuel, the son that Milkah bore to Nahor." [25] And she added, "We have plenty of straw and fodder, as well as room for you to spend the night."

[26] Then the man bowed down and worshiped the Lord, [27] saying, "Praise be to the Lord, the God of my master Abraham, who has not abandoned his kindness and faithfulness to my master. As for me, the Lord has led me on the journey to the house of my master's relatives."

²⁸ *The young woman ran and told her mother's household about these things.* ²⁹ *Now Rebekah had a brother named Laban, and he hurried out to the man at the spring.* ³⁰ *As soon as he had seen the nose ring, and the bracelets on his sister's arms, and had heard Rebekah tell what the man said to her, he went out to the man and found him standing by the camels near the spring.* ³¹ *"Come, you who are blessed by the Lord," he said. "Why are you standing out here? I have prepared the house and a place for the camels."*

The servant finds out to his delight that not only is Rebekah related to the family, she has room to put him up for the night. He praised God while she ran ahead to prepare. Her brother, Laban, takes one look at the bling on her arms and immediately asks the stranger why he's standing outside. Come in! Cha-ching!

We're going to hear much more about Laban and his gold-digging later on.

Giving Praise to God

³² *So the man went to the house, and the camels were unloaded. Straw and fodder were brought for the camels, and water for him and his men to wash their feet.* ³³ *Then food was set before him, but he said, "I will not eat until I have told you what I have to say."*

"Then tell us," Laban said.

³⁴ *So he said, "I am Abraham's servant.* ³⁵ *The Lord has blessed my master abundantly, and he has become wealthy. He has given him sheep and cattle, silver and gold, male and female servants, and camels and donkeys.* ³⁶ *My master's wife Sarah has borne him a son in her old age, and he has given him everything he owns.* ³⁷ *And my master made me swear an oath, and said, 'You must not get a wife for my son from the daughters of the Canaanites, in whose land I live,* ³⁸ *but go to my father's family and to my own clan, and get a wife for my son.'*

³⁹ *"Then I asked my master, 'What if the woman will not come back with me?'*

⁴⁰ "He replied, 'The Lord, before whom I have walked faithfully, will send his angel with you and make your journey a success, so that you can get a wife for my son from my own clan and from my father's family. ⁴¹ You will be released from my oath if, when you go to my clan, they refuse to give her to you—then you will be released from my oath.'

⁴² "When I came to the spring today, I said, 'Lord, God of my master Abraham, if you will, please grant success to the journey on which I have come. ⁴³ See, I am standing beside this spring. If a young woman comes out to draw water and I say to her, "Please let me drink a little water from your jar," ⁴⁴ and if she says to me, "Drink, and I'll draw water for your camels too," let her be the one the Lord has chosen for my master's son.'

⁴⁵ "Before I finished praying in my heart, Rebekah came out, with her jar on her shoulder. She went down to the spring and drew water, and I said to her, 'Please give me a drink.'

⁴⁶ "She quickly lowered her jar from her shoulder and said, 'Drink, and I'll water your camels too.' So I drank, and she watered the camels also.

⁴⁷ "I asked her, 'Whose daughter are you?'

"She said, 'The daughter of Bethuel son of Nahor, whom Milkah bore to him.'

"Then I put the ring in her nose and the bracelets on her arms, ⁴⁸ and I bowed down and worshiped the Lord. I praised the Lord, the God of my master Abraham, who had led me on the right road to get the granddaughter of my master's brother for his son. ⁴⁹ Now if you will show kindness and faithfulness to my master, tell me; and if not, tell me, so I may know which way to turn."

⁵⁰ Laban and Bethuel answered, "This is from the Lord; we can say nothing to you one way or the other. ⁵¹ Here is Rebekah; take her and go, and let her become the wife of your master's son, as the Lord has directed."

The servant launches into a lengthy retelling of the story so far. Note that he won't take a bite or take his ease until he has fulfilled his purpose. He's not making this journey for his own comfort, but to fulfill his vow to his master.

In the explanation the servant is careful to detail God's role in all of this. It's an important point. Most of us assume credit for ourselves when things go well and only remember God when we're in need. It's a form of betrayal, a missed opportunity. How will people learn that God is good unless we also speak of him that way?

Personally I'm not fond of the "finger pointed skyward after touchdown" phenomenon. I don't think you can witness effectively to that many people in that short a time by any means, let alone a brief wag of your digits. (I always wonder what fans of the opposing team think. "Well, I guess God had it in for us on that one. Cornerback fell down.") The same holds true when people tack, "Praise God!" at the end of random sentences as if the story was really the point and their praise a quick formality. I file all these things in the "theologically tacky" folder.

But sometimes when you're relaying your story among people you actually know, it wouldn't be so bad to explore how you see God working for good in your life. Those conversations are usually amazing and we never have them. Being petrified into silence because we fear what others will think is just as bad as being theologically tacky and not caring what anyone else thinks. Both are forms of self-absorption. When we're willing to be vulnerable enough to share our thoughts on God in a non-anxious manner, we give permission for others to do so as well.

The servant's description of God's goodness certainly had the right effect in this story. Rebekah's relatives looked at each other, shrugged, and said, "What can we do? This is from God. Take her to your master's son."

Wishing Well for Others

⁵² When Abraham's servant heard what they said, he bowed down to the ground before the Lord. ⁵³ Then the servant brought out gold and silver jewelry and articles of clothing and gave them to Rebekah; he also gave costly gifts to her brother and to her mother. ⁵⁴ Then he and the men who were with him ate and drank and spent the night there.

When they got up the next morning, he said, "Send me on my way to my master."

⁵⁵ But her brother and her mother replied, "Let the young woman remain with us ten days or so; then you may go."

⁵⁶ But he said to them, "Do not detain me, now that the Lord has granted success to my journey. Send me on my way so I may go to my master."

⁵⁷ Then they said, "Let's call the young woman and ask her about it." ⁵⁸ So they called Rebekah and asked her, "Will you go with this man?"

"I will go," she said.

⁵⁹ So they sent their sister Rebekah on her way, along with her nurse and Abraham's servant and his men. ⁶⁰ And they blessed Rebekah and said to her,

"Our sister, may you increase
    to thousands upon thousands;
may your offspring possess
    the cities of their enemies."

Despite the assurances of the night before, the morning brought hemming and hawing, more in line with what would be expected in such a situation. Abraham's servant wanted to leave right away, fulfilling his mission. Rebekah's family wanted her to remain 10 days or so, perhaps getting a chance to say goodbye, perhaps hoping some more jewelry would be coming their way, or perhaps because they didn't necessarily intend to let her go at all now that they thought about it.

In the end they left it to Rebekah, who decided to go. Her family gave her with a blessing that mirrored the covenant God spoke to Abraham earlier, "May you increase in numbers and may your offspring conquer their enemies."

We've lost the sense of blessing in our modern society. We've replaced it with the brief and sterile, "Good luck!" or the all-encompassing, "May all your dreams come true!" Blessing is supposed to convey more than generic good wishes. Blessing someone is a sign that you know someone, understand their desires, and care about both.

We've given up on blessings because we like to be quick and we like to be right. People don't want to be heard wishing for things that might not come true. We equate someone saying, "Well, that blessing didn't work" with them bringing back the blender we gave them for Christmas because it broke on December 26th. We make our well-wishes nebulous and non-specific to avoid this.

That was never the point of blessing, though. Neither blessing-giver nor blessing-receiver gets to control the outcome (unless the giver happens to be God). But we can still affirm each other, encourage each other, let others know that we care about them.

If we spend a little time getting to know our friends and family, blessing each other becomes easy. Instead of saying, "Good luck!" next time someone's heading off to their driving exam, try, "You've put so much work into this. May all you've learned come back to you as you take your test and may every traffic light be green." Show you've paid attention. Show that their well-being is important to you too. It won't matter if every light doesn't actually turn green, the person you blessed will still remember you and be encouraged.

The Lovers Meet

61 Then Rebekah and her attendants got ready and mounted the camels and went back with the man. So the servant took Rebekah and left.

GARDEN TO DESERT

⁶² Now Isaac had come from Beer Lahai Roi, for he was living in the Negev.⁶³ He went out to the field one evening to meditate, and as he looked up, he saw camels approaching. ⁶⁴ Rebekah also looked up and saw Isaac. She got down from her camel ⁶⁵ and asked the servant, "Who is that man in the field coming to meet us?"

"He is my master," the servant answered. So she took her veil and covered herself.

⁶⁶ Then the servant told Isaac all he had done. ⁶⁷ Isaac brought her into the tent of his mother Sarah, and he married Rebekah. So she became his wife, and he loved her; and Isaac was comforted after his mother's death.

The caravan returned, bride in tow, until in a moment worthy of film Isaac looked up one day and saw them approaching across the fields. Rebekah's heart caught as she uttered, "My, my, who IS that man?" Then the servant told Isaac how nifty Rebekah was and how he had managed to find her. The two became man and wife shortly after and Isaac was complete again after the death of his mother.

That's it. No deep theological crescendo here, no serpent hiding under the tent. Sometimes things just work out the way they're supposed to. We should treasure those moments when we get them.

What We Leave Behind

25 Abraham had taken another wife, whose name was Keturah. ² She bore him Zimran, Jokshan, Medan, Midian, Ishbak and Shuah. ³ Jokshan was the father of Sheba and Dedan; the descendants of Dedan were the Ashurites, the Letushites and the Leummites. ⁴ The sons of Midian were Ephah, Epher, Hanok, Abida and Eldaah. All these were descendants of Keturah.

⁵ Abraham left everything he owned to Isaac. ⁶ But while he was still living, he gave gifts to the sons of his concubines and sent them away from his son Isaac to the land of the east.

It seems typical that when a man loses his wife, he remarries quickly. Abraham did this, wedding Keturah and fathering several more sons. Their names are listed in Genesis 25:2 but the more important events happen in verses 3-4. All these sons would become fathers of their own peoples: Ashurites, Midianites, Letushites, Leummites. These tribes will appear later in the Old Testament, sometimes as allies of Israel, sometimes as enemies. Abraham became not only the father of a great nation, but the father of multiple nations.

Understanding the difficulties likely to arise between his heirs after his death, Abraham gave gifts to all his sons who were not Isaac, then sent them away to the east so Isaac would inherit his land without contest. This is not recommended among your children today (blended family or otherwise) but having a clear will and bequests does go a long way towards easing family stress after a parent passes.

Everybody loves their children and most children love each other, but the pressures inherent in trying to follow mom's or dad's wishes when nobody really knows what those wishes are is too much for any family to bear. Small items take on outsized importance. Huge fights develop over insignificant things. "That was mom's favorite toothbrush holder! She kept her toothbrush in it every night!"

Everybody with children should have a clear, concise document detailing their final wishes and stating explicitly that anything not named in the document is unimportant…that it can be thrown away, donated, buried, burned, split up, or sent to the moon for all you care, you just want your children to be there for each other in that time and not worry about it. Failing to do this is abdicating one of the solemn responsibilities of parenthood.

The Death of Abraham

⁷ Abraham lived a hundred and seventy-five years. ⁸ Then Abraham breathed his last and died at a good old age, an old man and full of years; and he was gathered to his people. ⁹ His sons Isaac and Ishmael buried *him in the cave of Machpelah near Mamre, in the field of Ephron son of Zohar the Hittite, ¹⁰ the field Abraham had bought from the Hittites. There Abraham was buried with his wife Sarah.*

The Bible says Abraham died at a "good old age...full of years", implying satisfaction with his life overall. Nobody could wish for more than that. Though it was not perfect, by most standards his was a good life. May we all be blessed to say the same at our time of passing.

Note the touching moment when Isaac and Ishmael reunite to bury their dad. Some things in life are more important than our divisions. In the end we all hope we're part of the same human family, beloved by God, no matter our differences.

Generation to Generation

¹¹ After Abraham's death, God blessed his son Isaac, who then lived near Beer Lahai Roi.

God continued to bless Isaac as he had blessed Abraham. We may die, but God's goodness never does. His promise endures from age to age. Each of us gets to see a part of it, but none of our lives can contain the whole.

Mortality is a tricky thing. We cannot celebrate it but we dare not fear it either. The temptation to define this as, "MY time" and then attempt to make it last forever is too strong. We shut out other generations, other viewpoints, and a host of wonderful lessons life tries to teach us when we do not acknowledge that we are mortal.

Life is movement. Death is the lack of movement. Your physical body attests to this. When your heart stops moving, you die.

When we fear death, we try to move forward as little as possible, locking ourselves into certain places, times, and perceptions. Ironically by not moving we are cementing ourselves into death rather than delaying or avoiding it. We die before we die.

Abraham hardly ever stopped moving. His descendants' lives would be full of motion as well. This was appropriate and necessary.

But how many churches, spiritual heirs of Abraham's family, invest all their effort into not moving? The church is a building with deep foundations and high walls made of stone to regulate who comes in and out. Practices and traditions are set in stone as well; God forbid anyone should change anything. They give up their place as temples of Life, becoming monuments to the fear of death.

If we all see only a part of God, centering a community around "not moving" is the same as calling our part of God the whole thing…a form of idolatry. We pretend as if God is no bigger than our culture, our time, and our viewpoint. We claim that he will not outlast them.

"Kids nowadays! The world is going to hell in a handbasket!" Your grandma thought that about your generation too. The world managed to survive mini-skirts and Elvis wiggling his hips. It'll probably survive Justin Bieber too. God is still here, and he's still operating in ways that no single generation can hope to encompass or understand.

Abraham was the father and founder of our faith, the guy at the top of the genealogy lists, maybe the most important figure in the Old Testament. Abraham also died. And God blessed Isaac after him.

We do not celebrate our mortality and we must not fear it, but we can understand it. We are temporary, but mortality is temporary as well. It's an important part of our story, one we dare not ignore, but it's neither the end of the story nor its most important facet. It's a small piece of an infinitely big puzzle which is not complete without it, but refuses to be dominated by it.

5 ISAAC AND HIS SONS

Feisty Twins

After a brief interlude to detail Ishmael's lineage, recounting how his offspring lived in hostility towards all those around him, Genesis 25 continues with the story of Isaac's twin sons.

19 This is the account of the family line of Abraham's son Isaac.

Abraham became the father of Isaac, 20 and Isaac was forty years old when he married Rebekah daughter of Bethuel the Aramean from Paddan Aram and sister of Laban the Aramean.

21 Isaac prayed to the Lord on behalf of his wife, because she was childless. The Lord answered his prayer, and his wife Rebekah became pregnant. 22 The babies jostled each other within her, and she said, "Why is this happening to me?" So she went to inquire of the Lord.

23 The Lord said to her,

"Two nations are in your womb,
*   and two peoples from within you will be separated;*
one people will be stronger than the other,
*   and the older will serve the younger."*

24 When the time came for her to give birth, there were twin boys in her womb. 25 The first to come out was red, and his whole body was like a hairy garment; so they named him Esau. 26 After this, his brother came out, with his hand grasping Esau's heel; so he was named Jacob. Isaac was sixty years old when Rebekah gave birth to them.

Like her mother-in-law, Rebekah had trouble conceiving children. Isaac prayed on her behalf and she conceived, bearing twins. But an interesting thing happened on the way to the delivery room. The twins began fighting and jostling inside the womb. No doubt massively uncomfortable, Rebekah cried to the heavens asking, "Why???" God gave her an interesting answer.

He explained that "two different nations" were in her womb. Her babies would grow to lead separate tribes. God also inverted the usual order of things, claiming that the elder child would serve the younger. The contest between them was already underway, before they were even born. All babies kick in the womb; these two were kicking each other.

The struggle continued as Rebekah went through labor. Esau came out red and covered with hair, but Jacob wasn't letting his brother get ahead. His first moments of life were spent clutching Esau's heel, unwilling to let the older brother get the upper hand. This was the opening bell in a bout that would last well into Jacob and Esau's adulthood.

Playing Favorites

27 The boys grew up, and Esau became a skillful hunter, a man of the open country, while Jacob was content to stay at home among the tents. 28 Isaac, who had a taste for wild game, loved Esau, but Rebekah loved Jacob.

29 Once when Jacob was cooking some stew, Esau came in from the open country, famished. 30 He said to Jacob, "Quick, let me have some of that red stew! I'm famished!" (That is why he was also called Edom.)

31 Jacob replied, "First sell me your birthright."

32 "Look, I am about to die," Esau said. "What good is the birthright to me?"

33 But Jacob said, "Swear to me first." So he swore an oath to him, selling his birthright to Jacob.

34 Then Jacob gave Esau some bread and some lentil stew. He ate and drank, and then got up and left.

So Esau despised his birthright.

You may have noticed that Genesis takes up wonderful, age-old themes. It does so again here as each boy develops qualities that endear him to a particular parent. Esau is a manly man; Dad loves him best. Jacob is more of a mama's boy. In these lads we feel the tension between warlike hunter and domestic settler, the strapping football player versus the clever chess champion.

In this tale Esau came back to camp from his wanderings with his stomach empty. He found Jacob cooking a savory stew. Esau demanded food from his brother.

Jacob, showing himself to be crafty (his name means "trickster" or "deceitful one") said he'd happily fork over the stew in return for Esau's birthright. This represented the duty to carry on the family name plus the land and wealth that accompanied it, usually a 2/3 share of the property. In Isaac's family it also represented the covenant that God had established with Abraham and pledged to propagate throughout all the generations of his offspring.

The text gives no indication that Esau understood the deeper implications of his birthright, nor that he was thinking of anything at all besides his stomach. He's portrayed as a headstrong bumbler, aware of what's in front of him and not much more.

Jacob, meanwhile, knew that but for a shove or two in the birth canal, he would have emerged first of the twins and inherited the family's greatest honors. Able to think many steps ahead, he saw a chance to rectify what seemed like a cruel injustice to him.

Jacob took the offer to trade stew for the family birthright dead seriously. Esau probably saw it as a joke. "If I die from hunger, what good is an inheritance?" This is less a serious statement than an exaggeration mirroring the incredible demand his brother had put forth.

Jacob pushed farther, demanding an oath which made the matter serious. Esau was likely still joking when he swore it. From that moment on, Jacob considered the family birthright as his while Esau thought the moment meant nothing.

A relationship therapist would probably sit the boys down and tell them they were talking past each other. Each assumed his own interpretation of events held sway. Neither bothered to correct the other. This was bound to cause trouble.

The phrase "So Esau despised his birthright" sticks out at the end of the passage. We usually take "despise" to mean "hate", but here it has a different meaning: neglect. Esau didn't hate his birthright, he just didn't take it seriously, didn't pay attention to its importance. He figured the birthright was something he could play around with.

We justify not treating people as we should by saying, "I don't *hate* them, I just don't pay attention to them." Long-term spouses are the prime candidates for this treatment, but coworkers, people who do services for us, and sometimes entire races or political parties fall under this umbrella too. You don't have to feel hate for someone to despise them. If you're not giving them attention, you're reducing them to something less than they're meant to be. You might be better off hating them. At least then they'd exist.

We all have to remember that *our* birthright is love. We can put many names on it: grace, mercy, forgiveness, salvation, but it all boils down to the same thing. God is love. Every moment we spend being anything less than the most loving we can be towards everyone we meet is a moment spent despising our birthright and neglecting our purpose.

Worse than that, we trade our birthright for bowls of stew every day, making wealth or power, possessions or prestige the center of our universe instead of love. Like Esau, we say, "I'm going to act this way because it's expedient at the moment. Who cares about the big picture? Give me my stew!"

These passages invite us to see Esau as a Neanderthal, a cretin who can't think past the rumbling of his own stomach to see what's really valuable. And we're all Esau. Most of us aren't even ashamed of it. If the reward smells good enough, we'll despise anything in order to get it.

Living With the Philistines

***26** Now there was a famine in the land—besides the previous famine in Abraham's time—and Isaac went to Abimelek king of the Philistines in Gerar.² The Lord appeared to Isaac and said, "Do not go down to Egypt; live in the land where I tell you to live. ³ Stay in this land for a while, and I will be with you and will bless you. For to you and your descendants I will give all these lands and will confirm the oath I swore to your father Abraham. ⁴ I will make your descendants as numerous as the stars in the sky and will give them all these lands, and through your offspring all nations on earth will be blessed, ⁵ because Abraham obeyed me and did everything I* *required of him, keeping my commands, my decrees and my instructions." ⁶ So Isaac stayed in Gerar.*

⁷ When the men of that place asked him about his wife, he said, "She is my sister," because he was afraid to say, "She is my wife." He thought, "The men of this place might kill me on account of Rebekah, because she is beautiful."

⁸ When Isaac had been there a long time, Abimelek king of the Philistines looked down from a window and saw Isaac caressing his wife Rebekah. ⁹ So Abimelek summoned Isaac and said, "She is really your wife! Why did you say, 'She is my sister'?"

Isaac answered him, "Because I thought I might lose my life on account of her."

¹⁰ Then Abimelek said, "What is this you have done to us? One of the men might well have slept with your wife, and you would have brought guilt upon us."

¹¹ So Abimelek gave orders to all the people: "Anyone who harms this man or his wife shall surely be put to death."

Finally, a king who doesn't fall for the Abraham Family Scam!

You can almost see old Abe up in heaven, slapping his forehead and saying, "No, son! You can't caress her until AFTER you get the sheep and camels and servants! Didn't I teach you anything?"

Meanwhile God reiterates the Abrahamic covenant to Isaac, passing it to the next generation. Plus God's people survive another famine. This time they don't have to journey all the way to Egypt, but stay right next door in the land of the Philistines.

Cue Abraham again, hands cupped around his mouth and yelling down from heaven, "You have it EASY! When I was your age we walked all the way to Egypt and back! Uphill! Both ways!"

Enduring Faithfully

¹² Isaac planted crops in that land and the same year reaped a hundredfold, because the Lord blessed him. ¹³ The man became rich, and his wealth continued to grow until he became very wealthy. ¹⁴ He had so many flocks and herds and servants that the

Philistines envied him. ¹⁵ So all the wells that his father's servants had dug in the time of his father Abraham, the Philistines stopped up, filling them with earth.

¹⁶ Then Abimelek said to Isaac, "Move away from us; you have become too powerful for us."

¹⁷ So Isaac moved away from there and encamped in the Valley of Gerar, where he settled. ¹⁸ Isaac reopened the wells that had been dug in the time of his father Abraham, which the Philistines had stopped up after Abraham died, and he gave them the same names his father had given them.

¹⁹ Isaac's servants dug in the valley and discovered a well of fresh water there. ²⁰ But the herders of Gerar quarreled with those of Isaac and said, "The water is ours!" So he named the well Esek, because they disputed with him. ²¹ Then they dug another well, but they quarreled over that one also; so he named it Sitnah. ²² He moved on from there and dug another well, and no one quarreled over it. He named it Rehoboth, saying, "Now the Lord has given us room and we will flourish in the land."

Isaac found that sticking with God is a good thing, as he multiplied his agricultural investment by 100 in a year of famine. He continued to work and serve until he had generated enough wealth to make his hosts, the Philistines, jealous. They ran around the countryside filling in all the wells that Abraham had commissioned, leaving Isaac without the means to support himself. Then King Abimelek kicked him out.

Isaac unstopped the wells and even dug some new ones, but every time he found water, the locals claimed it as theirs. He had to dig three wells before he could access one unmolested.

Endurance is an underrated aspect of faith. It's hard to do what's right. It's even harder when you do what's right and only get grief for it. Feedback can be a reliable guide, but is not always. If you're trying to do something right and get thwarted, you shouldn't give up easily. Sometimes you just have to try until it goes right.

We like to celebrate folks who achieve splashy, obvious success. We should probably celebrate folks who keep at it every day for the sake of righteousness, never knowing if their efforts will bear fruit but continuing anyway.

God Ain't Bad

23 From there he went up to Beersheba. 24 That night the Lord appeared to him and said, "I am the God of your father Abraham. Do not be afraid, for I am with you; I will bless you and will increase the number of your descendants for the sake of my servant Abraham."

25 Isaac built an altar there and called on the name of the Lord. There he pitched his tent, and there his servants dug a well.

26 Meanwhile, Abimelek had come to him from Gerar, with Ahuzzath his personal adviser and Phicol the commander of his forces. 27 Isaac asked them, "Why have you come to me, since you were hostile to me and sent me away?"

28 They answered, "We saw clearly that the Lord was with you; so we said, 'There ought to be a sworn agreement between us'—between us and you. Let us make a treaty with you 29 that you will do us no harm, just as we did not harm you but always treated you well and sent you away peacefully. And now you are blessed by the Lord."

30 Isaac then made a feast for them, and they ate and drank. 31 Early the next morning the men swore an oath to each other. Then Isaac sent them on their way, and they went away peacefully.

32 That day Isaac's servants came and told him about the well they had dug. They said, "We've found water!" 33 He called it Shibah, and to this day the name of the town has been Beersheba.

In these passages Isaac continues his father's tradition of talking with the Lord and building altars to him. He also strikes another well, allowing him to grow and prosper.

In between those two events his old friends the Philistines show up, the folks who had just filled in all his wells and booted him out of the country. Greeted with understandable suspicion, the visitors explain that it's evident God is with Isaac and they want no enmity with him because of it. The two parties sign a treaty of non-aggression.

You don't always have to convince people to believe like you do in order to show them God's power. As we saw several times with Abraham and now see with Isaac, working for righteousness is its own witness. Even if people around you don't come begging you for theological advice, you've still done something if you show them that God isn't all that bad…allowing them to make their own treaty of non-aggression with you and, by extension, with the God you serve.

"Non-aggression" sounds like a pretty modest thing to ask, but in this day and age it's a big deal.

Churches have spent a lot of time teaching "God stuff" that isn't scriptural at all. "Sit down and keep your mouth shut kid, plus listen to what I say and agree with me or else God will send you to hell" is found nowhere in scripture. But a couple generations have absorbed that message from "Christian" folks now and it's taken hold. I can't say the words "God" or "Christian" without a dozen bad connotations popping to mind. Therefore when I meet someone outside the church, I don't try to convert them. Instead I spend a lot of time quietly trying to show them that God isn't bad.

It doesn't help that almost every widespread depiction of the Christian faith is pure garbage. We live in the age where the only people seen on camera are complete crackpots. This is true of most "Christians" beamed into our living rooms as well. Add in dehumanizing billboards that assume the same words will fit every reader, bumper stickers that reduce complex scripture to four words in huge font, and the occasional street corner preacher screaming out damnation and you can see why the public perception of God is suffering.

We should do more to fight against this as people of faith…at the very least calling out the crackpots instead of assuming they're on "our side" just because they label themselves "Christian". Last I checked we're not supposed to have a side, let alone claim ownership of it. But if that's too hard, we should at least be working every day to model a faith that testifies against the inflammatory atrocities so routinely spoken in God's name.

The good news is, when you walk with God people *do* tend to see it, not because you shove it in their faces but because faith uplifts and supports them as well as you. Our God won't be confined. As his Spirit travels with you it'll overflow onto other people through the kindness, support, and mercy you share with them. Experiencing God through you should be a good experience for those around you. When they see that faith uplifts and supports people instead of tearing them down, they'll be more inclined to be cool towards God and his people.

Looking Through Proper Eyes

³⁴ When Esau was forty years old, he married Judith daughter of Beeri the Hittite, and also Basemath daughter of Elon the Hittite. ³⁵ They were a source of grief to Isaac and Rebekah.

Because the only thing worse than your son marrying one annoying daughter-in-law is your son marrying two of them.

As Esau's wives were Hittites, we may assume the grief caused to Isaac and Rebekah was not just personal, but theological. Foreign gods and idols brought in through intermarriage would become a constant problem for Abraham's descendants, eventually leading to their doom. It was the one issue they never seemed able to fix.

Besides the obvious warning to be careful who you marry, the passage points out the difference between traveling through an environment and becoming enmeshed in it. The line is fine and none of us tread it perfectly. At one time or another all of us find ourselves stuck in something we wish we hadn't been. The progress is so gentle, each step so sensible, that we ease ourselves into bad situations.

The worst thing we can do is presume that we know how to avoid this trap. As soon as we're sure we have it mastered--that we know the difference between right and wrong, between "just enough" and "too much"—we find ourselves married to our own Beeris and Basemaths.

The best we can do is try to keep faith in front of us each day, lifting up something besides ourselves and our own judgment. Forget whether doing this thing would make sense in our eyes. Would it make sense in God's eyes, in light of infinite love and goodness? If not it's probably better left undone no matter how much sense it seems to make.

Oceans 11,000 B.C.

27 When Isaac was old and his eyes were so weak that he could no longer see, he called for Esau his older son and said to him, "My son."

"Here I am," he answered.

2 Isaac said, "I am now an old man and don't know the day of my death. 3 Now then, get your equipment—your quiver and bow—and go out to the open country to hunt some wild game for me. 4 Prepare me the kind of tasty food I like and bring it to me to eat, so that I may give you my blessing before I die."

5 Now Rebekah was listening as Isaac spoke to his son Esau. When Esau left for the open country to hunt game and bring it back, 6 Rebekah said to her son Jacob, "Look, I overheard your father say to your brother Esau, 7 'Bring me some game and prepare me some tasty food to eat, so that I may give you my blessing in the presence of the Lord before I die.' 8 Now, my son, listen carefully and do what I tell you: 9 Go out to the flock and bring me two choice young goats, so I can prepare some tasty food for your father, just the way he likes it. 10 Then take it to your father to eat, so that he may give you his blessing before he dies."

Oh dear.

The time has finally come for Isaac to bestow his blessing and inheritance on one of his sons. At this crucial moment we see the flaw in Jacob's plan. Jacob may think Esau's stew-trading agreement is binding and may believe wholeheartedly that the inheritance is his, but he's not the one making the decisions. If Isaac doesn't believe it's valid, it's not valid. Dad gets to bless whomever he wishes.

Let's pause the story for a second and admit that we've all been where Jacob is, believing in something strongly without the power to enact it. Feeling like an injustice is being done but lacking the ability to correct it is one of the most frustrating things in the world, especially when the injustice hurts us or people we love.

We may not agree with the scheme Rebekah and Jacob are cooking up, but we can understand it. When you feel like the course of your life is being altered by forces beyond your control, almost any way you can find to correct that course seems fair.

Whether it's actually fair? That'll probably remain unresolved until we all get to heaven. Meeting injustice with more injustice doesn't satisfy, but neither does meeting injustice with surrender. The best we can do is remember that none of us are truly just. Isaac isn't the only blind man making decisions. We're all blind in one way or another.

The worst decisions inevitably come when the person making them is convinced they're right. When we have the power to enforce our will we must remember that we're bound to enforce it wrongly in some ways. When someone else's will is enforced wrongly on us we must protest but also remember that our view isn't perfect either. Life works better when we suspect ourselves as much as possible and give all the leeway we can to those who disagree with us. It's the opposite of the world's path to power, but it leaves more room for understanding between us. This creates better relationships and a better world.

I've been in positions of power many times in my life. My first instinct is to get as many opinions as possible before making decisions, so I know what's at stake and for whom. Understanding that any decision I make is going to disadvantage someone, I try to take special care of those who have been hurt by what I've done…making up for the injustice of a decision even when I know it's the right decision to make.

Neither Isaac nor Rebekah seemed to be following this path. Isaac loved Esau best while Rebekah favored Jacob. This is not in the Manual of Healthy Parenting. The struggle between Esau and Jacob blossomed into a struggle between Isaac and Rebekah as well. Everyone felt they were justified in choosing as side; nobody built a bridge.

In the end, Isaac's decision about the inheritance became one of power and tradition untampered by compassion. No doubt Isaac cared for both his sons, but functionally it would not show in this particular circumstance. Perceiving that power ruled over compassion, Rebekah and Jacob felt justified usurping that power for themselves in a just cause.

Every one of us should remember this lesson. When we make decisions by power—well-meaning or not—we will always run into someone who, by trickery or force, will take that power from us. When we make decisions with compassion we will find a wealth of compassion flowing back to us from the people around us.

In Isaac's case, the people about to seize power were his younger son and wife. They had a very cunning plan…

The Smell of Success

11 Jacob said to Rebekah his mother, "But my brother Esau is a hairy man while I have smooth skin. 12 What if my father touches me? I would appear to be tricking him and would bring down a curse on myself rather than a blessing."

13 His mother said to him, "My son, let the curse fall on me. Just do what I say; go and get them for me."

14 So he went and got them and brought them to his mother, and she prepared some tasty food, just the way his father liked it. 15 Then Rebekah took the best clothes of Esau her older son, which she had in the house, and put them on her younger son Jacob. 16 She also covered his hands and the smooth part of his neck with the goatskins. 17 Then she handed to her son Jacob the tasty food and the bread she had made.

18 He went to his father and said, "My father."

"Yes, my son," he answered. "Who is it?"

19 Jacob said to his father, "I am Esau your firstborn. I have done as you told me. Please sit up and eat some of my game, so that you may give me your blessing."

20 Isaac asked his son, "How did you find it so quickly, my son?"

"The Lord your God gave me success," he replied.

21 Then Isaac said to Jacob, "Come near so I can touch you, my son, to know whether you really are my son Esau or not."

22 Jacob went close to his father Isaac, who touched him and said, "The voice is the voice of Jacob, but the hands are the hands of Esau." 23 He did not recognize him, for his hands were hairy like those of his brother Esau; so he proceeded to bless him. [24] *"Are you really my son Esau?" he asked.*

"I am," he replied.

[25] *Then he said, "My son, bring me some of your game to eat, so that I may give you my blessing."*

Jacob brought it to him and he ate; and he brought some wine and he drank. [26] *Then his father Isaac said to him, "Come here, my son, and kiss me."*

[27] *So he went to him and kissed him. When Isaac caught the smell of his clothes, he blessed him and said, "Ah, the smell of my son*
   is like the smell of a field
   that the Lord has blessed.
[28] *May God give you heaven's dew*
   and earth's richness—
   an abundance of grain and new wine.
[29] *May nations serve you*
   and peoples bow down to you.
Be lord over your brothers,
   and may the sons of your mother bow down to you.
May those who curse you be cursed
   and those who bless you be blessed."

Rebekah dressed her younger son in the guise of the older. Jacob put on Esau's clothes and covered his hands and neck in old goatskins. Rebekah put the stew in his hands, patted his head, and sent him into blind, old Isaac's tent.

Jacob presented the meal to his father, who was instantly suspicious. The voice wasn't right. He asked how Esau had gotten his game so quickly and Jacob made bold, pulling the Lord into the equation. He claimed that God had blessed him with an easy hunt. Then Isaac beckoned him closer. He felt the goat hair on the hands, sniffed the odor of a fertilized field in the clothes. If it feels like a goat and smells like manure, it must be Esau.

This story justifies mothers of 8-13 year old boys everywhere. Had Esau bothered to bathe every once in a while, this wouldn't have happened.

Despite having tested Jacob three times over, Isaac was still fooled. We must beware our own perceptions. Sometimes no matter how hard we try, we're just not going to get it right.

Isaac blessed Jacob with abundance of crops, with the promise that nations would bow down before him, with the headship of the family over all his brothers, and with the Abrahamic invocation that anyone who cursed him would himself be cursed. The family birthright—material and spiritual— had been passed. Jacob now had his fondest desire.

No Blessings to Give

30 After Isaac finished blessing him, and Jacob had scarcely left his father's presence, his brother Esau came in from hunting. 31 He too prepared some tasty food and brought it to his father. Then he said to him, "My father, please sit up and eat some of my game, so that you may give me your blessing."

32 His father Isaac asked him, "Who are you?"

"I am your son," he answered, "your firstborn, Esau."

33 Isaac trembled violently and said, "Who was it, then, that hunted game and brought it to me? I ate it just before you came and I blessed him—and indeed he will be blessed!"

34 When Esau heard his father's words, he burst out with a loud and bitter cry and said to his father, "Bless me—me too, my father!"

35 But he said, "Your brother came deceitfully and took your blessing."

36 Esau said, "Isn't he rightly named Jacob? This is the second time he has taken advantage of me: He took my birthright, and now he's taken my blessing!" Then he asked, "Haven't you reserved any blessing for me?"

37 Isaac answered Esau, "I have made him lord over you and have made all his relatives his servants, and I have sustained him with grain and new wine. So what can I possibly do for you, my son?"

38 Esau said to his father, "Do you have only one blessing, my father? Bless me too, my father!" Then Esau wept aloud.

[39] *His father Isaac answered him,*

"Your dwelling will be
  away from the earth's richness,
  away from the dew of heaven above.
[40] *You will live by the sword*
  and you will serve your brother.
But when you grow restless,
  you will throw his yoke
  from off your neck."

No sooner had Jacob left the tent than the other shoe dropped. Esau came in with his own stew, ready to receive what was his. Except it wasn't his anymore. Isaac had bestowed the birthright and the blessing. It could not be undone. It wasn't Isaac's to give anymore. It was Jacob's.

Esau asked what was left for him. Isaac struggled to find a single important thing he hadn't already bestowed on Jacob. This speaks of the favoritism Isaac intended to show to Esau in the first place…why Jacob and Rebekah felt the whole deal was unfair. Had things gone unchecked, Esau would have ruled and Jacob would have ended up with nothing.

Still Esau begged. His father gave a "non-blessing" blessing that sounded more like a directive. "You're not going to get the fertile fields. You're not going to get heaven's showers. But you have a sword and you're subservient to your brother who has stolen all the things you want. When you get tired of that, you'll figure out some way to throw his yoke off your neck." (Strong implication: by using that sword to remove his head from his.)

Just as Rebekah had played her hand fully with Jacob, now Isaac seemed intent on pushing his power to the limit with Esau. As is typical of intense family fights, nobody was backing down here.

Esau's Plan

[41] *Esau held a grudge against Jacob because of the blessing his father had given him. He said to himself, "The days of mourning for my father are near; then I will kill my brother Jacob."*

⁴² When Rebekah was told what her older son Esau had said, she sent for her younger son Jacob and said to him, "Your brother Esau is planning to avenge himself by killing you. ⁴³ Now then, my son, do what I say: Flee at once to my brother Laban in Harran. ⁴⁴ Stay with him for a while until your brother's fury subsides. ⁴⁵ When your brother is no longer angry with you and forgets what you did to him, I'll send word for you to come back from there. Why should I lose both of you in one day?"

Esau may have been a bit of a donkey, following his wild urges over wisdom and good sense, but for once instinct and intellect aligned perfectly. He was upset at his brother's trickery. He also knew that inheritances are only enjoyed by the living. If his father was gone and his brother was gone, he was next in line for the family wealth. The solution seemed simple: wait until his father passed, then kill his brother and take everything for himself.

But Esau let his plan leak. Somebody told Rebekah, who counseled her favorite son to flee. She urged him to go back to her homeland, where Abraham's servant found her by a well long ago. He could stay with her brother Laban until all this blew over.

An Agreement

⁴⁶ Then Rebekah said to Isaac, "I'm disgusted with living because of these Hittite women. If Jacob takes a wife from among the women of this land, from Hittite women like these, my life will not be worth living."

28 So Isaac called for Jacob and blessed him. Then he commanded him: "Do not marry a Canaanite woman. ² Go at once to Paddan Aram, to the house of your mother's father Bethuel. Take a wife for yourself there, from among the daughters of Laban, your mother's brother. ³ May God Almighty bless you and make you fruitful and increase your numbers until you become a community of peoples. ⁴ May he give you and your descendants the blessing given to Abraham, so that you may take possession of the land where you now reside as a foreigner, the land God gave to Abraham." ⁵ Then Isaac sent Jacob on his way, and he went to Paddan Aram, to Laban son of Bethuel the Aramean, the brother of Rebekah, who was the mother of Jacob and Esau.

Finally Isaac and Rebekah find something they can agree on. They hate the local girls, especially as marriage prospects for their sons. Rebekah used this truth to finally slide Isaac closer to her side. Seeking a proper wife gave Jacob an excuse to leave the camp. This kept him safe from Esau. It kept the covenant of Abraham pure for Isaac instead of cross-breeding it with local religions. It kept them both from having to deal with yet another Hittite wife in the camp. Sometimes win-win situations are possible. The couple found common bond again.

Mixed Up, But Blessed

⁶ Now Esau learned that Isaac had blessed Jacob and had sent him to Paddan Aram to take a wife from there, and that when he blessed him he commanded him, "Do not marry a Canaanite woman," ⁷ and that Jacob had obeyed his father and mother and had gone to Paddan Aram. ⁸ Esau then realized how displeasing the Canaanite women were to his father Isaac; ⁹ so he went to Ishmael and married Mahalath, the sister of Nebaioth and daughter of Ishmael son of Abraham, in addition to the wives he already had.

Esau, hearing that his parents had blessed Jacob and sent him out of reach, retaliated by going out and marrying yet another Canaanite woman just to tick them off. What a guy.

Sitting around one of our recent Bible Study tables I heard someone utter this wisdom: "Everybody knows that they're own family is a little off, crazy and messed up. Nobody realizes that everybody else's family is like that too. We all hide it because we're afraid that we're the only ones." Who among you does not see your family in Isaac and Rebekah, in tricky Jacob and strong-headed Esau? All of our families are messed up, including Biblical families.

Too often we teach that God chooses perfect people. When we read about a Noah or Abraham we ask, "What was so special about him? He must have had some amazing quality that I don't have." We teach our Sunday School students to be like these guys, extolling their virtues and ignoring their human weaknesses.

The message of the Bible isn't, "Be like these guys," it's, "You ARE like these guys." God doesn't choose perfect people to work through. He works through ordinary, messed-up people just like us.

You are reading about the family chosen to bear God's word and heritage down through the ages. Centuries later people would still be calling on "the God of Abraham, Isaac, and Jacob". Patriarchs and paragons were crazy just like your family. God made good come out of them anyway, just as he does in your household.

People often wonder what God's blessing means. It's simple. God's blessing means that your crazy, mixed-up stuff won't get in the way of goodness…at least not in the end. Whatever is wrong with you isn't nearly as powerful and enduring as what's right with you. The family of Isaac and Rebekah are in a screwed up situation here. That's going to continue, maybe even get worse. But ultimately the purpose for it wasn't misery, but joy and faith. That's the assurance for your family too.

My mother has passed on now. She was a difficult and wonderful woman. Our relationship was far too complex to delve into here, but let's just say she spurred me to greater heights than I would have reached alone and occasionally drug me to deeper depths as well. She never meant to do the latter. We couldn't come to a common ground on certain things because her ground was sometimes too unsteady to stand on and in the younger part of my life, so was mine. But my relationship with her gave me part of the understanding I need to be writing to you right now. And I know in heaven mom and I will be together without division or separation,. We'll be the people we wanted to be with each other instead of the people we ended up as. That's a powerful promise of faith and it holds true for all of us mixed-up souls in all of our mixed-up families that try to reach for goodness and never quite get there.

Esau's being a pill and marrying abrasive wives just for spite. God will end up making a great nation out of that pill and his wives and an equally great nation out of the people his choices are annoying. That's what God does. That's why he's God.

God's Ladder

¹⁰ Jacob left Beersheba and set out for Harran. ¹¹ When he reached a certain place, he stopped for the night because the sun had set. Taking one of the stones there, he put it under his head and lay down to sleep. ¹² He had a dream in which he saw a stairway resting on the earth, with its top reaching to heaven, and the angels of God were ascending and descending on it. ¹³ There above it stood the Lord, and he said: "I am the Lord, the God of your father Abraham and the God of Isaac. I will give you and your descendants the land on which you are lying. ¹⁴ Your descendants will be like the dust of the earth, and you will spread out to the west and to the east, to the north and to the south. All peoples on earth will be blessed through you and your offspring. [15] *I am with you and will watch over you wherever you go, and I will bring you back to this land. I will not leave you until I have done what I have promised you."*

[16] *When Jacob awoke from his sleep, he thought, "Surely the Lord is in this place, and I was not aware of it."* [17] *He was afraid and said, "How awesome is this place! This is none other than the house of God; this is the gate of heaven."*

[18] *Early the next morning Jacob took the stone he had placed under his head and set it up as a pillar and poured oil on top of it.* [19] *He called that place Bethel, though the city used to be called Luz.*

[20] *Then Jacob made a vow, saying, "If God will be with me and will watch over me on this journey I am taking and will give me food to eat and clothes to wear* [21] *so that I return safely to my father's household, then the Lord will be my God* [22] *and this stone that I have set up as a pillar will be God's house, and of all that you give me I will give you a tenth."*

Back in Chapter 25 when Rebekah was pregnant with her boys, the Lord told her that the older would serve the younger as each became the leader of a nation. Here God confirms that to Jacob himself as Jake pulls up a rock for a pillow (making chiropractors everywhere cringe) and has an amazing dream.

In this dream God speaks to Jacob as God's messengers travel up and down a stairway laid out between heaven and earth. God assures Jacob that he is the God of his father Isaac and grandfather Abraham. He repeats the promise given to Jacob's sires, that countless descendants would spread across the land, bringing blessings. In this case the blessings are magnified, bestowed upon all the people on earth in Jacob's name. God also promises to be with Jacob, to watch over him, and bring him back home someday.

What an incredible promise to a young man who is separated from his family, despised by his brother, on a journey away from everything he's ever known into a land he's never seen.

All of us make Jacob's journey at some point, though hopefully not under his exact circumstances. We graduate high school and go to college. We move away from home and get a job. We lose things behind us with no surety about what lies ahead. Our only hope in those moments is exactly the one Jacob had: that God will be with us, watching over us, making us and our life's work a blessing.

The striking symbolism of Jacob's vision has inspired spirituals, book and movie titles, and likely countless sermons. We must be careful when talking about "Climbing Jacob's Ladder", though. At no point did Jacob set foot on the thing. It wasn't really Jacob's ladder at all, but God's. The only motion in the scene is God sending messengers to earth. The vision may have changed Jacob, but that transformation happened not through his movement or will, but by the Word of God moving through him.

How quickly we want to appropriate for ourselves God's graceful gift, calling the ladder Jacob's and implying he climbed it. "Out of the way, God! That ladder is ours! We finally have a way to get to heaven through our own power!" (Munch, munch goes the garden fruit as hammers ring on the Tower of Babel.)

When Jacob saw this vision, he wasn't thinking about climbing. He was awed to the point of being afraid. He turned his impromptu stone pillow into an impromptu altar, following the tradition of his father and grandfather. He vowed that he would respond to God's goodness with honor and sacrifice.

Sometimes we forget how powerful God is. I often ask my Confirmation students how long they're able to look at the sun. The sun is just a star…one among billions of billions in the universe. Our eyes aren't equipped to deal with a single star, nor our skin to endure its rays for long, nor our bodies to stand its heat without shade. What would happen if God showed up in unfiltered form, more powerful and radiant than a galaxy of stars? We'd be groveling under a table, hiding our eyes, or just die on the spot.

This provides perspective on the question, "Why doesn't God just show up?" Answer: Because he's being nice to you! You can see why scripture has him coming in visions, through angels, in the person of Jesus, or through water, bread, and wine. We can handle all those things in a way we couldn't handle his pure being.

Even a vision-fueled glimpse of the Heavenly Father was enough to knock Jacob off his stride. Awe and wonder should always be part of the equation when we talk about our relationship with God. Otherwise we won't understand how astonishing it is that the being who created and exceeds the entire universe actually cares about us, changes plans for us, sent Son and Spirit to us to *serve* us just as he served poor, lonely Jacob.

We cannot hope to comprehend God, nor to merit his attention or favor. We can respond to it as Jacob did, however, with honor and sacrifice. This puts awe and wonder to productive use. "You bless me, you shelter me, you claim me as your own. I can't believe it, but I'll spend the rest of my life showing you and everybody else how much that means to me." Those same words could translate to the most important relationships of our life: marriage, the child-parent relationship, friendships, and the like. They all start with God. Knowing how he loves us and reacting to that love appropriately sets the pattern of our love for each other.

The Big Turn

29 *Then Jacob continued on his journey and came to the land of the eastern peoples.* ² *There he saw a well in the open country, with three flocks of sheep lying near it because the flocks were watered from that well. The stone over the mouth of the well was large.* ³ *When all the flocks were gathered there, the shepherds would roll the stone away from the well's mouth and water the sheep. Then they would return the stone to its place over the mouth of the well.*

⁴ *Jacob asked the shepherds, "My brothers, where are you from?"*

"We're from Harran," they replied.

⁵ *He said to them, "Do you know Laban, Nahor's grandson?"*

"Yes, we know him," they answered.

⁶ *Then Jacob asked them, "Is he well?"*

"Yes, he is," they said, "and here comes his daughter Rachel with the sheep."

⁷ *"Look," he said, "the sun is still high; it is not time for the flocks to be gathered. Water the sheep and take them back to pasture."*

⁸ *"We can't," they replied, "until all the flocks are gathered and the stone has been rolled away from the mouth of the well. Then we will water the sheep."*

⁹ *While he was still talking with them, Rachel came with her father's sheep, for she was a shepherd.* ¹⁰ *When Jacob saw Rachel daughter of his uncle Laban, and Laban's sheep, he went over and rolled the stone away from the mouth of the well and watered his uncle's sheep.* ¹¹ *Then Jacob kissed Rachel and began to weep aloud.* ¹² *He had told Rachel that he was a relative of her father and a son of Rebekah. So she ran and told her father.*

¹³ *As soon as Laban heard the news about Jacob, his sister's son, he hurried to meet him. He embraced him and kissed him and brought him to his home, and there Jacob told him all these things.* ¹⁴ *Then Laban said to him, "You are my own flesh and blood."*

Jacob finds a warm welcome as he returns to his family's land of origin. He discovers shepherds able to tell him that his uncle is well. Then his uncle's daughter, Rachel, arrives with the family flocks. Gallant Jacob rolls the stone away from the well for her, then waters the sheep himself. After he identifies his family connection she runs home, bringing her father back to meet him. Laban claims Jacob as his own flesh and blood, confirming him as a member of the family.

Rolling the stone away from the well begins Jacob's resurrection story. Heretofore his path has been downward. He's succeeded at the things he's tried (mostly tricking his brother and father) but they haven't brought him goodness. The road ahead will be rocky, but it leads upward.

Here, too, we find Jacob eminently relatable. Most of us have had resurrection moments, sometimes more than once in our lives. In these moments we realize that our old path isn't taking us anywhere, that success is just bringing us more stress, pain, and worry. As the Brady Bunch taught us long ago, when it's time to change, then it's time to change.

All paths lead to eternity, but few are themselves eternal. Something that was good ten years ago may not be right anymore. Even so, it's hard to let go of old ways. They've protected us up to that point, given us identity and comfort. But sometimes you have to risk everything you're comfortable with to find the path you're supposed to be on.

Churches often get ensnared in this trap. Something works for them—or works for a few powerful people in the congregation—and they ordain it as THE thing to do. Usually they prescribe THE manner in which it shall be done as well, along with THE people to do it. (Then those people complain that they can't find anybody else to help them!)

The very first thing you should ask when somebody complains that nobody else is stepping up is, "Stepping up to what?" Have you defined the path so narrowly and kept it so much in your control that only you can walk it? Then you may rightly expect to be walking it the rest of your natural life with nobody to help. But that's not their fault, it's yours. The people around you might be trying to move a stone off a well while you're sitting on it, insisting that this is where it belongs.

The church I serve is steeped in tradition and we understand that structure and order are important. But the shape of that order changes with the needs of the congregation. We're not afraid to try new paths: new music, new people leading, new voices speaking up in Bible Study telling us new things about old books. We draw from our past, maintaining the path unbroken, but we're not afraid to forge the next section in a different direction. Whether we turn left or right, sing Hymn #444 or #362, the path continues.

Jacob carried his family history with him but began forging it in a new way in his uncle's house. Perhaps the vision on the road had done him some good. Perhaps the first sight of Rachel gave his life meaning and purpose he hadn't discovered before. Either way, things changed.

Jacob rolled the stone away from the well when the other shepherds wouldn't. He watered Rachel's sheep when it wasn't his job. He gave to others instead of grasping for himself.

This is the key to all change for the good. Taking the church example above, if somebody selfishly claims that one hymn is the best while another person selfishly demands that we sing another, nobody wins no matter which hymn we choose. We make a good turn when we stop asking who gets to be selfish over hymns today and start asking who we're going to give to and honor with our music. God and the scripture we're reading head that list, but we're also conscious of the people around us. The hymn you hate is someone else's favorite. We're up front about asking all our members to serve each other by lifting up their voices as best they can in every hymn regardless of whether they know and like it or not. We're there to give to each other and God, not demand our own way.

When Jesus would later talk about the blind leading the blind, he didn't mean people who couldn't see, he meant people who only saw themselves. When we forget about ourselves and serve others, our eyes open. They aren't cast down in front of us anymore, they're looking ahead for more opportunities for goodness. Looking outward makes the path forward far easier to discern.

Jacob was lost, then he was found. But he didn't discover a home because he found family, he discovered a home because of how he treated them.

A Love Story

After Jacob had stayed with him for a whole month, ¹⁵ *Laban said to him, "Just because you are a relative of mine, should you work for me for nothing? Tell me what your wages should be."*

¹⁶ *Now Laban had two daughters; the name of the older was Leah, and the name of the younger was Rachel.* ¹⁷ *Leah had weak eyes, but Rachel had a lovely figure and was beautiful.* ¹⁸ *Jacob was in love with Rachel and said, "I'll work for you seven years in return for your younger daughter Rachel."*

Ah…love. Jacob was smitten with Rachel from the start. When his uncle asked what he wanted his reward to be for all his hard work, Jacob asked nothing but to marry Laban's younger daughter.

This was somewhat unfortunate for the older daughter Leah. The designation of "weak eyes" is meant to conjure visions of a goofy, if not homely, face. Scripture isn't kind to the poor girl.

Wife Swap

¹⁹ *Laban said, "It's better that I give her to you than to some other man. Stay here with me."* ²⁰ *So Jacob served seven years to get Rachel, but they seemed like only a few days to him because of his love for her.*

21 Then Jacob said to Laban, "Give me my wife. My time is completed, and I want to make love to her."

22 So Laban brought together all the people of the place and gave a feast. 23 But when evening came, he took his daughter Leah and brought her to Jacob, and Jacob made love to her. 24 And Laban gave his servant Zilpah to his daughter as her attendant.

Well, an already weird family just got weirder.

After agreeing to let Jacob marry Rachel after years of toil, the ever-crafty Laban comes up with a scheme to turn the situation to his advantage. Jacob wants a wife; Laban is stuck with a somewhat-homely, less-than-marriageable older daughter. In a maneuver worthy of a soap opera script, Laban calls in Leah to pinch hit for her sister on her wedding day. Seven years in service to his uncle have flown by for Jacob because of his love for this girl. Now he's not getting her.

Apparently trickery runs in Jacob's family. Now Jacob knows what it feels like to be on the wrong end of it. It's never nice to discover what it feels like to be wronged as we've wronged others but it's often a part of our journey towards maturity.

People claim that what goes around, comes around. It's an overstatement. Actions and consequences never correspond exactly. But we do have the power to shape the environment around us. What we pour into each other flows back to us. Jesus wasn't just looking out for our neighbors when he told us to do unto others as we would have them do unto us. He was trying to save our fannies too.

Sticking With Your Purpose

25 When morning came, there was Leah! So Jacob said to Laban, "What is this you have done to me? I served you for Rachel, didn't I? Why have you deceived me?"

26 Laban replied, "It is not our custom here to give the younger daughter in marriage before the older one. 27 Finish this daughter's bridal week; then we will give you the younger one also, in return for another seven years of work."

²⁸ And Jacob did so. He finished the week with Leah, and then Laban gave him his daughter Rachel to be his wife. ²⁹ Laban gave his servant Bilhah to his daughter Rachel as her attendant. ³⁰ Jacob made love to Rachel also, and his love for Rachel was greater than his love for Leah. And he worked for Laban another seven years.

So now the truth comes out…sort of. Jacob is understandably outraged to find Leah in his bed in place of her sister. Not only is Leah not his love, he served all those years in order to marry Rachel. This was like working for most of a decade to earn a title to beachfront property and then finding out it's in the Upper Peninsula of Michigan.

When Jacob accosted his uncle with the ironic words, "Why have you deceived me?" Laban replied with a glib answer. "Well in our land we don't marry off the younger daughter until the older one is married as well." In a call back to an earlier chapter, that may have been *a* truth, but it wasn't *the* truth. Laban could have married Leah off to someone different. Laban could have told Jacob the deal. He didn't do either.

To be fair, he may have been legitimately afraid that he couldn't marry off his older daughter and was looking out for the family's best interests when foisting her off on Jacob. More likely he knew Jacob would continue pursuing Rachel, and it was in Laban's best interests to capitalize on Jacob's desire. He got seven more years of work out of his nephew through his sly chicanery. Not a bad deal.

So Rachel became Jacob's dream girl, Leah the spare tire along for the ride. Jacob ended up working 14 years for his uncle to earn his brides before getting to be his own man. Yet he did it. He served because, whatever Laban managed to twist out of him because of it, Jacob's eyes were still set on a goal beyond himself. He was holding course after his turn back at the well.

We cannot control how others perceive or use our ambitions. All we can do is plot a course as true as possible, then stick to it. Not all sacrifices are noble. Sometimes the world will extract a steep, even unfair, price for following your dreams. If you find a cause good enough, you do what Jacob did: pay it and keep heading onward.

A Blessing for Each

³¹ When the Lord saw that Leah was not loved, he enabled her to conceive, but Rachel remained childless. ³² Leah became pregnant and gave birth to a son. She named him Reuben, for she said, "It is because the Lord has seen my misery. Surely my husband will love me now."

³³ She conceived again, and when she gave birth to a son she said, "Because the Lord heard that I am not loved, he gave me this one too." So she named him Simeon.

³⁴ Again she conceived, and when she gave birth to a son she said, "Now at last my husband will become attached to me, because I have borne him three sons." So he was named Levi.

³⁵ She conceived again, and when she gave birth to a son she said, "This time I will praise the Lord." So she named him Judah. Then she stopped having children.

Thank God somebody was watching out for poor Leah in all this. Up until this point she's been nothing but the ugly, unloved sister. But with God's grace it turns out she has a gift…the most important gift a wife could have in those days. With a little assist from God she was able to crank out sons with regularity.

In our modern times we would (appropriately) shy away from the idea that the only value this woman had was to bring her husband's sons into the world. Reducing the worth of another human being to a single function is wrong.

There's a deeper lesson here, though…that just when it looked like she'd be left out forever, Leah was favored. God spends extra time and gives extra care to those who are worse off in any situation. If you want to know who you should befriend as a person of faith, start with whomever is being disadvantaged most. That person needs a friend most.

In Leah's time bearing sons would have been seen as a sign of blessing. If Jacob wasn't going to favor her, God sure was. You can hear Leah begging with every child, "Please…now will you love me?" She didn't end up getting what she wanted , but she was graced with her children and, at least for now, a higher status than her sister Rachel.

Some people will tell you that you should believe in God because then you'll get whatever you desire. I've not found that to be true, myself. Nobody gets *everything* they want. It's not possible, because we never stop wanting. Just when we think we're full, we find ourselves empty and needy again. Having everything in the world wouldn't satisfy us. Adam and Eve were living proof of that.

But that doesn't mean that you won't get *anything*. For everyone there's something. You may have to outlast depression, divorce, illness, death, poverty, or oppression to see it. It may be a small thing, a brief moment where you feel wanted or needed, gifted with your own purpose. You may not understand its importance when it happens. You may not see its full flower this side of heaven, but it will come. A blessing will be yours, just as it was Leah's.

Defining Life by the Negative

30 When Rachel saw that she was not bearing Jacob any children, she became jealous of her sister. So she said to Jacob, "Give me children, or I'll die!"

2 Jacob became angry with her and said, "Am I in the place of God, who has kept you from having children?"

3 Then she said, "Here is Bilhah, my servant. Sleep with her so that she can bear children for me and I too can build a family through her."

4 So she gave him her servant Bilhah as a wife. Jacob slept with her, 5 and she became pregnant and bore him a son. 6 Then Rachel said, "God has vindicated me; he has listened to my plea and given me a son." Because of this she named him Dan.

7 Rachel's servant Bilhah conceived again and bore Jacob a second son. 8 Then Rachel said, "I have had a great struggle with my sister, and I have won." So she named him Naphtali.

9 When Leah saw that she had stopped having children, she took her servant Zilpah and gave her to Jacob as a wife. 10 Leah's servant Zilpah bore Jacob a son. 11 Then Leah said, "What good fortune!" So she named him Gad.

¹² Leah's servant Zilpah bore Jacob a second son. ¹³ Then Leah said, "How happy I am! The women will call me happy." So she named him Asher.

The grass is always greener, isn't it? All Leah wants is for her husband to love her as much as he loves her sister. She can't get that, but she has a bunch of sons by him. All Rachel wants is sons. She can't get that. All she has is her husband's undying love. Each wants what the other has and each is unhappy.

Everybody's going to be unhappy about something. You will always carry emptiness with you and feel that you're lacking. That's what sin does to us. You have a choice each day. Are you going to focus on the things you lack or the things you have, on opportunities for unhappiness or opportunities for joy and peace?

We tell ourselves, "If I just get *this thing* the emptiness will be filled and I'll be happy." That's a lie. The hole inside us goes all the way through. No matter how many cookies you stick into a jar with no bottom, it will never be full. We try chocolate chip cookies for a while, then switch to peanut butter when that doesn't work, then figure maybe snickerdoodles will do the trick. The flavor of your desire doesn't matter. All of them fall right out the bottom, leaving you just as empty as before.

God's grace, mercy, and love are the only things that can fill up that hole. Infinite forgiveness, purpose, and joy cancel out bottomless longing. This is how God works. He turns the bombed-out, endless craters inside of us into repositories of goodness, fountains of everlasting life instead of symbols of everlasting pain.

If you're not happy today, you're probably not going to be happy tomorrow either. Happiness isn't circumstantial. It doesn't come because of things around you. It comes because you choose to concentrate on the good you have and the good you can do for others more than you concentrate on whatever is bothering you today.

This sounds presumptuous. I can already hear people saying, "Easy for you to say! I've got reason to be unhappy!" I get it. I do too. Some of those things are beyond my control and some I've even caused myself. Both Leah and Rachel had serious reasons to be unhappy too. They lacked HUGE things in their life: love and children respectively. Each also had reasons to be happy. Both of them lifted up the unhappy things more than the happy and it ended up tearing their family to shreds, bringing grief where love was meant to flourish.

Mind you, God still worked through them. He doesn't let our mindset thwart his determination that goodness has he final word. But it's easier to perceive him working when you understand and focus on that goodness he's aiming towards than it is when you lift up whatever you lack and long over.

This simple lesson can change our lives completely. Focusing on the good makes you a much more productive parent. It turns good teachers into the best teachers we ever had. It creates friends who lift each other up instead of tearing each other down. Don't even get me started on how much difference happiness and contentment make when dating. They help you fill up the people you love instead of draining them.

Another way to say this is that folks who live by the goodness in their lives are able to give to others, while folks who accentuate the negative can't see beyond it. They figure they'll start giving when they finally have enough, but they never get enough, so the giving never comes.

Everyone's going to feel unhappy sometimes. That's normal, even necessary considering how imperfect our world is. But feelings determine our reality less than how we choose to act on them.

You'd have thought having four healthy, wonderful boys (versus zero for her sister) would have been enough for Leah. It wasn't. You'd have thought the love of her husband would have been something for Rachel to build on. It wasn't. Instead the two engaged in a jealousy-fueled Baby Arms Race. Like opposing superpowers, they stockpiled weapons and measured themselves against each other. Except in this case their merit wasn't measured by missiles, but offspring.

Leah offered the opening salvo with her four sons. Then Rachel grabbed Jacob by the collar and said, "Give me children or I can't live anymore!" When Jacob sputtered that it wasn't his fault she wasn't fertile (bad move, by the way) Rachel decided to run the "Maid Option" and have her husband conceive a child with her servant.

After Rachel's maid gave birth to two children Leah started thinking this wasn't fair, so she threw *her* handmaid at her husband. Leah's maid had two sons of her own, bringing the total Son Count to eight.

Meanwhile both Leah and Rachel were naming these boys variations on, "Ha! Take that, sister!" Life was flourishing everywhere and everyone was bitter about it. What a mess.

More Anger and Bitterness

14 During wheat harvest, Reuben went out into the fields and found some mandrake plants, which he brought to his mother Leah. Rachel said to Leah, "Please give me some of your son's mandrakes."

15 But she said to her, "Wasn't it enough that you took away my husband? Will you take my son's mandrakes too?"

"Very well," Rachel said, "he can sleep with you tonight in return for your son's mandrakes."

16 So when Jacob came in from the fields that evening, Leah went out to meet him. "You must sleep with me," she said. "I have hired you with my son's mandrakes." So he slept with her that night.

17 God listened to Leah, and she became pregnant and bore Jacob a fifth son. 18 Then Leah said, "God has rewarded me for giving my servant to my husband." So she named him Issachar.

19 Leah conceived again and bore Jacob a sixth son. 20 Then Leah said, "God has presented me with a precious gift. This time my husband will treat me with honor, because I have borne him six sons." So she named him Zebulun.

21 Some time later she gave birth to a daughter and named her Dinah.

22 Then God remembered Rachel; he listened to her and enabled her to conceive. 23 She became pregnant and gave birth to a son and said, "God has taken away my disgrace." 24 She named him Joseph, and said, "May the Lord add to me another son."

Here we hear about of the rest of Jacob's sons (but one) being conceived plus a daughter, Dinah. By this point Jacob is just a tool to be hired out among his wives, who are still fighting over who is the best. The mandrake plants that Reuben found were an aid to infertility. Leah and Rachel were still angling to win the Arms Race. And from the sound of it ("Wasn't it enough that you took away my husband?" and "God has taken away my disgrace") nobody has forgiven or forgotten anything.

This is the problem with festering anger and bitterness. They reduce everyone around them, not just the angry, bitter people but those in relationship with them.

Purebred and Inbred

25 After Rachel gave birth to Joseph, Jacob said to Laban, "Send me on my way so I can go back to my own homeland. 26 Give me my wives and children, for whom I have served you, and I will be on my way. You know how much work I've done for you."

27 But Laban said to him, "If I have found favor in your eyes, please stay. I have learned by divination that the Lord has blessed me because of you." 28 He added, "Name your wages, and I will pay them."

29 Jacob said to him, "You know how I have worked for you and how your livestock has fared under my care. 30 The little you had before I came has increased greatly, and the Lord has blessed you wherever I have been. But now, when may I do something for my own household?"

31 "What shall I give you?" he asked.

"Don't give me anything," Jacob replied. "But if you will do this one thing for me, I will go on tending your flocks and watching over them: 32 Let me go through all your flocks today and remove from them every speckled or spotted sheep, every dark-colored lamb and every spotted or speckled goat. They will be my wages. 33 And my honesty will testify for me in the future, whenever you check on the wages you have paid me. Any goat in my possession that is not speckled or spotted, or any lamb that is not dark-colored, will be considered stolen."

34 "Agreed," said Laban. "Let it be as you have said." 35 That same day he removed all the male goats that were streaked or spotted, and all the speckled or spotted female goats *(all that had white on them) and all the dark-colored lambs, and he placed them in the care of his sons. ³⁶ Then he put a three-day journey between himself and Jacob, while Jacob continued to tend the rest of Laban's flocks.*

Meanwhile, out in the fields, Jacob was ready for a change. He had stayed in this land long enough. He was ready to take his family and go home.

Uncle Laban wasn't so willing. He knew that Jacob was making him a profit; Laban's nephew was good at his job and God favored him. Laban had prospered because of Jacob's blessing.

Laban asked Jacob to name his price to stay. Jacob pointed out how much Laban had gained off of his labor and asked when he would become his own master instead of the son-in-law, a glorified hired hand.

Again Laban asked what Jacob wanted. Jacob refused to take any wages, but offered up a simple deal. If Laban would give him all the spotted or speckled livestock, he'd tend both his herds and Laban's. This seemed like a good deal because purebred stock was generally considered better than mixed breeds. To Laban it was as if Jacob was asking for the factory seconds. He happily agreed.

Jacob had a plan in mind, though. The trickster in him hadn't died entirely, though in his defense his request that Laban let him go should have been honored. When Jacob says, "You'll easily be able to tell I'm not stealing from you because not one of your light-colored lambs will be in my flock," we should assume a sly smile crossing his face.

Laban agreed and Jacob left no doubt by putting a three-day walk between his livestock and his uncle's.

Today we know that mixed breeds tend to be hardier than purebreds. We'd probably see through Jacob's agricultural trick. When it comes to theological breeding, though, we still hold to Laban's ways.

Different viewpoints and ideas make for a hardier, more well-rounded theology, not because you adopt them, but because they help you see the weaknesses in your own view. Churches get stronger when diverse voices are heard and followed. Yet we spend an inordinate amount of time and energy making sure nobody says anything we disagree with in church and that things are done the way they always have been.

Leaves aren't meant to twist in the wind, but neither are they meant to deny that the wind blows. (Recall that we learned in Genesis 1 that wind and Spirit are the same word.) Churches that insist on a purebred theology and spotless congregation without offering even the slightest possibility of hearing anything different become weak and inbred. Better to have a slightly mottled church that's dynamic than a carefully cultivated one that's stagnant and won't outlast its own generation.

Strength and Weakness

37 Jacob, however, took fresh-cut branches from poplar, almond and plane trees and made white stripes on them by peeling the bark and exposing the white inner wood of the branches. 38 Then he placed the peeled branches in all the watering troughs, so that they would be directly in front of the flocks when they came to drink. When the flocks were in heat and came to drink, 39 they mated in front of the branches. And they bore young that were streaked or speckled or spotted. 40 Jacob set apart the young of the flock by themselves, but made the rest face the streaked and dark-colored animals that belonged to Laban. Thus he made separate flocks for himself and did not put them with Laban's animals. 41 Whenever the stronger females were in heat, Jacob would place the branches in the troughs in front of the animals so they would mate near the branches, 42 but if the animals were weak, he would not place them there. So the weak animals went to Laban and the strong ones to Jacob. 43 In this way the man grew exceedingly prosperous and came to own large flocks, and female and male servants, and camels and donkeys.

Long before Mendel, Jacob demonstrates a keen grasp of genetics here. He knows plants that stimulate the mating urge, either from long practice in the field or from long practice as the test subject of his wives and their maids.

When it came time to breed livestock, it didn't really matter whose animals belonged to whom. The timing of the mating between them was key. Jacob encouraged his flocks to mate when stronger animals were in heat, Laban's to mate when weaker ones were. He incorporated the resulting strong, speckled young into his herd, leaving all those lesser, unblemished offspring to his uncle. By skillful application of his primitive genetics program, Jacob prospered.

In general this is true with faith as well. Strong is strong, no matter what color or flavor it comes in. Weak is weak even when it looks pretty. Most people equate strength with being right or, more regrettably, being loud. Nothing could be further than the truth. Love is strength. Love comes in many guises, among young and old, people of all races and convictions, even among those who claim to oppose God. I've met loving atheists whom I consider much closer to God's truth than some of the people of supposedly "strong" faith I've known.

We need to breed strength in our lives. Our job as Christians isn't to police the world to make sure everybody thinks like us. That's weakness parading as strength, putting ourselves and our beliefs in the place of God. When we see goodness in the world we need to respond to that goodness, knowing God is there even if the people perpetuating the good don't. Like Jacob, we're supposed to care less about the color of the sheep or who claims ownership of it than about what the sheep does for the flock.

Similarly we are to shun weakness, moving three days away from it and keeping our herd separate from it. Except weakness is not defined by doubt or impurity, sin or unorthodoxy, but by self-centered manipulation of power as Laban practiced over Jacob.

This holds true even if weakness parades around in Christian guise. Many times I've found myself saying, "There's strength in God's name, but not the way you're using it." God works through imperfect vessels. We're all weak, when it comes down to it. But there's a difference between admitting one's own weakness and hoping God corrects for it and labeling one's own weakness as godly in order to profit off of it. We're called to embrace the former, flee from the latter.

The Litmus Test of Love

31 Jacob heard that Laban's sons were saying, "Jacob has taken everything our father owned and has gained all this wealth from what belonged to our father." 2 And Jacob noticed that Laban's attitude toward him was not what it had been.

3 Then the Lord said to Jacob, "Go back to the land of your fathers and to your relatives, and I will be with you."

The problem with Jacob's scheme was that it worked too well. It wasn't long before everybody in the region knew that Jacob's flocks were prospering and Laban's dying. This included Laban's sons, who stood to inherent a tidy sum due to Jacob's prior work for their father but now were in danger of losing it all as their agricultural bubble burst.

Laban, too, looked at his nephew with suspicion. When the profit ran dry, so did his love.

You can tell those who love truly by their attitude when things are down, particularly when they're not pleased. This is the litmus test. Anyone can love people who make them feel good. Few love those who disappoint them.

Yet this is exactly the kind of love God has for us. That's the reason he's our Savior. We did everything we could think of to break his world, mess up, and displease him--including nailing Jesus to a cross--and still he loves us, sticks by us, claims us as family.

Our love for each other should reflect God's love for us. Faith isn't about profit, it's about commitment and endurance.

In Genesis 31:3 God announced to Jacob: "It's time." The final part of the promise was about to be fulfilled. Jacob would return to the land of his fathers and inhabit it with God by his side.

Means to an End

4 So Jacob sent word to Rachel and Leah to come out to the fields where his flocks were. 5 He said to them, 'I see that your father's attitude toward me is not what it was before, but the God of my father has been with me. 6 You know that I've worked for your father with all my strength, 7 yet your father has cheated me by changing my wages ten times. However, God has not allowed him to harm me. 8 If he said, 'The speckled ones will be your wages,' then all the flocks gave birth to speckled young; and if he said, 'The streaked ones will be your wages,' then all the flocks bore streaked young. 9 So God has taken away your father's livestock and has given them to me.

10 "In breeding season I once had a dream in which I looked up and saw that the male goats mating with the flock were streaked, speckled or spotted. 11 The angel of God said to me in the dream, 'Jacob.' I answered, 'Here I am.' ¹² *And he said, 'Look up and see that all the male goats mating with the flock are streaked, speckled or spotted, for I have seen all that Laban has been doing to you.* ¹³ *I am the God of Bethel, where you anointed a pillar and where you made a vow to me. Now leave this land at once and go back to your native land.'"*

¹⁴ *Then Rachel and Leah replied, "Do we still have any share in the inheritance of our father's estate?* ¹⁵ *Does he not regard us as foreigners? Not only has he sold us, but he has used up what was paid for us.* ¹⁶ *Surely all the wealth that God took away from our father belongs to us and our children. So do whatever God has told you."*

It was time for a little family huddle out in the fields where Jacob and his wives couldn't be overheard. Jacob told Leah and Rachel that their father was no longer well-disposed towards him, but God still was. God had blessed him with an effective breeding program, allowed him to succeed through it, and supported him despite living under Laban's injustices. But enough was enough. The same God who was looking out for his success said it was now time to go. Would his wives, Laban's daughters, follow him?

Leah and Rachel had their share of difficulties with each other, but both were practical and knew where their interests lie. They'd seem their own father put his interests over family ties. Laban had foisted Leah off, treating her like she was of no account. Laban had polluted the waters of Rachel's true love. He had traded them both for years of farm work, like they were wages to a hired worker. And now that neither were a source of potential profit to him, Laban treated his daughters like strangers. Their future hopes of prosperity and respect lay not with their father, but with their sons. Both of them were willing to follow Jacob and his God even if that meant leaving dad behind.

People are not means to an end. Laban never understood this. In order to justify using people for our purposes, we view them as tools to get us what we want. No practice could be farther from faith.

In the early parts of my life I worked in retail sales. I was decent at it and might have ended up great, except I could never get over the sense of using others and being used in turn. I wanted to help people, to make them happy. Ideally that's what a retail relationship should be. But it quickly devolved into sales statistics and dollars generated per hour…fine and necessary metrics, but hardly a reason for being (or even, in my view, a sufficient reason for working). The company used me to move product. I used the customer's desires to convert as much of that product into cash as quickly as possible. Some of the customers used me as a target to vent their frustrations on, or used the power of cash in hand to wheedle what they could. We were all using each other, each of us a means to the other's end.

How many churches view other people as means to an end as well? We've all but ruined the concept of evangelism by viewing neighbors as potential converts instead of complex, integral children of God. Churches view members a means of generating operating expenses. We worry about Sunday morning attendance numbers more than who's actually there, why they're there, and what message the Spirit is bestowing on us all that day. The church has become Laban with dozens of Jacobs putting in their years of labor to please the boss.

Scratch beneath the practices and assumptions your church instinctively operates under—parse out things said casually and accepted as "truth" in meetings and Bible Studies—and you're going to find a healthy dose of "means to an end" thinking. It's just as wrong for us as it was for Jacob's uncle. As long as we practice it, people are more than justified packing up their tents and leaving us too.

Idols and Lies

[17] Then Jacob put his children and his wives on camels, [18] and he drove all his livestock ahead of him, along with all the goods he had accumulated in Paddan Aram, to go to his father Isaac in the land of Canaan.

[19] When Laban had gone to shear his sheep, Rachel stole her father's household gods. [20] Moreover, Jacob deceived Laban the Aramean by not telling him he was running away. [21] So he fled with all he had, crossed the Euphrates River, and headed for the hill country of Gilead.

[22] On the third day Laban was told that Jacob had fled. [23] Taking his relatives with him, he pursued Jacob for seven days and caught up with him in the hill country of Gilead. [24] Then God came to Laban the Aramean in a dream at night and said to him, "Be careful not to say anything to Jacob, either good or bad."

Jacob took his wives and children out to the field, stuck them on camels, gathered up his flocks, and got out of Dodge. On her way out the door Rachel stole all the family "gods" or idols. In those days it was not uncommon for households to have personal deities, nor for them to invest wealth into various depictions of their gods, kept on the family altar. Likely Laban's altar was decorated with valuables, which Rachel saw fit to slip into her handbag before she left.

The idea of "family gods" seems odd to us in a world where religion is defined corporately. We're fine saying we follow one of the commonly-accepted religions or saying we have no god at all. We're tempted to laugh behind our hands at the idea of idols sitting on a shelf in our family room. Theists and atheists alike find themselves too sophisticated for such a thing.

Except we're not.

We tend to define "god" as "that which we formally worship". Worship means to going to a building and participating in rituals. If we don't sing hymns to it, we don't consider it our god. Defining things this way convinces us that we don't practice idolatry when really it's all around us.

Your "god" is the thing you trust in to support you, fulfill you, make you feel safe. Participating in formal worship is not required to make a god. If you buy into the construct under which your god operates, if you define your life and beliefs by its assumptions, then functionally you have a god.

We all have family gods. They might be political parties, bank accounts, family traditions, or career paths. You don't have to own your own business for long before you start believing that whatever is good for that business is good empirically. Rooting for a sports franchise bends people's vision dramatically. A disinterested observer will see a referee's call one way, the true fanatic will see the same call completely differently. It's perfectly possible to make a god out of your religion or church as well, depending on belonging to a particular denomination or holding a correct belief to save you instead of God.

The people of the Old Testament never shook themselves free from idolatry and neither have we. We all believe *something* will make us happy. That "something" quickly becomes our family deity. It happens so deep within us that we're blind to it. We walk around claiming we have this God or that god or no god at all when in reality half a dozen "gods" have hold of us in ways we can't even begin to understand. We bend ourselves to their rules, live by their precepts, buy into the systems that support their importance.

When we read of Rachel stealing her father's family gods we shouldn't be thinking, "Sheesh! What primitives!" Instead we should read that as, "Rachel snuck in and stole her father's favorite football jersey," or the autographed photo of his political hero, or his big-screen TV, or his checkbook. Whatever we depend on or dream about to make our lives complete, that's what Rachel stole.

When Laban realized that Jacob, Jacob's vast herds, and the family gods had all flown the coop together, he gathered up the men of the family and chased after his fleeing son-in-law.

Since herds don't move very fast, catching him was only a matter of time. But the night before Laban was to confront Jacob and his family, God saved Jacob's bacon Joe Pesci style, coming to Laban in a dream and saying, "Be careful how you talk to him." Implied: "Because he's a close, personal friend of mine, and you don't want to make me angry."

The Gravity of Self-Interest

⁵Jacob had pitched his tent in the hill country of Gilead when Laban overtook him, and Laban and his relatives camped there too. ²⁶ Then Laban said to Jacob, "What have you done? You've deceived me, and you've carried off my daughters like captives in war. ²⁷ Why did you run off secretly and deceive me? Why didn't you tell me, so I could send you away with joy and singing to the music of timbrels and harps? ²⁸ You didn't even let me kiss my grandchildren and my daughters goodbye. You have done a foolish thing. ²⁹ I have the power to harm you; but last night the God of your father said to me, 'Be careful not to say anything to Jacob, either good or bad.' ³⁰ Now you have gone off because you longed to return to your father's household. But why did you steal my gods?"

Notice how quickly Laban becomes the aggrieved father here. The guy who treated his daughters like foreigners, who from the day they met used his son-in-law to line his own pockets, suddenly cares about kisses and tambourines and proper send-offs. He is wounded to the quick that Jacob and company should leave his house without a proper farewell.

Oh…and Jacob stole the family gods. They're worth big bucks. Where are they? At this point Laban knows he's not getting Jacob to stay. He may not even get goodbye kisses and hugs. But at least he wants his money back.

You may remember that when we first met him back in Chapter 24, Laban was drawn to the jewelry that Abraham's servant put on Rebekah's arms. Now he's concerned about his property and wealth as we part company with him. Some people will never change.

Selfishness is like flypaper to our souls. Dip a toe into it and you're going to stick. Every time we step down that path we become a little blinder, less able to see alternatives, more enmeshed in a mindset that will overcome us and break all our relationships. Eventually we find ourselves unable to see things any other way. The people around us can no longer reach us, nor we them, because everything they say or do gets filtered through the lens of our self-interest. Attempting to save ourselves, we lose ourselves and everything that's good about life.

31 Jacob answered Laban, "I was afraid, because I thought you would take your daughters away from me by force. 32 But if you find anyone who has your gods, that person shall not live. In the presence of our relatives, see for yourself whether there is anything of yours here with me; and if so, take it." Now Jacob did not know that Rachel had stolen the gods.

33 So Laban went into Jacob's tent and into Leah's tent and into the tent of the two female servants, but he found nothing. After he came out of Leah's tent, he entered Rachel's tent. 34 Now Rachel had taken the household gods and put them inside her camel's saddle and was sitting on them. Laban searched through everything in the tent but found nothing.

35 Rachel said to her father, "Don't be angry, my lord, that I cannot stand up in your presence; I'm having my period." So he searched but could not find the household gods.

Jacob was able to answer Laban with righteous indignation because he didn't know what his wife had done. Sometimes ignorance is bliss. The story would have had a sad ending had Laban found his idols but Rachel, showing herself as tricky as all the men in her life, sat on the goods and claimed to be too indisposed to rise and reveal them.

We might be tempted to think less of Rachel because this whole thing seems…well…less than kosher. Certainly we can't advocate robbing your father on the way out the door of his house. But let's not lose track of the other side of the story too. What was Laban looking for? What did he see when he entered that tent? He should have seen his daughter, his own flesh and blood, a beloved and precious human being. He wasn't looking for that. He only cared about hunks of metal or stone or wood. He cared about nothing else.

What do you look for when you go into your local store? Do you see people in the aisle, at the checkout counter, on the street? Or do you just see what you want to see…which is whatever you hope to procure from the store at that moment? Every one of those people is somebody's son or daughter. Every one of them has value. Not to our eyes, though. We want what we want and view people as aids or obstacles to getting it. That's pretty sad. That's exactly how Laban viewed Rachel at that moment.

The ironic thing is, were one of those other store patrons to lift our wallet or purse, we'd feel hurt and violated. We'd wonder why they didn't see us as human beings, whether they understood the real damage they had caused to our soul by robbing us. We'd wish the world were a better place, a place where people cared about each other more than this. But when we walked into that store, we were thinking of everybody else in the same, impersonal, means-to-an-end way as the pickpocket. That we didn't actually steal anything doesn't make our philosophical outlook any nobler. We and the thief view the world the same way. We just use different means to achieve our ends.

We think God asks so much of us: perfection or holiness or sainthood. I suspect he'd settle for us not being such constant jerks to each other…at least *trying* to view other people with a little charity and goodwill instead of objectifying them.

Sadly, neither Rachel nor Laban viewed each other with anything more than practicality. Each wanted the same thing: those idols. Rachel got it, Laban didn't.

It's not the most heartwarming tale but if everybody's going to think like a thief, this is what you have to expect. I guess you end up rooting for the person who achieved their aim. That was Rachel.

Productive Confrontation

36 Jacob was angry and took Laban to task. "What is my crime?" he asked Laban. "How have I wronged you that you hunt me down? 37 Now that you have searched through all my goods, what have you found that belongs to your household? Put it here in front of your relatives and mine, and let them judge between the two of us.

38 "I have been with you for twenty years now. Your sheep and goats have not miscarried, nor have I eaten rams from your flocks. 39 I did not bring you animals torn by wild beasts; I bore the loss myself. And you demanded payment from me for whatever was stolen by day or night. 40 This was my situation: The heat consumed me in the daytime and the cold at night, and sleep fled from my eyes. 41 It was like this for the twenty years I was in your household. I worked for you fourteen years for your two daughters and six years for your flocks, and you changed my wages ten times. 42 If the God of my father, the God of Abraham and the Fear of Isaac, had not been with me, you would surely have sent me away empty-handed. But God has seen my hardship and the toil of my hands, and last night he rebuked you."

43 Laban answered Jacob, "The women are my daughters, the children are my children, and the flocks are my flocks. All you see is mine. Yet what can I do today about these daughters of mine, or about the children they have borne? 44 Come now, let's make a covenant, you and I, and let it serve as a witness between us."

45 So Jacob took a stone and set it up as a pillar. 46 He said to his relatives, "Gather some stones." So they took stones and piled them in a heap, and they ate there by the heap. 47 Laban called it Jegar Sahadutha, and Jacob called it Galeed.

48 Laban said, "This heap is a witness between you and me today." That is why it was called Galeed. 49 It was also called Mizpah, because he said, "May the Lord keep watch between you and me when we are away from each other. 50 If you mistreat my daughters or if you take any wives besides my daughters, even though no one is with us, remember that God is a witness between you and me."

⁵¹ Laban also said to Jacob, "Here is this heap, and here is this pillar I have set up between you and me. ⁵² This heap is a witness, and this pillar is a witness, that I will not go past this heap to your side to harm you and that you will not go past this heap and pillar to my side to harm me. ⁵³ May the God of Abraham and the God of Nahor, the God of their father, judge between us."

So Jacob took an oath in the name of the Fear of his father Isaac. ⁵⁴ He offered a sacrifice there in the hill country and invited his relatives to a meal. After they had eaten, they spent the night there.

⁵⁵ Early the next morning Laban kissed his grandchildren and his daughters and blessed them. Then he left and returned home.

Jacob does something powerful here. Fed up with his uncle's self-centered manipulation, he speaks the truth as he knows it. Ironically, he's not entirely right. His wife actually did steal Laban's goods. But Jacob's lack of knowledge matters less than his willingness to reveal his perspective.

None of us can claim to know the complete truth in any situation. Even our strongest-held beliefs are seeded with mistakes and misperceptions. But honest relationships don't depend on infallible knowledge. They require us to be forthright enough to speak what we believe and courageous enough to hear what other people think in turn.

Confrontation has gotten a bad rap over the last couple decades. Most people will walk miles out of their way to avoid it. Confrontation was not intended to be a bad thing. In a world where nobody's right it becomes a necessary part of our growth process. Two people lay out the truth as they see it, those truths grind against each other, and each person emerges with a new perspective. The weaker parts of our viewpoints get whittled away leaving the stronger parts intact.

That fine theory falls apart in practice because confrontation requires making oneself vulnerable to criticism, a risk most folks prefer not to take. We're used to viewing the world in black and white, designating winners and losers in any argument. We fear that if we lose a point in an argument we'll also lose our identity and credibility. We don't enter an argument unless we're sure we'll win.

Sadly, that surety usually comes from the tactics we use more than the integrity of our view. We're willing to do anything to make sure we'll win, including shouting down other people, exaggerating, attacking them personally instead of considering their points, and talking behind their backs instead of speaking with them personally. Rather than make ourselves vulnerable we make ourselves invincible. We never lose but we never learn anything either.

Fear of just such a scenario causes us to steer clear of confrontation even when it's necessary. A bus driver headed towards a cliff doesn't need his passengers to remain silent for fear of offending him or getting yelled at. Some things are worth getting yelled at for. In service to the 40 other people on the bus and the driver himself, somebody needs to speak up before the tires leave the pavement.

Look at Jacob in this scenario. He and Laban didn't see eye to eye. Nor did Jacob have a reasonable expectation that Laban would agree with his point of view. Still Jacob took the risk. He spoke the truth plainly…or as much of the truth as he knew anyway. His uncle listened…not because he was on Jacob's side, but because putting yourself out there as Jacob did tends to make people feel closer to you even when they don't necessarily like what you're saying.

In the end, Laban relented. He and Jacob made peace. Between the two of them they piled up rocks at a place they called, "The Heap of Witness". Laban told Jacob to treat his daughters well and make them his only wives…their children his only heirs. Laban and Jacob pledged not to harm each other. Neither would pass to the other side of the Witness Heap with intent to harm. They called upon the God of their common relative Abraham to judge them should either break their oath. Jacob offered a sacrifice, they ate together, and spent the night in peace. The next morning Laban and Jacob separated, Laban returning to his fields and Jacob traveling onward to destiny.

At no point did Laban change his ways or his views. Uncle and nephew never ended up on the same side. The Heap of Witness was more of a demilitarized zone than a family reunion spot. But neither man had to give in to the other or win the argument in order to come to an accord. Where truth is spoken and heard, productive confrontation follows and after that usually comes peace.

The Holy Angels

32 Jacob also went on his way, and the angels of God met him. ² When Jacob saw them, he said, "This is the camp of God!" So he named that place Mahanaim.

The first people Jacob met on his way home were God's angels. God was with Jacob from the start and he remained so here.

Whenever one reads a text like this there's a temptation to say, "Hey! Where's my angels? Why don't I ever get visions and visitations like that?"

I wonder if we recognize them when we see them.

"The Camp of God", or Mahanaim, was a real place. It had rocks, dust, and insects. The sun shone on it; when it rained it got wet. We can't anticipate the places where God will work. They don't come with neon signs and velvet ropes. Up until the very moment the angels appeared, you wouldn't have known Mahanaim from any other ordinary-seeming patch of dirt.

Are we sure we know where and when angels will appear, or won't?

No doubt some angels appear in heavenly guise, shining white and showing off wings. But as we've said, the word "angel" also means "messenger". Just as you'd never have recognized Mahanaim before the angels showed up in it, you can't recognize God's messengers before you meet them. They often look ordinary; they turn out to be anything but.

I've met angels—God's messengers—in the form of 99-year-old women and 5-year-old boys. I've met angels of both genders, various races, inside and outside the church, even a couple who claimed other religions besides mine. Some will cry heresy at this…I prefer to think of it as God being bigger than I imagine, able to work through people who don't know they're his messengers.

Sometimes these angels have brought me good news, other times wisdom. Occasionally they've scolded me or called me to reform myself. Many of them have changed my life.

I have seen living rooms, church tables, playgrounds, bowling alleys, classrooms, and car seats transformed into Mahanaim. One moment you're just walking, the next you realize that you're standing on holy ground speaking with someone who's transforming you with their message.

It's not so hard to see angels if you have your eyes right. You have to understand God is speaking to you in every moment, sometimes using the faces and voices of those around you. You have to listen as people speak, crediting them with the possibility of speaking holy truth even before you know what they're going to say. You also have to be willing to change in response to others, or else God's message will bounce right off you.

The easiest way to avoid perceiving angels is to only listen to people who say what you already agree with, only crediting people with truth when they tell you what you already know. That will limit the entire universe to the size of your head. But if you understand God works in ways you don't expect, speaks through people you don't anticipate, and you are willing to grow your perception of him in response to others, you'll find that angels are everywhere. The smallest utterance of a holy 2nd grader can change your life. I've had it happen to me.

No Easy Roads

³ Jacob sent messengers ahead of him to his brother Esau in the land of Seir, the country of Edom. ⁴ He instructed them: "This is what you are to say to my lord Esau: 'Your servant Jacob says, I have been staying with Laban and have remained there till now. ⁵ I have cattle and donkeys, sheep and goats, male and female servants. Now I am sending this message to my lord, that I may find favor in your eyes.'"

⁶ When the messengers returned to Jacob, they said, "We went to your brother Esau, and now he is coming to meet you, and four hundred men are with him."

⁷ In great fear and distress Jacob divided the people who were with him into two groups, and the flocks and herds and camels as well. ⁸ He thought, "If Esau comes and attacks one group, the group that is left may escape."

By the time Jacob journeyed back to his homeland, he was in tune with himself, his environment, and his mission. The manipulative trickster was, for the most part, gone...replaced by a truth-speaker, a man used to listening to and depending on God. He heard God's messengers all around him as he walked; a camp of angels surrounded him.

The message he sent to his brother reflected this. It was simple and truthful. "I ran away claiming I was Lord of the family. I return as your servant. I don't need to grasp at the things I once did, nor to take anything away from you. I just want to come home and find favor in your eyes."

Keep in mind that Jacob was talking to a brother he had never known peace with, the man with whom he had struggled in their mother's womb. Yet he was willing to put aside everything he once claimed as his own to make the relationship good. The man who once broke apart his family to trick his brother out of their father's land and title now acquiesced without a struggle.

When Jacob's messengers returned, though, it appeared the fight was not done from Esau's point of view. He approached with 400 armed men. In fear, Jacob made the best plan he could. He split his flocks in two, hoping that if Esau attacked one, the other would survive.

Nobody's road is easy, even the most centered, humble, and reformed among us. Our best plans are half-measures. As Esau's might descended upon him, Jacob must have wondered if all his toil had bought him a little more life eked out of an inevitable progression towards death, a few battles won in a war that he'd already lost. If Esau were to descend upon him in war, Jacob couldn't save his property and maybe not even his family. At best he could preserve half of them for a while. Frustration and futility reigned as Jacob divided the fruits of his life's work into separate groups, knowing everything might disappear in an instant should Esau prove vengeful.

The Beautiful Prayer

9 Then Jacob prayed, "O God of my father Abraham, God of my father Isaac, Lord, you who said to me, 'Go back to your country and your relatives, and I will make you prosper,' 10 I am unworthy of all the kindness and faithfulness you have shown your servant. I had only my staff when I crossed this Jordan, but now I have become two camps. 11 Save me, I pray, from the hand of my brother Esau, for I am afraid he will come and attack me, and also the mothers with their children. 12 But you have said, 'I will surely make you prosper and will make your descendants like the sand of the sea, which cannot be counted.'"

In this passage Jacob prayed in words both touching and self-aware. He began his prayer by naming God as Lord of his family. He spoke of the mission God had set before him, to return home.

Then in Genesis 32:10 he made a confession so pure that one can hardly credit it to the same man who once put on goat skins to trick his own father. "I don't deserve the kindness you've shown me, God. Without you I had nothing, with you I now have everything." Jacob condensed our entire relationship with God into a couple sentences. We mess up and don't deserve help, but we need help, so we ask for it anyway. Our heavenly Obi-Wan, God is our only hope.

Return again to Adam and Even in the garden. Had they confessed as Jacob did, they wouldn't have broken the world. "You are my only hope" is the exact opposite of, "You've held back from me and now I want to take your place."

After this Jacob named his deepest fear. He was worried Esau will slaughter his children. Then he reminded God of God's own promise to him. This seems cheeky, as God hardly needed the reminder, but in practice it's a statement of faith. "I trust you when you say you'll deliver me." It reminds us what we believe in more than it reminds God what he said.

Hearing these things would make any father's heart melt. "Dad, you've given me everything even though I didn't always deserve it. I'm so afraid of it all coming to nothing. Can you help?" Who among us would not be at our son's side instantly?

We spend far too much time trying to look perfect in front of each other and God. Not only is the attempt futile, it's not necessary. Jacob wasn't perfect, but these words show that he was in harmony with the world and its Creator in a way fear could not overcome. Peace doesn't come from everything going right, it comes when even the worst of wrongs can't shake you from your purpose or trust in God.

Showing Who You Are

13 He spent the night there, and from what he had with him he selected a gift for his brother Esau: 14 two hundred female goats and twenty male goats, two hundred ewes and twenty rams, 15 thirty female camels with their young, forty cows and ten bulls, and twenty female donkeys and ten male donkeys. 16 He put them in the care of his servants, each herd by itself, and said to his servants, "Go ahead of me, and keep some space between the herds."

17 He instructed the one in the lead: "When my brother Esau meets you and asks, 'Who do you belong to, and where are you going, and who owns all these animals in front of you?' 18 then you are to say, 'They belong to your servant Jacob. They are a gift sent to my lord Esau, and he is coming behind us.'"

19 He also instructed the second, the third and all the others who followed the herds: "You are to say the same thing to Esau when you meet him. 20 And be sure to say, 'Your servant Jacob is coming behind us.'" For he thought, "I will pacify him with these gifts I am sending on ahead; later, when I see him, perhaps he will receive me." 21 So Jacob's gifts went on ahead of him, but he himself spent the night in the camp.

After his beautiful prayer, Jacob practiced generous behavior. When he was pressured in the old days, Jacob's instinct was to trick, to take. Here he decided to give instead. To his brother he sent goats and sheep, camels and cows, then some donkeys for good measure. Each herd was a gift, showing God's blessings and his willingness to share them.

People often struggle with self-expression. We want to show the world who we are but we can't find the right voice and venue. We fear being rejected, mocked, even attacked. We don't realize that fear is a sure sign that we're thinking of ourselves more than those we want to share with.

Most of our self-expression comes in the form of taking: listen to my music, let me speak now, read my t-shirt. We engage in an unspoken tug-of-war with everyone else who is trying to do the same. You've probably seen Open Mic Nights where everybody's waiting for their turn in the spotlight, not really caring when others are up. Everybody knows the artist who walks around art shows sniffing, "Hmmph. I could do better than that."

Perhaps we're right to fear rejection. When we interact with the world this way, that's probably what we deserve.

The one form of self-expression that never needs explanation and is seldom rejected is generosity. If we go out into the world to give instead of to draw attention to ourselves, we break the selfish pattern and create a new one. No longer is my "self" about what I can take from you, it's about what I can render…what we can share together. Instead of drawing you in to view me a museum piece, I pour out myself and you see me at work in your life. Both ways demonstrate who I am, but the first hardly matters while the second means everything.

You don't have to think that deeply in order to show yourself to the world. Just do what Jacob did. Give generously to the people in your life. You don't have to bestow livestock or money upon them. Whatever you have, share and make good use of it to help others. Then people will not only see who you are, but appreciate it. They might even stop to listen to your Open Mic music or buy a piece of your art!

Wrestling With God

[22] That night Jacob got up and took his two wives, his two female servants and his eleven sons and crossed the ford of the Jabbok. [23] After he had sent them across the stream, he sent over all his possessions. [24] So Jacob was left alone, and a man wrestled with him till daybreak. [25] When the man saw that he could not overpower him, he touched the socket of Jacob's hip so that his hip was wrenched as he wrestled with the man. [26] Then the man said, "Let me go, for it is daybreak."

But Jacob replied, "I will not let you go unless you bless me."

[27] The man asked him, "What is your name?"

"Jacob," he answered.

[28] Then the man said, "Your name will no longer be Jacob, but Israel, because you have struggled with God and with humans and have overcome."

[29] Jacob said, "Please tell me your name."

But he replied, "Why do you ask my name?" Then he blessed him there.

³⁰ So Jacob called the place Peniel, saying, "It is because I saw God face to face, and yet my life was spared."

³¹ The sun rose above him as he passed Peniel, and he was limping because of his hip. ³² Therefore to this day the Israelites do not eat the tendon attached to the socket of the hip, because the socket of Jacob's hip was touched near the tendon.

Jacob's journey climaxes with one of the most poignant, thoughtful stories in all of scripture disguised as a WWE main event. Fearing Esau's wrath, Jacob sent his wife, children, and all his possessions over the Jabbok river, remaining behind alone. Suddenly he felt himself grabbed by an unknown assailant, perhaps a robber in the night.

All night Jacob wrestled with his opponent until the sun was about to rise. Then the attacker pulled a dirty trick, wrenching out Jacob's hip socket in a move that would leave him with a pronounced limp. Still Jacob would not concede.

"Let me go," said the man.

"Not until you bless me," Jacob replied.

"What is your name?"

"Jacob." It meant trickster.

"No longer will your name be Jacob, but Israel." Israel means "Wrestles with God".

Jacob tried once again to find out the identity of his assailant but came up empty handed. He did, however, get his blessing. Between the name change, the supernatural strength and endurance, and the mystery left behind, Jacob had a pretty good idea who he'd been struggling with. He named the spot "Peniel", meaning "Face of God". After years of chatting, Jacob and his creator finally met in person.

The story arc of Jacob practically begs for this moment. Here was a man dissatisfied since before he was born, never knowing peace. He fought against his brother for an inheritance, fought against his father for a blessing, fought against his uncle for possessions and independence, then watched his wives fight against each other for primacy and children. His life had been a long, continuous struggle. Every time he seemed to get the upper hand, another event or circumstance would plunge him back into turmoil.

During this long struggle Jacob also fought to carve out an identity. Was he the trickster, the mama's boy, the put-upon nephew, the smart agriculturalist, the harried husband, or the family head? No title ever stuck. At no point was he able to be sure about himself or his place.

Finally, at the end of his journey, having grown and fought through all these experiences, Jacob realized he'd spent his whole life contesting not just with the world, his family, or himself, but God. God always had a destiny for him, yet Jacob spent his life flailing, trying to find his own way, until this night when he came face to face with his God.

At no point did Jacob have a hope of winning this fight. As God demonstrated, a single divine touch was enough to cripple him, giving God the upper hand. So Jacob did the only thing he could…he held on and wouldn't let go.

At no point do we have a hope of winning our battle against God either. We go astray, see things wrong, work for our own selfish gain just as Jacob did. When we come up against ultimate righteousness, pure justice, and infinite love, we find ourselves hopelessly outmatched. Even our best impulses seem silly and vain.

If you take faith seriously at all, you're going to run smack dab into the futility of it all. We're called to do good while at the same time knowing we'll never understand goodness completely this side of the grave. We know that perfection exists somewhere and that we're called to follow it, but we can't get to it. The precise moment when we think we have it all solved, that we're perfectly right, that we have no sin, we're the most wrong we've ever been.

Practicing faith is like walking on a treadmill. You put in effort, sweat, and passion knowing that you're not going to get to a destination you can be satisfied with. The more you discover, the farther you have left to go. All you can hope for is to get better at walking. You don't get to win. The finishing line comes when you lie down into God's hand at the moment of death, not a second before. Meanwhile you get up tomorrow and walk that treadmill again.

The only thing you can do in this situation is hold on…keep doing what you're supposed to be doing and pray you'll see the reason for it someday. That's faith in its purest form: not winning, not being right, not feeling good or vindicated or happy. Faith is holding on one more day, trusting one more time in a world full of violence and greed and cancer and racism and poverty and starvation and war and peril. Faith is holding onto the love, the community, the Word…holding onto God.

The single greatest utterance in all our life of faith is, "I need you, Lord." The second, right behind it, is simply, "I won't let go."

That's exactly what Jacob went through that night…and all his life, really. He didn't let go. Through all the mistakes and turmoil and ultimately wrestling with an opponent he couldn't overcome, he didn't let go.

And God blessed him.

God changed his name from Jacob the Trickster to "Israel, Wrestles with God". This would be the name that God's people—the long-promised descendants of Abraham, Isaac, and Jacob—would be known by forevermore.

God did not name Jacob and his people "They Who Were Right" or "The Ones Who Made It" or "The Folks Who Always Felt Blessed and Happy". God called them the people who wrestle with him. Wrestling implies close contact, maybe even common purpose with an opponent, but also a perpetual contest. How else could our relationship with God be in a fallen world?

Many times over in this book I've talked about the foolishness of judgmental Christianity. Too often people who appropriately reject this interpretation of faith swing into another equally inaccurate rendition: "Everybody is OK. I don't judge." We're not OK. The world is broken and we're broken too. "Everybody and everything is OK" tells just as much of a lie about our relationship with God as, "I'm OK and you're not" does.

Every time God is near us he has to struggle with us, our mistaken ways and unjust deeds. God has to fight as hard to be with us as we do to be with him. By rights the Lord of Perfection would refuse to be anywhere near us. But God's love overcomes need for justice. He does stay with us, even if he has to wrestle with us to do it.

Faith provides no easy answers. We wrestle through tears and doubts, through beauty and pain, through right and wrong and all the ups and downs of life. We wrestle because we're not capable of greeting God in peace, because we're loved far too much to walk away. Sometimes we get our hips broken as our best-laid plans go astray. Sometimes we're blessed and receive new identities. Through it all we cling to God and the process because that's all we've got.

There is no greater honor or purpose in life than to wrestle with God. There is no greater accomplishment than to hold on.

That's all Jacob had that night, alone with the Maker against whom he'd struggled since the womb. He limped as he walked away from the encounter, but he finally found the peace he had been searching for. His old struggles were ended. New ones would arise—as they do for us all--but they would no longer find Jacob lost and blowing every which way in response to his desires. Instead they'd find Israel, a man whose imperfections were filled up and washed away through a Godly identity that allowed him to deal with the world in a new and better way.

United at Last

33 Jacob looked up and there was Esau, coming with his four hundred men; so he divided the children among Leah, Rachel and the two female servants. 2 He put the female servants and their children in front, Leah and her children next, and Rachel and Joseph in the rear. 3 He himself went on ahead and bowed down to the ground seven times as he approached his brother.

4 But Esau ran to meet Jacob and embraced him; he threw his arms around his neck and kissed him. And they wept. 5 Then Esau looked up and saw the women and children. "Who are these with you?" he asked.

Jacob answered, "They are the children God has graciously given your servant."

⁶ Then the female servants and their children approached and bowed down. ⁷ Next, Leah and her children came and bowed down. Last of all came Joseph and Rachel, and they too bowed down.

⁸ Esau asked, "What's the meaning of all these flocks and herds I met?"

"To find favor in your eyes, my lord," he said.

⁹ But Esau said, "I already have plenty, my brother. Keep what you have for yourself."

¹⁰ "No, please!" said Jacob. "If I have found favor in your eyes, accept this gift from me. For to see your face is like seeing the face of God, now that you have received me favorably. ¹¹ Please accept the present that was brought to you, for God has been gracious to me and I have all I need." And because Jacob insisted, Esau accepted it.

¹² Then Esau said, "Let us be on our way; I'll accompany you."

¹³ But Jacob said to him, "My lord knows that the children are tender and that I must care for the ewes and cows that are nursing their young. If they are driven hard just one day, all the animals will die. ¹⁴ So let my lord go on ahead of his servant, while I move along slowly at the pace of the flocks and herds before me and the pace of the children, until I come to my lord in Seir."

¹⁵ Esau said, "Then let me leave some of my men with you."

"But why do that?" Jacob asked. "Just let me find favor in the eyes of my lord."

¹⁶ So that day Esau started on his way back to Seir. ¹⁷ Jacob, however, went to Sukkoth, where he built a place for himself and made shelters for his livestock. That is why the place is called Sukkoth.

¹⁸ After Jacob came from Paddan Aram, he arrived safely at the city of Shechem in Canaan and camped within sight of the city. ¹⁹ For a hundred pieces of silver, he bought from the sons of Hamor, the father of Shechem, the plot of ground where he pitched his tent. ²⁰ There he set up an altar and called it El Elohe Israel.

The first person to benefit from Jacob's new identity was his brother Esau. Gone was the conniving, grasping lad whom Esau had wanted to strangle so badly. In his place was a man talking about grace, about family, about generous giving. Jacob bestowed part of his herds upon his brother, making up for the attempted hijacking of their father's inheritance. Suddenly the brothers who had been doing nothing but taking from each other were arguing about which of them would accept gifts.

The family did not reunite entirely. Esau did not travel with Jacob, nor did the two end up living in the same place. But in that moment when the two brothers embraced and wept, we find a peaceful ending to a long and bitter feud. Wrestling with God ultimately ends in reunion and paradise. We get a foretaste of that destiny as we make peace with each other.

Again note that Jacob did not find peace with his brother by demanding peace, but by giving it. The language of power asks who will give in first and how far they'll bend. The language of love gives without being asked. Its power comes from lifting others instead of wringing concessions from them and feeling superior for doing so. Jacob's way proved the stronger. He changed Esau and his entire family dynamic by changing himself, walking in faith instead of selfishness.

A Story That Must Speak for Itself

34 Now Dinah, the daughter Leah had borne to Jacob, went out to visit the women of the land. 2 When Shechem son of Hamor the Hivite, the ruler of that area, saw her, he took her and raped her. 3 His heart was drawn to Dinah daughter of Jacob; he loved the young woman and spoke tenderly to her. 4 And Shechem said to his father Hamor, "Get me this girl as my wife."

5 When Jacob heard that his daughter Dinah had been defiled, his sons were in the fields with his livestock; so he did nothing about it until they came home.

6 Then Shechem's father Hamor went out to talk with Jacob. 7 Meanwhile, Jacob's sons had come in from the fields as soon as they heard what had happened. They were shocked and furious, because Shechem had done an outrageous thing in Israel by sleeping with Jacob's daughter—a thing that should not be done.

8 But Hamor said to them, "My son Shechem has his heart set on your daughter. Please give her to him as his wife. 9 Intermarry with us; give us your daughters and take our daughters for yourselves. 10 You can settle among us; the land is open to you. Live in it, trade in it, and acquire property in it."

¹¹ Then Shechem said to Dinah's father and brothers, "Let me find favor in your eyes, and I will give you whatever you ask. ¹² Make the price for the bride and the gift I am to bring as great as you like, and I'll pay whatever you ask me. Only give me the young woman as my wife."

¹³ Because their sister Dinah had been defiled, Jacob's sons replied deceitfully as they spoke to Shechem and his father Hamor. ¹⁴ They said to them, "We can't do such a thing; we can't give our sister to a man who is not circumcised. That would be a disgrace to us. ¹⁵ We will enter into an agreement with you on one condition only: that you become like us by circumcising all your males. ¹⁶ Then we will give you our daughters and take your daughters for ourselves. We'll settle among you and become one people with you. ¹⁷ But if you will not agree to be circumcised, we'll take our sister and go."

¹⁸ Their proposal seemed good to Hamor and his son Shechem. ¹⁹ The young man, who was the most honored of all his father's family, lost no time in doing what they said, because he was delighted with Jacob's daughter. ²⁰ So Hamor and his son Shechem went to the gate of their city to speak to the men of their city. ²¹ "These men are friendly toward us," they said. "Let them live in our land and trade in it; the land has plenty of room for them. We can marry their daughters and they can marry ours. ²² But the men will agree to live with us as one people only on the condition that our males be circumcised, as they themselves are. ²³ Won't their livestock, their property and all their other animals become ours? So let us agree to their terms, and they will settle among us."

²⁴ All the men who went out of the city gate agreed with Hamor and his son Shechem, and every male in the city was circumcised.

²⁵ Three days later, while all of them were still in pain, two of Jacob's sons, Simeon and Levi, Dinah's brothers, took their swords and attacked the unsuspecting city, killing every male. ²⁶ They put Hamor and his son Shechem to the sword and took Dinah from Shechem's house and left. ²⁷ The sons of Jacob came upon the dead bodies and looted the city where[a] their sister had been defiled. ²⁸ They seized their flocks and herds and donkeys and everything else of theirs in the city and out in the fields. ²⁹ They carried off all their wealth and all their women and children, taking as plunder everything in the houses.

³⁰ Then Jacob said to Simeon and Levi, "You have brought trouble on me by making me obnoxious to the Canaanites and Perizzites, the people living in this land. We are few in

number, and if they join forces against me and attack me, I and my household will be destroyed."

³¹ But they replied, "Should he have treated our sister like a prostitute?"

Genesis 34 may be full of theological meaning. I'm not sure. Here's what I do know: A woman was raped.

Whenever I'm tempted to treat this chapter like the others we've talked about so far, I feel the burden of being a man in a society that far too often has minimized the crime and agony of sexual assault against women. Some will cry, "Well you talked about Abel getting killed a few chapters ago! That was murder!" We haven't made a cottage industry over the years of justifying murder. Everybody will agree that killing your brother out of jealousy is wrong. Nobody is going to ask what Abel was wearing like they ask sexual assault survivors.

With the weight of that reality in front of me, I feel like further theological analysis—especially that which would shift the focus away from what happened to Jacob's daughters in favor of what happened with his sons—would be a betrayal. Earlier in this book we discussed how the word "but" can invalidate everything that comes before it. Theologically speaking, me pursuing this story would be the equivalent of saying, "A woman was raped, but here's what it really means."

I will say that I don't believe the response of Dinah's brothers was an appropriate one in the case of rape, nor do I think the aftermath of rape should focus on the injury done to males, whether related to the victim or the perpetrator. Beyond that, though, I would refer you to people more qualified to handle this subject theologically and sociologically. I would suggest starting with any number of female theologians who have approached this text with more sensitivity and nuance than I possibly could. That would be one way to honor the gravity of the events in this chapter while exploring its meaning.

As for me, my heart goes out to all survivors of sexual assault. I cannot imagine how hard it must be sometimes to hold on. I pray that you may find strength and courage on your journey.

Leaving the Past Behind

35 Then God said to Jacob, "Go up to Bethel and settle there, and build an altar there to God, who appeared to you when you were fleeing from your brother Esau."

2 So Jacob said to his household and to all who were with him, "Get rid of the foreign gods you have with you, and purify yourselves and change your clothes. 3 Then come, let us go up to Bethel, where I will build an altar to God, who answered me in the day of my distress and who has been with me wherever I have gone." 4 So they gave Jacob all the foreign gods they had and the rings in their ears, and Jacob buried them under the oak at Shechem.5 Then they set out, and the terror of God fell on the towns all around them so that no one pursued them.

6 Jacob and all the people with him came to Luz (that is, Bethel) in the land of Canaan. 7 There he built an altar, and he called the place El Bethel, because it was there that God revealed himself to him when he was fleeing from his brother.

After the horrible events of Chapter 34, God urges Jacob to remove himself from the place, returning to Bethel, where Jacob had seen the vision of God's messengers ascending and descending. One translation of Bethel is "House of God".

As Jacob made the move he commanded his family to divest themselves of all foreign gods, to ritually cleanse themselves, even leaving their old clothes behind. They buried all those things, giving them back to the land that spawned them. They needed a new start.

Most of us have experienced times when we had to leave behind something we knew was bad for us and begin again. Such changes often herald a return to the "house of God". If we don't revisit the church itself at least we resolve to lead a more godly, upright life.

In the initial stages of such transformations divesting is as important as investing. We dare not delude ourselves that we can carry old wrongs into a new place without becoming bent towards them again. Blaming our environment for our ills is easy, sometimes accurate. But the wrong was inside us to begin with and remains inside us no matter where we go. Environmental factors can make pursuing our weaknesses easier or harder, but the transgression is still ours. Until we admit that, we cannot be free of it.

A popular treatment program for alcoholism encourages people to say, "I am an alcoholic and I remain one. I don't drink right now but if I were to take another sip, I'd be right back down the same road." That lesson applies to us as well. We're "sinoholics". We're bent to enjoy the taste, sound, smell, feel, and sight of it. Sin draws us. The temptation to trust in other things besides God for our happiness is overwhelming. Anyone who thinks otherwise is like the reformed alcoholic walking through bars 24 hours a day claiming he can handle it. He may not be slipping yet, but the future doesn't look bright.

We have no hope of being free from sin altogether, at least not by our own will. Most of us would settle for being free of a particular, destructive sin that has held us down throughout our lives. Whatever the sin is, whenever we make the transformation, we have to leave the signs, symbols, and hallmarks of wrongdoing behind. They belong buried in the land in which we found them, inaccessible and remote idols to a different us in a different place and time. If we fail to do this it doesn't matter whose house we run to, the old desires will follow.

Another Passage

[8] *Now Deborah, Rebekah's nurse, died and was buried under the oak outside Bethel. So it was named Allon Bakuth.*

In the midst of the family transformation Rebekah's nurse Deborah dies…creating yet another place name but also reminding us of the passage of time. Jacob and his wives aren't "the kids" anymore. They're getting on in years and life is changing around them.

Our culture demands that we embrace youth. From moisturizers to mid-life crises, we play hide-and-seek with aging and our own mortality. We never succeed in reversing the clock. Mostly we end up looking stupid, wasting the time we do have chasing after time we don't.

God's intention for us is infinite life. We can stop worrying on that score. 60 seems like a large fraction of 90. It's barely a speck of a billion billion, which itself is an even smaller portion of infinity. We don't need to pursue youth or time; they're already ours.

We do need to remember that our time here is finite, not to cause fear but to make better use of it. Rebekah's nurse died. Eventually so did Rebekah, Jacob and his wives, their children, and everyone we're reading about. Does anyone now remember how many wrinkles Rachel had? What will people remember us for when we're gone? If we want it to be anything more than foolish vanity, we need to acknowledge that time always runs faster than we think and begin doing the things that are important to us now.

Beginning With Another Covenant

9 After Jacob returned from Paddan Aram, God appeared to him again and blessed him. 10 God said to him, "Your name is Jacob, but you will no longer be called Jacob; your name will be Israel." So he named him Israel.

11 And God said to him, "I am God Almighty; be fruitful and increase in number. A nation and a community of nations will come from you, and kings will be among your descendants. 12 The land I gave to Abraham and Isaac I also give to you, and I will give this land to your descendants after you." 13 Then God went up from him at the place where he had talked with him.

14 Jacob set up a stone pillar at the place where God had talked with him, and he poured out a drink offering on it; he also poured oil on it. 15 Jacob called the place where God had talked with him Bethel.

As always, Jacob's new start—new creation, if you will--is accompanied by a fresh covenant from God. In this case it's a brief renewal of the promise God gave to Abraham and Isaac, now confirmed in Jacob their descendant. Multiplicity of children (easier to see in Jacob's case than in his father's or grandfather's), the land and nation…everything is there. God has bestowed his full promise upon Israel.

It's not alluded to here, but Christians might hearken to their own baptismal covenant when they hear the story of these promises. Baptism is a new creation, the old self drowned in chilly waters as a new self rises to new life. Baptism imparts God's promise to dwell with us, washing away our sin and making us new continually, claiming us as part of his family and bringing us to everlasting life. What God did for Abraham, Isaac, and Jacob he also does for you. Genesis isn't just their story, it's your story too.

Each day is meant to be a new creation for us in which God's promises are renewed and God's covenant lived out. It's amazing how often we wake up without remembering the purpose for our waking. Like Jacob's family we wander in a foreign land. We find ourselves distracted, tempted to prioritize emptiness over faith. We're called to wake up remembering God's promise to us, viewing the night's rest as an ending and the morning as rising to new life. That which burdened us yesterday is gone, washed away in a flood of grace. All that sustained us yesterday is redoubled. Today we get another chance to live the life we were meant to live, with God leading the way.

Rachel Dies

16 Then they moved on from Bethel. While they were still some distance from Ephrath, Rachel began to give birth and had great difficulty. 17 And as she was having great difficulty in childbirth, the midwife said to her, "Don't despair, for you have another son." 18 As she breathed her last—for she was dying—she named her son Ben-Oni. But his father named him Benjamin.

19 So Rachel died and was buried on the way to Ephrath (that is, Bethlehem). 20 Over her tomb Jacob set up a pillar, and to this day that pillar marks Rachel's tomb.

Sadly, Jacob would lose his favored wife as she fulfilled her dream of having more children. "Ben-Oni" means "son of trouble", likely referring to the difficulty of this particular birthing. Benjamin means "child of my right hand", in other words "strong and favored child that I depend upon".

Our dreams don't always end up as we imagined. Sometimes they don't bring us happiness, but woe. This is the litmus test of any desire, not whether you think it will make you happy, but whether it's worth sacrificing yourself for. In the end, Rachel gave her life bringing another child into the world. It was a sad thing, also something most mothers would deem as worth any sacrifice. Jacob would end up treasuring the son just as much as he treasured the mother.

21 Israel moved on again and pitched his tent beyond Migdal Eder. 22 While Israel was living in that region, Reuben went in and slept with his father's concubine Bilhah, and Israel heard of it.

Jacob had twelve sons:

23 The sons of Leah:
Reuben the firstborn of Jacob,
Simeon, Levi, Judah, Issachar and Zebulun.
24 The sons of Rachel:
Joseph and Benjamin.
25 The sons of Rachel's servant Bilhah:
Dan and Naphtali.
26 The sons of Leah's servant Zilpah:
Gad and Asher.
These were the sons of Jacob, who were born to him in Paddan Aram.

In contrast to the newly-arrived Benjamin, one of the sons of Leah was not endearing himself to Jacob very much. Reuben, Jacob's first born, had relations with one of his stepmothers. Chosen people or not, this family never seems to get very far away from trouble.

Nevertheless, with Benjamin the list of Jacob's sons is complete. These men will give their names to the 12 tribes of the nation of Israel. You can find their names throughout the Old Testament and sometimes in the New Testament as well.

The juxtaposition of abhorrent act and magnificent calling in these verses summarizes the human condition perfectly. The names of our greatest leaders echo throughout history. Inevitably those leaders are also fallible. Only one king in history was without blemish. When he showed up, we nailed him to a cross. Humanity cannot experience goodness without sadness and sin interfering.

Isaac Dies

27 Jacob came home to his father Isaac in Mamre, near Kiriath Arba (that is, Hebron), where Abraham and Isaac had stayed. 28 Isaac lived a hundred and eighty years. 29 Then he breathed his last and died and was gathered to his people, old and full of years. And his sons Esau and Jacob buried him.

At this time Isaac finally breathes his last, to be buried by his sons Esau and Jacob in a mirror image of Isaac and Ishmael burying their father Abraham. Despite his frailties, Isaac lived long enough to see his family reunited, an unexpected but welcome blessing.

Genesis 36 recounts the descendants of Esau, who became a mighty nation next to Israel. Like all the other cousins of the chosen line, the Edomites would become enemies of Israel from time to time, though descended from a common ancestor.

6 JOSEPH AND HIS BROTHERS

Favored Son

37 Jacob lived in the land where his father had stayed, the land of Canaan.

² This is the account of Jacob's family line.

Joseph, a young man of seventeen, was tending the flocks with his brothers, the sons of Bilhah and the sons of Zilpah, his father's wives, and he brought their father a bad report about them.

³ Now Israel loved Joseph more than any of his other sons, because he had been born to him in his old age; and he made an ornate robe for him. ⁴ When his brothers saw that their father loved him more than any of them, they hated him and could not speak a kind word to him.

You would think that after all the trouble Jacob had witnessed because of his parents picking favorites among their children, he'd be able to avoid it among his own sons. But you'd think wrong.

We're not as smart as we think we are. We can overcome any obstacles the world throws at us--tornadoes, diseases, gravity itself—but we can't seem to get over ourselves. The wisest people among us still fall prey to their own weaknesses.

In my denomination anybody who wants to become a pastor has to serve a semester as a hospital chaplain, visiting and ministering to folks who are sick. The chaplaincy training supervisor at my hospital was an ex-nun battle-axe with a voice that ran razors up your backbone and a stare that could pickle cucumbers. She needed to be, too. She had the task of turning (mostly) able-bodied, (mostly) men who thought they were hot stuff (and definitely weren't experiencing terminal illnesses) into compassionate people who would be of service to patients in their lowest, most vulnerable moments.

For the record, I loved her and I appreciate every moment of wringer-twisting she put me through. I was an idiot. Still am, in some ways. But she made me slightly less of one. I am forever grateful for this.

My supervisor's main goal, as she described it, was to get us away from the preconceptions we came in with and give us ministry options we'd never thought of before. Every one of us carried a toolkit loaded with assumptions about the way life worked, the way people related, definitions of "good" and "evil", and a hundred other things. There was nothing wrong with our toolkits per se. They served us well. But not everybody was like us. Some people needed different approaches.

Before we met the Battle Axe we just assumed our tools fixed everything. Because they had covered every situation we had encountered prior to that time, we were using them instinctively and automatically, not even realizing it was a choice. To us, that's just the way things were. People were broken, we fixed them.

Our supervisor didn't try to take our tools from us. Instead she made us realize that they were one option among many…most of which we had no clue about yet. As we were about to learn, the way we *assumed* life worked wasn't the way life *actually* worked.

Every time we came back from visiting a patient the Battle Axe grilled us hard, asking us again and again why we were doing things that we had always assumed were not only right, but necessary.

"Why did you choose to pray with the person in Room 221?"

"Uh…because that's what you do?"

"Who says? Not everybody does it. I didn't pray with him. The nurse and doctor didn't pray with him. Why did you pray with him?"

"Because I'm the chaplain!" (Yay! Got one right!)

"OK, you know who you are. So who is that guy in 221?"

"He's the patient?"

"I know what he's doing here! I asked who he *is!* What's his faith background? Does he like prayer? Did he want prayer? Is he Buddhist? Atheist? Did his dad use to quote prayers while beating him with a switch so now he shudders every time somebody prays out loud in his vicinity?

Did you bother to find out ANYTHING about the guy or did you just start praying because 'You're the Chaplain' and you were only thinking about YOURSELF when he's lying there dying in that bed??? Were you there to make him feel better or to make you feel better?"

"Permission to crawl under the table, m'am?"

Her point was, if we don't realize our instincts are actually choices, we have no power to make choices about them. We just follow blindly what we've been taught by our experiences. This is how faults get passed from one generation to the next. We just assume those faults are "the way things are". Our limitations rule us. We lose the power to transcend them when the need arises. Jacob's parents play favorites with him, he plays favorites with his sons.

Until we realize that our sight is limited, we take our perception as reality and pass on our shortcomings to the world as "truth", without remorse or filter. Being more conscious of our own limits won't stop us from making mistakes but it might allow us to admit that they're mistakes and open up the possibility of choosing differently. Just because our parents or bosses or friends treated us a certain way doesn't mean we have to treat others the same. We can take power and choose a new path. It'll still be flawed, but at least it'll be flawed in ways that are easier for us to see and compensate for.

We fear that admitting we're imperfect will make us weaker. Instead it makes us stronger and gives us far more insight into our life and our choices.

A Prophetic Dream

⁵ Joseph had a dream, and when he told it to his brothers, they hated him all the more. ⁶ He said to them, "Listen to this dream I had: ⁷ We were binding sheaves of grain out in the field when suddenly my sheaf rose and stood upright, while your sheaves gathered around mine and bowed down to it."

⁸ His brothers said to him, "Do you intend to reign over us? Will you actually rule us?" And they hated him all the more because of his dream and what he had said.

⁹ Then he had another dream, and he told it to his brothers. "Listen," he said, "I had another dream, and this time the sun and moon and eleven stars were bowing down to me."

¹⁰ When he told his father as well as his brothers, his father rebuked him and said, "What is this dream you had? Will your mother and I and your brothers actually come and bow down to the ground before you?" ¹¹ His brothers were jealous of him, but his father kept the matter in mind.

Throughout the Bible dreams are seen as divine messages. Joseph's was a doozy. He dreamed that he was working in the field with his brothers and his wheat stood up straight while the others gathered around and bowed to it. Then he dreamed that the sun and moon plus 11 stars (representing father, mother, and the exact number of his brothers) were bowing down to him. These were clear signs of dominance, primacy in his family.

You may remember that Jacob angered his twin brother to the extreme by suggesting that he, the younger (but only by seconds) would rule the family. Joseph had 11 brothers, most of whom were older than him by a wide margin. Plus he threw daddy and mama in there as well. This would not go over well.

Even dad had a hard time swallowing this prophecy. Joseph's brothers were downright furious. They had experienced all they wanted to of this young whippersnapper. Joseph's mom had been dad's favorite wife, edging out their mothers. Joseph was dad's favorite son. He had already tattled on them once in verse 2. Now he was trying to take away the one advantage they had: a superior position over him by virtue of age.

If I were Joseph I would have kept my mouth shut about the whole dream thing. Revealing his vision wasn't the most politically savvy move. But Joseph possessed an innocence and forthrightness that would hold him in good stead through trying times. We don't get the impression that he was being mean or bragging. He was clueless about his brothers' true feelings towards him. He trusted them when he shouldn't have.

As much as his brothers didn't want to admit it, Joseph's story would show that his youthful dreams were divinely inspired. God sometimes tells us things we don't like to hear. I always tell my congregation that if we aren't doing something that makes you upset or nervous at least once a year, we're probably not doing anything important. Any god who only tells you what you're comfortable with is not a god at all, just an extension of you. We cannot belong to communities that teach the opposite of what we believe, but residing in a community that doesn't challenge us at all is just as big of a problem.

The jealous, angry, hateful reaction of Joseph's brothers should also be a caution to us. Perhaps you've heard that the things you hate most viscerally about other people are the things you secretly hate most about yourself. This was true of Joseph's brothers. They were furious at what they perceived as Joseph's power grab because they wanted power for themselves. They weren't willing to let God or anyone else tell them they couldn't have it, nor point out their fault in wanting it. The fact that they *hated* Joseph for his dreams should have been a clue that something was wrong in *them*, not just in Joseph. Instead they followed their hatred blindly, with predictably horrible results.

Down the Well

12 Now his brothers had gone to graze their father's flocks near Shechem, 13 and Israel said to Joseph, "As you know, your brothers are grazing the flocks near Shechem. Come, I am going to send you to them."

"Very well," he replied.

14 So he said to him, "Go and see if all is well with your brothers and with the flocks, and bring word back to me." Then he sent him off from the Valley of Hebron.

When Joseph arrived at Shechem, 15 a man found him wandering around in the fields and asked him, "What are you looking for?"

16 He replied, "I'm looking for my brothers. Can you tell me where they are grazing their flocks?"

17 "They have moved on from here," the man answered. "I heard them say, 'Let's go to Dothan.'"

So Joseph went after his brothers and found them near Dothan. 18 But they saw him in the distance, and before he reached them, they plotted to kill him.

19 "Here comes that dreamer!" they said to each other. 20 "Come now, let's kill him and throw him into one of these cisterns and say that a ferocious animal devoured him. Then we'll see what comes of his dreams."

21 When Reuben heard this, he tried to rescue him from their hands. "Let's not take his life," he said. 22 "Don't shed any blood. Throw him into this cistern here in the wilderness, but don't lay a hand on him." Reuben said this to rescue him from them and take him back to his father.

23 So when Joseph came to his brothers, they stripped him of his robe—the ornate robe he was wearing— 24 and they took him and threw him into the cistern. The cistern was empty; there was no water in it.

Not imagining the depth of his sons' hatred for poor Joseph, Jacob sent his favorite boy out into the fields to check up on their work. You may recall that the last report Joseph gave to his father about his brothers' work ethic was not favorable. His brothers certainly remembered that as they saw Joseph coming over the horizon.

Joseph did not find family and flocks in the expected spot. After wandering farther than anticipated, he walked straight into a trap. His brothers saw him coming and plotted to kill him, putting the blame on wild animals.

Then Reuben, heretofore made to look like the worst of the brothers, got his moment in the sun. He convinced his brothers to delay killing Joseph, planning to rescue him and return him home at a later time.

There was a limit to Reuben's nobility; the brothers did strip Joseph of his coat and throw him down a well. But it goes to show that you can never anticipate what part a person will play in the grand story. Sometimes people we dislike end up saving our bacon in ways we never expect.

Every church has at least one or two super annoying people. Pastors know this intimately. You can't get rid of them. Every pastor is tempted to think, "If only this person would leave, the congregation would be perfect." But when that person actually does leave, somebody else who used to be wonderful (or at least pleasantly neutral) steps up to take their place. It's a universal law. There must be at least one thorn in your side in every setting. You never know who it will be, just that there will be one.

Thorns exist for a reason, though. Everybody has their gifts. Some people's gifts come wrapped in garish packaging, but certain gifts lend themselves to that. What you call annoying, someone else may call practical, forthright, and honest. Chances are you'll need those qualities in your life at some point. When you do, those formerly-annoying people become your salvation.

Had it not been for Mr. Jealous-As-Heck, Slept-With-Stepmom Reuben, Joseph's tale may have had a different, far more tragic ending. Be careful what you assume about people; they may just surprise you.

Sold As A Slave

25 As they sat down to eat their meal, they looked up and saw a caravan of Ishmaelites coming from Gilead. Their camels were loaded with spices, balm and myrrh, and they were on their way to take them down to Egypt.

26 Judah said to his brothers, "What will we gain if we kill our brother and cover up his blood? 27 Come, let's sell him to the Ishmaelites and not lay our hands on him; after all, he is our brother, our own flesh and blood." His brothers agreed.

28 So when the Midianite merchants came by, his brothers pulled Joseph up out of the cistern and sold him for twenty shekels of silver to the Ishmaelites, who took him to Egypt.

Opportunity presented itself to Joseph's brothers in the form of distant cousins, headed to sell goods to the Egyptians. The traders weren't above peddling a slave or two. The sons of Jacob just happen to have a spare brother to sell them.

The warmth with which Judah terms Joseph, "our brother, our own flesh and blood" in verses 26-27 is touching. "How could we *possibly* kill him? Let's sell him into slavery instead!" It sounds crazy when you read it from the outside, but the first casualty of sin is our ability to perceive right and wrong.

If we understood where the wrong paths would take us, we'd never set foot on them. Too often we consider these things too late. More than one person has gotten trapped in something awful by taking a series of "reasonable" steps. Each stride leads to the next. Soon you don't realize how far down the path you've gone. You end up doing things that you never would have imagined back at the trailhead, things that would have seemed crazy to you back then but somehow make sense in your current, messed up context.

Eventually the "sunk cost" fallacy comes into play. You perceive that you've invested so much walking down the wrong path that you might as well see it through. It's too late to reverse. You could never undo all those steps.

Of course it's never too late. We don't have to reverse our way back through a path in order to get off it. All we need to do is step sideways and refuse to keep walking it. Repairing the damage and finding a better way may take a while or they may be as simple as, "I'm sorry." Either way, turning off of a bad road throws everything back in proper perspective. We're never as stuck as we think we are. The consequences of leaving the path are seldom as great as the consequences of seeing it through.

I've seen this happen in churches countless times. Congregations engage in group-think and steer themselves wrong. Their plan doesn't work but they feel committed to keep at it…a sad kind of corporate stubbornness. The danger gets magnified when a few, powerful people make decisions for the entire church. Pride gets in the way of good sense and suddenly the whole church is careening pell-mell towards disaster.

I've seen a single, small voice turn a church around in situations like this. Somebody raises a hand and says, "Why are we doing this? I'm not comfortable with it." Then everybody breathes a sigh of relief because they were all thinking the same thing but nobody was saying it. It's a good argument for encouraging free sharing and/or debate over everything—including scripture—in communities of faith.

Joseph's brothers either didn't get that voice or didn't listen to it, depending on how sympathetic you are to Reuben. They sold their brother for 8 ounces of silver…about enough to hammer into a nice-sized ring for each of them. That's what family was worth to them.

The Worth of a Brother

²⁹ When Reuben returned to the cistern and saw that Joseph was not there, he tore his clothes. ³⁰ He went back to his brothers and said, "The boy isn't there! Where can I turn now?"

³¹ Then they got Joseph's robe, slaughtered a goat and dipped the robe in the blood. ³² They took the ornate robe back to their father and said, "We found this. Examine it to see whether it is your son's robe."

³³ He recognized it and said, "It is my son's robe! Some ferocious animal has devoured him. Joseph has surely been torn to pieces."

³⁴ Then Jacob tore his clothes, put on sackcloth and mourned for his son many days. ³⁵ All his sons and daughters came to comfort him, but he refused to be comforted. "No," he said, "I will continue to mourn until I join my son in the grave." So his father wept for him.

³⁶ Meanwhile, the Midianites sold Joseph in Egypt to Potiphar, one of Pharaoh's officials, the captain of the guard.

Ahhh…Reuben. His brother goes missing, killed for all he knows, and his first thought is, "Well, I'm screwed now." His selflessness lasted about a half-dozen verses.

Instead of actually fixing the *problem* by running after the Midianites and getting their brother back, Jacob's sons tried to mitigate the *consequences*. They dipped Joseph's pretty robe in goat blood, put on their super-sad faces, and shuffled back to their dad. They didn't even have to lie. Jacob saw the blood on the robe and jumped to his own conclusion. His son was dead, causing him a wound that he'd carry with him to the grave.

Fixing consequences instead of the underlying problem doesn't often work. Problems are usually systemic and cyclical. You may avoid their worst effects once or twice but eventually they'll catch up to you.

Consequences are feedback. They encourage us to pursue good paths and abandon bad. Slicing the consequences away from a bad path doesn't encourage people to get off it any quicker. It just robs them of the information necessary to do so.

These verses reveal another truth about ducking consequences: they don't just disappear when you dodge them; somebody else ends up paying instead. Jacob mourned his son for years because of the actions of Reuben, Judah, and company. They avoided punishment but their dad had to carry all the pain they would have experienced and then some.

As Jacob was crying his eyes out, his supposedly-dead son was being sold to a high official in Egypt named Potiphar. Even now his brothers could have done something, trying to locate him somehow, but they didn't. In their eyes the potential inconvenience of admitting the truth seemed far greater than the agony their brother and father were experiencing.

Self-centered living is often described as "blindness" in scripture. Neither their brother's plight nor their own father's grief registered with Jacob's sons. They had eyes only for themselves. We, too, become blind when we judge the world by how it affects us without any sense of the greater good. We're called to make political, economic, and social decisions from a broader foundation than our own self-interest. Effects on other people matter as much as benefit or pain to us. As soon as we lose sight of that we've thrown our brothers and sisters down a well and sold them up the river to preserve ourselves and our desired way of life. No matter how we justify it, our words carry no more weight than did Judah's or any of Joseph's brothers.

Justice for All

38 At that time, Judah left his brothers and went down to stay with a man of Adullam named Hirah. ² There Judah met the daughter of a Canaanite man named Shua. He married her and made love to her; ³ she became pregnant and gave birth to a son, who was named Er. ⁴ She conceived again and gave birth to a son and named him Onan. ⁵ She gave birth to still another son and named him Shelah. It was at Kezib that she gave birth to him.

⁶ Judah got a wife for Er, his firstborn, and her name was Tamar. ⁷ But Er, Judah's firstborn, was wicked in the Lord's sight; so the Lord put him to death.

⁸ Then Judah said to Onan, "Sleep with your brother's wife and fulfill your duty to her as a brother-in-law to raise up offspring for your brother." ⁹ But Onan knew that the child would not be his; so whenever he slept with his brother's wife, he spilled his semen on the ground to keep from providing offspring for his brother. ¹⁰ What he did was wicked in the Lord's sight; so the Lord put him to death also.

¹¹ Judah then said to his daughter-in-law Tamar, "Live as a widow in your father's household until my son Shelah grows up." For he thought, "He may die too, just like his brothers." So Tamar went to live in her father's household.

¹² After a long time Judah's wife, the daughter of Shua, died. When Judah had recovered from his grief, he went up to Timnah, to the men who were shearing his sheep, and his friend Hirah the Adullamite went with him.

¹³ When Tamar was told, "Your father-in-law is on his way to Timnah to shear his sheep," ¹⁴ she took off her widow's clothes, covered herself with a veil to disguise herself, and then sat down at the entrance to Enaim, which is on the road to Timnah. For she saw that, though Shelah had now grown up, she had not been given to him as his wife.

¹⁵ When Judah saw her, he thought she was a prostitute, for she had covered her face. ¹⁶ Not realizing that she was his daughter-in-law, he went over to her by the roadside and said, "Come now, let me sleep with you."

"And what will you give me to sleep with you?" she asked.

¹⁷ "I'll send you a young goat from my flock," he said.

"Will you give me something as a pledge until you send it?" she asked.

¹⁸ He said, "What pledge should I give you?"

"Your seal and its cord, and the staff in your hand," she answered. So he gave them to her and slept with her, and she became pregnant by him. ¹⁹ After she left, she took off her veil and put on her widow's clothes again.

²⁰ Meanwhile Judah sent the young goat by his friend the Adullamite in order to get his pledge back from the woman, but he did not find her. ²¹ He asked the men who lived there, "Where is the shrine prostitute who was beside the road at Enaim?"

"There hasn't been any shrine prostitute here," they said.

²² So he went back to Judah and said, "I didn't find her. Besides, the men who lived there said, 'There hasn't been any shrine prostitute here.'"

²³ Then Judah said, "Let her keep what she has, or we will become a laughingstock. After all, I did send her this young goat, but you didn't find her."

²⁴ About three months later Judah was told, "Your daughter-in-law Tamar is guilty of prostitution, and as a result she is now pregnant."

Judah said, "Bring her out and have her burned to death!"

²⁵ As she was being brought out, she sent a message to her father-in-law. "I am pregnant by the man who owns these," she said. And she added, "See if you recognize whose seal and cord and staff these are."

²⁶ Judah recognized them and said, "She is more righteous than I, since I wouldn't give her to my son Shelah." And he did not sleep with her again.

²⁷ When the time came for her to give birth, there were twin boys in her womb. ²⁸ As she was giving birth, one of them put out his hand; so the midwife took a scarlet thread and tied it on his wrist and said, "This one came out first." ²⁹ But when he drew back his hand, his brother came out, and she said, "So this is how you have broken out!" And he was named Perez. ³⁰ Then his brother, who had the scarlet thread on his wrist, came out. And he was named Zerah.

The Bible is not sewn from whole cloth, nor is Genesis a continuous narrative from a single source. Right in the middle of our beautiful, redemptive Joseph story we get…well…this. It's like, "Did we accidentally switch the station to Cinemax? Turn it back!"

The story of Tamar and Judah shows concern with the Law, particularly the procedures governing inheritance and creating progeny during trying times. In an age where harsh conditions caused husbands to die early, leaving their wives without vital connection to family or community, the law provided for a way to keep the husband's name alive and the wife's purpose intact.

Should a husband die without heir, it was the responsibility of his nearest male relative—often a brother—to father a child with his widow. This child would then be considered the offspring of the deceased husband, raised by the widow whose relationship to her dead husband's family was now preserved.

In this story Judah, one of Jacob's sons, married a Canaanite woman who gave him three sons. Er, the eldest, married Tamar. But Er was a wicked man and did not live long.

Once Er died it was the responsibility of his brother, Onan, to give Tamar a child to raise in Er's name. But Onan was unwilling to father a child that would not be his in name as well as genetic makeup. To all appearances he fulfilled his duty to the family and to the Law, sleeping with Tamar. But each time at the moment of truth, Onan practiced the "pull out" method of contraception, spilling his seed on the ground and producing no children.

Just as Er had been wicked (read: selfish and not fulfilling his duty) so, too, Onan was found lacking. God ended his life as well.

After two sons who had intercourse with Tamar died, Judah began to ponder whether she might not be bad luck. Instead of sending his third son to fulfill the law's demand, Judah sent Tamar home to her family of origin and told her to wait until the third son was grown and ready. He protected his own interests but cheated this woman, Tamar, of her due under the law.

Let's count. Er (Judah's first son) was wicked and did not do right by his wife…if nothing else because he behaved so badly that he got himself killed. Onan (the second son) cheated that same wife out of the chance to be redeemed by bearing a child for the family, leaving her out in the cold and alone. Then Judah (the dad) cheated her again by sending her out into the cold, hoping her birth family would take her back after marrying her off. By the law and the standards of the time, all three men did her wrong.

Time passed, Judah's wife died, and still he showed no signs of doing the right thing by his daughter-in-law Tamar. He had abandoned her in her family's house, leaving her without recourse or a way forward. So she took matters into her own hands.

When Judah was on his way to her town, Tamar went and sat by the town gate, covering her face as would a prostitute. While members of the "oldest profession" are seldom the most respected citizens in any town, people then did not hold the same puritan morality as we regarding the trade.

Prostitution would have been one of the ways an unattached, yet unmarriageable, woman could have supported herself. In theory Tamar was still attached to Judah's family and therefore shouldn't have engaged in such practices, but practically speaking Judah wasn't doing anything about that attachment and wasn't supporting her in any way. He was already treating her as women who turned to prostitution were treated.

When Judah walked by and saw the "prostitute" at the town gate, he decided to indulge. They haggled about price and Judah promised to send her a young goat. She demanded surety for the promise…after all he might just leave afterwards and never return to pay her. When asked what kind of pledge she wanted, Tamar requested Judah's seal (kind of like his ID card) and his staff, to be returned when the old goat finally sent a young goat in payment. Judah agreed and the deal was consummated.

Except later when Judah sent his friend to town with the payment, the "prostitute" was nowhere to be found. Then three months later Tamar showed evidence of being pregnant. This sent Judah into a fit, as his daughter-in-law, the wife of his deceased son, was not supposed to do such a thing! He was ready to burn her at the stake.

Then came the climatic reveal. Tamar showed Judah his own seal and staff, indicating that he was the father of her child. This jarred him back to reality. He realized that in killing her he'd kill another of his sons, this one as yet unborn. He expressed shame because he did not follow the law. He had forced Tamar to take from him by deceit and prostitution what he should have given to her freely.

Tamar bore twin sons, one named for breaking out of the womb and another named for his scarlet color.

Carrying modern sensibilities, we're tempted to paint this story as a sex scandal. It certainly rivals any tabloid article ever written. But this story doesn't center around sex. Any intercourse Tamar had with her husband Er and his brother Onan were within the bounds of the law. Sex with Judah was more in the gray area but it was understandable given the circumstances. Tamar had no other way to get what was due to her under the law.

That's the focus of the story. It's not about sex, but injustice and the rights of those ignored and oppressed. These men were supposed to do what was right by Tamar and none of them did. Through guile and sacrifice she forced them to. She was vindicated twice over by the sons she bore. She was the only one in the whole story who ended up righteous, more righteous indeed than Judah himself, a fact he admits with his own lips.

Some people—particularly people whom society regards as less-favored—cannot get justice. When they're suffering they cannot wait for it to be given. Sometimes they have to reach out and take it by whatever means are available to them. This is accounted as righteous even if those means are not standard. After all, the definition of "standard" is "that which benefits the majority"…the dominant culture that refuses to give justice in the first place.

Being unjust to people and then condemning the means they use to rectify the situation is an old trick. It's like an older brother locking the younger brother in a closet so he can have all the cookies, then accusing the younger of thievery when he swipes one of those cookies himself. Maybe he stole one but you stole the whole box! And you're pointing the finger at him? As Jesus would later say, take the plank out of your own eye before removing the speck in your neighbor's.

If Judah had been just in the first place, if he had followed the law and cared about Tamar's future the way he was supposed to, there would have been no need for trickery or fake prostitution or sleeping with her father-in-law. His unrighteousness caused the situation. She just made do with what she had to work with.

Judah's near-callous disregard for the relationship he was supposed to have with Tamar was unrighteous. He denied her for verse after verse until finally it advantaged him to remember her in verse 24, when he thought he'd been wronged. He forgot their connection entirely when he owed her, then recalled their bond when he thought she had wronged him.

How many people in our lives do we treat exactly like this? We neglect and forget, ignore and exclude people of different races, cultures, religions, and genders until we perceive they've done something to offend us. Then we're more than willing to talk about them (negatively) and demand that they honor our relationship (by owning up to their injustice). We filter out every possible good thing about them, every chance we have to grow in love and understanding, every courtesy and respect and credit for being human that we owe them. We only let in the bad stuff, the accusations, the evening news stories, the moments when we feel wronged. That's no more right for us than it was for Judah.

I can already hear cries of, "Respect is earned!" and, "Why should I have a good relationship with people I don't agree with, with people different than I, with people who might even oppose me?" We love to justify our ills as righteous.

How have you earned God's respect? Either you've messed up or you think you're so good that you've never sinned. Neither earns you respect in God's eyes.

Do you think God agrees with you? Do you think he's the *same* as you? How often have you opposed God, wallowing in a world full of sin to which you contribute?

What if God took the attitude that respect is earned, that good and giving relationships were only for people we agree with, who are the same as we, who don't oppose us in any way? If God took that approach with us, where would we be now? We'd be doomed. I don't see any way to argue otherwise.

What God has first done for us, we are called to do for each other. When Judah didn't do it for Tamar, that was his failing, not hers. When we don't do it for our neighbors that's our failing, not theirs.

Serving in Every Circumstance

39 Now Joseph had been taken down to Egypt. Potiphar, an Egyptian who was one of Pharaoh's officials, the captain of the guard, bought him from the Ishmaelites who had taken him there.

² The Lord was with Joseph so that he prospered, and he lived in the house of his Egyptian master. ³ When his master saw that the Lord was with him and that the Lord gave him success in everything he did, ⁴ Joseph found favor in his eyes and became his attendant. Potiphar put him in charge of his household, and he entrusted to his care everything he owned. ⁵ From the time he put him in charge of his household and of all that he owned, the Lord blessed the household of the Egyptian because of Joseph. The blessing of the Lord was on everything Potiphar had, both in the house and in the field. ⁶ So Potiphar left everything he had in Joseph's care; with Joseph in charge, he did not concern himself with anything except the food he ate.

We return to Joseph's story just in time to see him sold to the Captain of Pharaoh's Guard, Potiphar.

It's impossible to read this story without envisioning the emotional devastation which had to accompany these events for Joseph. He was his father's pride and joy, loved and cared for since he was young. That he was naïve about his brothers' feelings towards him only makes the shock of being sold into slavery worse. There's no way he could have been prepared for these unimaginable circumstances. Rising fear and despair must have threatened to crush him.

Yet the Lord was with Joseph…even here, even now. Like his father before him in Laban's fields, everything Joseph touched in this strange land turned to good. When Potiphar saw that Joseph was blessed, he advanced the young man to head of the household, entrusting him with everything he owned. God blessed Potiphar's house through Joseph; all involved prospered.

An age-old strain of faith claims that circumstances are evidence of God's blessings. Those with the best circumstances (wealth, power, fame, etc.) are considered the most favored by God. Today we call this "prosperity gospel". Most popular televangelists preach some version of it.

Jesus spoke against this idea in the Beatitudes, saying, "Blessed are the poor…the meek…those who mourn…those who are reviled." We see Jesus' message here in the person of Joseph. You cannot get closer to "nothing" than being sold into slavery by your own brothers and bought like a piece of property by a foreigner. And yet God was with Joseph, favoring him so demonstrably that even the Egyptians noticed.

Experiencing only good things in life is neither a goal nor a result of faith. Prosperity preaching puts us perilously close to idolatry as we invest trust in our wealth and its fruits instead of in God. Inevitably just when we set up our idol and think we've managed it perfectly (and thus are perfectly safe) something comes along to tip it over: the market crashes, we lose a job, or we die. Everything we try to master, we lose.

Faith in God doesn't mean controlling our circumstances to gain more wealth. Faith in God means that even when we're out of control and experiencing the worst circumstances—even when everything else we rely on is gone--he's still there loving us. We continue loving God and our neighbors no matter what the environment around us is like, whether we have a billion dollars or only debt to our name. That's faith.

In this way people of faith become a blessing to others even when they don't feel blessed themselves. Potiphar neither believed in nor knew about Joseph's God. Yet Joseph trusted and served. Through Joseph Potiphar's household experienced goodness.

We abhor slavery today, but we still bear the responsibility to serve each other…not just people we're comfortable with, but foreigners and strangers as well. The duty of a person of faith is the same no matter who around them believes or doesn't. God's love, mercy, and goodness are infinite. We are an embodiment of his Spirit, a place where he touches the world. If you aren't satisfied that someone believes until you've harangued them into admitting they think like you, you're giving the impression that God's Spirit and goodness are less than infinite. You're withholding God and your service until the people around you have met your criteria. This is not how God treats you. Jesus didn't consult an opinion poll before he died on the cross for us.

We're supposed to give freely to the people around you no matter what your circumstance or theirs. This is the only way to show God's goodness. Service becomes its own testimony…far better than any of our imperfect demands of each other. If you wish people to know love, love them. If you wish people to experience goodness, be good to them. If you want people to trust in mercy, be merciful to them.

Joseph did a hundred good things in Potiphar's household and that's how his master came to know about his God…not by Joseph demanding some kind of conversion experience, but by Joseph showing who he was and who God is. Doing this under such dire circumstances was an amazing testimony. Then again, as soon as he did it the circumstances became less dire.

God's Will Revisited

Now Joseph was well-built and handsome, [7] and after a while his master's wife took notice of Joseph and said, "Come to bed with me!"

[8] But he refused. "With me in charge," he told her, "my master does not concern himself with anything in the house; everything he owns he has entrusted to my care. [9] No one is greater in this house than I am. My master has withheld nothing from me except you, because you are his wife. How then could I do such a wicked thing and sin against God?" [10] And though she spoke to Joseph day after day, he refused to go to bed with her or even be with her.

[11] One day he went into the house to attend to his duties, and none of the household servants was inside. [12] She caught him by his cloak and said, "Come to bed with me!" But he left his cloak in her hand and ran out of the house.

[13] When she saw that he had left his cloak in her hand and had run out of the house, [14] she called her household servants. "Look," she said to them, "this Hebrew has been brought to us to make sport of us! He came in here to sleep with me, but I screamed. [15] When he heard me scream for help, he left his cloak beside me and ran out of the house."

[16] She kept his cloak beside her until his master came home. [17] Then she told him this story: "That Hebrew slave you brought us came to me to make sport of me. [18] But as soon as I screamed for help, he left his cloak beside me and ran out of the house."

[19] When his master heard the story his wife told him, saying, "This is how your slave treated me," he burned with anger. [20] Joseph's master took him and put him in prison, the place where the king's prisoners were confined.

But while Joseph was there in the prison, [21] the Lord was with him; he showed him kindness and granted him favor in the eyes of the prison warden. [22] So the warden put Joseph in charge of all those held in the prison, and he was made responsible for all that was done there. [23] The warden paid no attention to anything under Joseph's care, because the Lord was with Joseph and gave him success in whatever he did.

Well, circumstances became less dire for a minute, anyway. No sooner had Joseph gotten his feet under him than Potiphar's wife got the hots for him.

Did you ever notice how often trouble arises because somebody wants these apparently-irresistible Israelites? Must be a burden to be that good looking compared to your neighbors.

Joseph remained faithful to his master and to God, refusing Mrs. Potiphar's advances. This only made her angry. One day when she had the chance, she betrayed him. Turning the tables, she accused Joseph of making advances towards *her*. Potiphar had to believe his wife over his slave. He threw Joseph in jail.

Twice now Joseph has been at the top of his little corner of the world only to be dashed to the uttermost depths. Yet God remains with Joseph even in jail. God makes Joseph favorable in the sight of the prison warden and Joseph is put in charge of the pokey, responsible for everything and everyone in the warden's stead.

People have tried to describe God's will in various ways. To me, it's like a wave at the ocean. You can dig in and stand against it; you might even hold your ground for a while. You can push and it appears to yield. You can move into it and appear to make progress. But if you stand there and observe long enough you realize that the ocean is going to do what the ocean is going to do. You may have disrupted this tiny section of the wave, but it's thousands of feet long. Even as you break it, it's reforming right behind you and heading on in. Even as you try to stand firm and still, it's moving the sand beneath your feet. Most importantly of all, the waves come in again…and again…and again. Stand there for more than a minute and you realize that the soft, repetitive insistence of those waves will do you in eventually. You can stand against them for a while, but not forever. You might as well surf or fish or do something productive because every moment you spend fighting the ocean only makes it look stronger in the end.

We should read Joseph's story like waves curling into the beach. Everybody around him is pushing him against the tide. Every time he comes floating back.

We often misinterpret God's will as micromanaging control. "God wants me to have this career and marry this person and live in this place." Those are just possible points at which you intersect the wave. You can choose any of a million of them. Whether you're 5 feet from the left hand edge or 50 feet or 500 feet from it, it's all the same wave. God is less concerned with what career you choose than you bringing good into the world through it. He's less concerned with who you marry than you honoring and cherishing that person, bringing more love into the world thereby. Where you live is immaterial when he's with you in all places. All of these things are significant, but none of them comprise the entirety of the wave.

The real power of the wave, the force that pushes you towards shore no matter where you intersect it, is God's choice to love you. He redeems you, helps you stand through imperfections, and brings you eternal life in joy and peace. Where you're standing as the wave hits you is far less important than its endlessly-insistent push towards destiny.

This is exactly what Joseph found. God's will was working for him and the collective decisions of the powerful people around him weren't going to interfere for long.

More Dreams

40 Some time later, the cupbearer and the baker of the king of Egypt offended their master, the king of Egypt. ² Pharaoh was angry with his two officials, the chief cupbearer and the chief baker, ³ and put them in custody in the house of the captain of the guard, in the same prison where Joseph was confined. ⁴ The captain of the guard assigned them to Joseph, and he attended them.

After they had been in custody for some time, ⁵ each of the two men—the cupbearer and the baker of the king of Egypt, who were being held in prison—had a dream the same night, and each dream had a meaning of its own.

⁶ When Joseph came to them the next morning, he saw that they were dejected. ⁷ So he asked Pharaoh's officials who were in custody with him in his master's house, "Why do you look so sad today?"

⁸ "We both had dreams," they answered, "but there is no one to interpret them."

Then Joseph said to them, "Do not interpretations belong to God? Tell me your dreams."

⁹ So the chief cupbearer told Joseph his dream. He said to him, "In my dream I saw a vine in front of me, ¹⁰ and on the vine were three branches. As soon as it budded, it blossomed, and its clusters ripened into grapes. ¹¹ Pharaoh's cup was in my hand, and I took the grapes, squeezed them into Pharaoh's cup and put the cup in his hand."

¹² "This is what it means," Joseph said to him. "The three branches are three days. ¹³ Within three days Pharaoh will lift up your head and restore you to your position, and you will put Pharaoh's cup in his hand, just as you used to do when you were his cupbearer. ¹⁴ But when all goes well with you, remember me and show me kindness; mention me to Pharaoh and get me out of this prison. ¹⁵ I was forcibly carried off from the land of the Hebrews, and even here I have done nothing to deserve being put in a dungeon."

¹⁶ When the chief baker saw that Joseph had given a favorable interpretation, he said to Joseph, "I too had a dream: On my head were three baskets of bread. ¹⁷ In the top basket were all kinds of baked goods for Pharaoh, but the birds were eating them out of the basket on my head."

¹⁸ "This is what it means," Joseph said. "The three baskets are three days. ¹⁹ Within three days Pharaoh will lift off your head and impale your body on a pole. And the birds will eat away your flesh."

You may recall that Joseph had some facility with dreams. A couple of visions got him into this mess to begin with and a couple more were about to get him out.

Two servants of Pharaoh had angered their master. As a result the king's wine steward and chief baker both found themselves in jail, where they got to know Joseph. One morning he noticed that they looked put out. Upon asking why, he found that they had each had experienced a memorable dream but could not figure out what it meant. Since dreams were regarded as visions from heaven and predictive of the future, this was disturbing.

Joseph offered them a solution. If any god could tell them the meaning of their visions, the One who watched over him could.

Pharaoh's servants confided in Joseph. The wine steward saw a three-branched vine, which he harvested and served to Pharaoh. Joseph found this simple. In three days the steward would return to Pharaoh's side and serve him again. The now-hopeful baker had goods for his master as well, but in his dream birds were eating them before he could deliver. Joseph had to tell the poor guy that he'd be executed in three days and the birds would eat his remains. I do not believe Joseph received a tip from his client for this prediction.

Joseph asked one thing of the servant who was going to live: that he mention Joseph to Pharaoh. Nobody had undergone more suffering more unjustly than Joseph. He wanted a chance to plead his case to the highest authority. Please, could the chief cupbearer just do this one thing? Please???

Our Faulty Memory

[20] Now the third day was Pharaoh's birthday, and he gave a feast for all his officials. He lifted up the heads of the chief cupbearer and the chief baker in the presence of his officials: [21] He restored the chief cupbearer to his position, so that he once again put the cup into Pharaoh's hand— [22] but he impaled the chief baker, just as Joseph had said to them in his interpretation.

[23] The chief cupbearer, however, did not remember Joseph; he forgot him.

The chief cupbearer could not.

As soon as things started going well for him again, Pharaoh's servant forgot Joseph. This is typical. When we're doing well, we credit ourselves. When things go poorly we turn to God. When things return to normal, we forget him again, along with all the pledges and resolutions we made in the down times.

Many people of faith talk about the virtues of handling adversity, but handling prosperity is just as important (and far more often botched). We're never in so much danger of seeing things wrongly and messing up as we are when things are going well for us. Prosperity clouds our vision and enslaves us.

The cupbearer didn't realize how his shift in perception was injuring Joseph. We tend to think of harming people as an intentional act. We associate it with violence and malice. Not always. We also harm people by forgetting them, especially when they're in need. Jesus called people like Joseph to our attention by saying, "As you do unto the least of these, you do unto me." Those who remember others remember God. Those who forget others also forget him.

Every person who's ever had to transition to an assisted living facility understands the truth of these words. People forgotten while in jail, sick in the hospital, mourning death or divorce, and those suffering from mental illness understand them too. The first thing an abuser does to control his victim is isolate them, attempting to make them forget anyone else exists and vice versa. Forgetting can do just as much harm as injuring a person with intent.

When Pharaoh's chief cupbearer needed Joseph he kept up the relationship. When he started doing well on his own he abandoned the young man. Heartbreak was Joseph's constant companion.

Opportunity Arises

41 When two full years had passed, Pharaoh had a dream: He was standing by the Nile, 2 when out of the river there came up seven cows, sleek and fat, and they grazed among the reeds. 3 After them, seven other cows, ugly and gaunt, came up out of the Nile and stood beside those on the riverbank. 4 And the cows that were ugly and gaunt ate up the seven sleek, fat cows. Then Pharaoh woke up.

5 He fell asleep again and had a second dream: Seven heads of grain, healthy and good, were growing on a single stalk. 6 After them, seven other heads of grain sprouted—thin and scorched by the east wind. 7 The thin heads of grain swallowed up the seven healthy, full heads. Then Pharaoh woke up; it had been a dream.

8 In the morning his mind was troubled, so he sent for all the magicians and wise men of Egypt. Pharaoh told them his dreams, but no one could interpret them for him.

9 Then the chief cupbearer said to Pharaoh, "Today I am reminded of my shortcomings. 10 Pharaoh was once angry with his servants, and he imprisoned me and the chief baker in the house of the captain of the guard. 11 Each of us had a dream the same night, and each dream had a meaning of its own. 12 Now a young Hebrew was there with us, a servant of the captain of the guard. We told him our dreams, and he interpreted them for us, giving each man the interpretation of his dream. ¹³ And things turned out exactly as he interpreted them to us: I was restored to my position, and the other man was impaled."

¹⁴ So Pharaoh sent for Joseph, and he was quickly brought from the dungeon. When he had shaved and changed his clothes, he came before Pharaoh.

Joseph spent two full years in jail waiting for his former cellmate to remember him. Fate must have seemed cruel. But a vision granted to Pharaoh jogged the cupbearer's memory. Pharaoh had a disturbing and memorable dream just as his servants had 24 months earlier. Not a soul in the kingdom could tell him what it meant. At this moment his cupbearer finally piped up. He had tried to forget the whole jail incident, but he did remember a man who was especially adept at interpreting dreams. Could Pharaoh use such a man now?

Pharaoh could.

Even when things look darkest, opportunity awaits. Problems will always dog us; new openings always lie before us. Even death, the insurmountable difficulty at the end of our lives, has been handled. The smaller deaths we experience along the way eventually will give way to resurrection as well. Clinging to our difficulties is just another way of dying. We have to acknowledge them; they weigh down our back every day. But they eyes of faith look forward, reaching towards the next thing rather than bowing to the last. We dare not become so comfortable with our trials that we cannot let them go. Anticipating the next step, the next identity, in some ways even the next set of problems (because at least they're different than the ones we have now) keeps us in motion towards eventual perfection, freeing us from our bondage to today's imperfection.

Joseph couldn't see a way out of jail. He had been betrayed, abandoned, and left to rot. But when the situation changed he was ready to change with it, focusing not on the bitterness of his past but his next opportunity to serve.

The Purpose of Our Gifts

¹⁵ Pharaoh said to Joseph, "I had a dream, and no one can interpret it. But I have heard it said of you that when you hear a dream you can interpret it."

16 "I cannot do it," Joseph replied to Pharaoh, "but God will give Pharaoh the answer he desires."

The moment Joseph heard of Pharaoh's dilemma his heart soared. He could help!

How greatly Joseph must have been tempted to use his ability for his own gain. He could have bartered with Pharaoh for his release. He might have insisted that Pharaoh hear his story before he heard Pharaoh's dream. Joseph did neither of these things. He asked for no surety. The first words out of his mouth were, "I, myself, cannot do this, but God can. I'm not here representing me, but him."

What an amazing statement of trust. For all Joseph knew Pharaoh might have heard his interpretation and then tossed him right back in jail. It didn't matter. He was not going to claim that his God-given gift was all about him. His gifts and talents were meant for the good of the world. Joseph was merely a mouthpiece, a voice daring to speak words that God wanted to say to the king when nobody else would or could.

I experience something similar, though in a smaller way, in my work as a pastor. People come to pastors expecting answers. Half the time they genuinely want one, half the time they dare you to come up with one. They stand poised, ready to call you a genius or a fool. Except that's not what it's about. I don't have many answers. The ones I do have mostly work for me. Since I'm different than you, your mileage may vary. Making ministry about oneself or one's gifts is a sure way to fail.

Instead I try to do as Joseph did. God is already speaking to the people I talk to. Most of the time they know the answer to their dilemma long before they approach me. They come to my office because they're having a hard time processing the message they're already getting. My job isn't to give them my answer or show off my brilliant wisdom, but to help them listen to what they're asking God and what he's telling them in return. Whatever answer they find isn't about me, it's about them and their relationship with God and the world.

In the art world people often ask who gets to interpret a given piece of art. As a piece of art is being designed it lies in control of the artist, the creator.

Once the piece goes on display the artist places it in the hands of the viewer, who then gets to add their own interpretation. Which is more important, the painting or the eye that sees it?

The answer is "neither". Artistic magic doesn't happen on canvas or within the eye, but in the space in between them. The relationship between viewer and art creates something new entirely. As viewers discuss their perceptions, more relationships are created between them. A 3x4 painting and a few pounds of brain matter fill up entire rooms and the beyond.

Our relationship with God works in similar fashion. It's not about us. ("Will I get to heaven?") God has never made it about him either. Grace, love, and beauty happen in the space between us as we interact. God, the Artist, creates them but we grow and develop as we receive them, talk about them, and live them out with each other. In the end, they fill the world.

Joseph understood his gifts not as personal possessions, but as part of his living, growing relationship with God and the people around him. For a few moments he became the work of art, standing in the space between Artist and viewer, facilitating the living relationship between them. It was for such moments that his gifts were given in the first place.

Each of us has gifts of some sort, things peculiar to us that we share with the world. Too many of us regard getting something in return for our gifts as confirmation that they're real or valuable. What we get for them is incidental. The real honor is to give in such a way that makes life more than it was for another person, helping them understand their relationship with the Infinite a little more clearly so they can find their place in the story too.

A good friend of mine makes a living as an auto mechanic. He's a holy man, though I'm sure he doesn't realize it. I don't know much about cars beyond how to change the oil and other "Idiot's Guide" things. When my car isn't working right, I'm stressed. It affects everything I do. Having someone I can trust to take my car to makes a huge difference. I don't have to worry about whether I'm sending my wife and kids out in a four-wheeled death trap. I don't have to fear getting jacked for my life savings trying to fix it. I don't have to worry if it'll be repaired right. When I visit my friend he talks about brake pads and gear ratios, but I hear, "It's OK. I'll take care of this so you can do the things you need to do." He makes my life better with his gift.

That's the purpose of the gift, why he's good at what he does. He creates life. That he makes a living doing it is incidental. Every day he gets chances to make people's lives better and he does it with honesty, trust, and care. When you know people like that, you don't forget them. I don't think he charges near enough! How many people can say that about their car mechanic?

This is exactly what Joseph did with Pharaoh. He'd get something from his gift, but the reward came at the tail end. His sole purpose as he walked into that room was sharing his talent, then helping the king understand that it wasn't from him, but from the same God who watched over them both.

The Promised Redemption

17 Then Pharaoh said to Joseph, "In my dream I was standing on the bank of the Nile, 18 when out of the river there came up seven cows, fat and sleek, and they grazed among the reeds. 19 After them, seven other cows came up—scrawny and very ugly and lean. I had never seen such ugly cows in all the land of Egypt. 20 The lean, ugly cows ate up the seven fat cows that came up first. 21 But even after they ate them, no one could tell that they had done so; they looked just as ugly as before. Then I woke up.

22 "In my dream I saw seven heads of grain, full and good, growing on a single stalk. 23 After them, seven other heads sprouted—withered and thin and scorched by the east wind. 24 The thin heads of grain swallowed up the seven good heads. I told this to the magicians, but none of them could explain it to me."

25 Then Joseph said to Pharaoh, "The dreams of Pharaoh are one and the same. God has revealed to Pharaoh what he is about to do. 26 The seven good cows are seven years, and the seven good heads of grain are seven years; it is one and the same dream. 27 The seven lean, ugly cows that came up afterward are seven years, and so are the seven worthless heads of grain scorched by the east wind: They are seven years of famine.

28 "It is just as I said to Pharaoh: God has shown Pharaoh what he is about to do. 29 Seven years of great abundance are coming throughout the land of Egypt, 30 but seven years of famine will follow them. Then all the abundance in Egypt will be forgotten, and the famine will ravage the land. ³¹ The abundance in the land will not be remembered, because the famine that follows it will be so severe. ³² The reason the dream was given to Pharaoh in two forms is that the matter has been firmly decided by God, and God will do it soon.

³³ "And now let Pharaoh look for a discerning and wise man and put him in charge of the land of Egypt. ³⁴ Let Pharaoh appoint commissioners over the land to take a fifth of the harvest of Egypt during the seven years of abundance. ³⁵ They should collect all the food of these good years that are coming and store up the grain under the authority of Pharaoh, to be kept in the cities for food. ³⁶ This food should be held in reserve for the country, to be used during the seven years of famine that will come upon Egypt, so that the country may not be ruined by the famine."

³⁷ The plan seemed good to Pharaoh and to all his officials. ³⁸ So Pharaoh asked them, "Can we find anyone like this man, one in whom is the spirit of God?"

³⁹ Then Pharaoh said to Joseph, "Since God has made all this known to you, there is no one so discerning and wise as you. ⁴⁰ You shall be in charge of my palace, and all my people are to submit to your orders. Only with respect to the throne will I be greater than you."

Pharaoh told Joseph his dream. Seven fat cows got eaten by seven skinny ones. Seven full heads of grain were devoured by seven parched ones. To Joseph this was a piece of cake. Egypt would know seven years of plenty followed by seven devastating years of famine.

Joseph even suggested a practical approach to dealing with this crisis: tax the abundant harvests heavily to store up grain in preparation for the famine. When the lean time came Egyptians could ride it out in style while everybody else scrambled for sustenance.

Hearing Joseph's interpretation, wisdom, and selflessness, Pharaoh sensed that Joseph was a man of God. He felt comfortable putting Joseph in charge of not only the grain storage plan, but everything and everyone save Pharaoh himself. This marked the third time that Joseph had been so promoted. Paralleling God's entire salvation story, each fall had paved the way for an even greater rise.

As Joseph walked through them, the events of his early life seemed horrible. Looking back, they were but steps to a destiny far bigger than he could have imagined back in the days when he sat next to his father in a multi-colored coat. That's how it is for all of us. We can't see the ultimate endpoint as we're making the journey. We struggle through life trying to make the best of it. In the end, we see how each moment—even the hard ones—created a relationship that led to something more amazing than we ever envisioned.

Sons and Profits

41 So Pharaoh said to Joseph, "I hereby put you in charge of the whole land of Egypt." 42 Then Pharaoh took his signet ring from his finger and put it on Joseph's finger. He dressed him in robes of fine linen and put a gold chain around his neck. 43 He had him ride in a chariot as his second-in-command, and people shouted before him, "Make way!" Thus he put him in charge of the whole land of Egypt.

44 Then Pharaoh said to Joseph, "I am Pharaoh, but without your word no one will lift hand or foot in all Egypt." 45 Pharaoh gave Joseph the name Zaphenath-Paneah and gave him Asenath daughter of Potiphera, priest of On, to be his wife. And Joseph went throughout the land of Egypt.

46 Joseph was thirty years old when he entered the service of Pharaoh king of Egypt. And Joseph went out from Pharaoh's presence and traveled throughout Egypt. 47 During the seven years of abundance the land produced plentifully. 48 Joseph collected all the food produced in those seven years of abundance in Egypt and stored it in the cities. In each city he put the food grown in the fields surrounding it. 49 Joseph stored up huge quantities of grain, like the sand of the sea; it was so much that he stopped keeping records because it was beyond measure.

50 Before the years of famine came, two sons were born to Joseph by Asenath daughter of Potiphera, priest of On. 51 Joseph named his firstborn Manasseh and said, "It is because God has made me forget all my trouble and all my father's household." 52 The second son he named Ephraim and said, "It is because God has made me fruitful in the land of my suffering."

53 The seven years of abundance in Egypt came to an end, 54 and the seven years of famine began, just as Joseph had said. There was famine in all the other lands, but in the whole land of Egypt there was food. *55 When all Egypt began to feel the famine, the people cried to Pharaoh for food. Then Pharaoh told all the Egyptians, "Go to Joseph and do what he tells you."*

56 When the famine had spread over the whole country, Joseph opened all the storehouses and sold grain to the Egyptians, for the famine was severe throughout Egypt. 57 And all the world came to Egypt to buy grain from Joseph, because the famine was severe everywhere.

As Pharaoh's right-hand man, Joseph carried out his tax-and-save plan until he had so much grain he could not account for it all. He married and had two sons whom he named, "I forget" [implied: what came before] and "I'm twice fruitful" [implied: now].

When the famine came Joseph was able to give the people just what they needed, returning the grain to them in measure. In the first ever documented case of insider trading, Joseph's foreknowledge allowed him to store enough grain that he was able to sell to the rest of the world, allowing Egypt to turn a profit when everybody else was down. He ended up being exactly the right person with exactly the right gifts in the right place and time. Those who listened to him were amply rewarded.

More Than We See

42 When Jacob learned that there was grain in Egypt, he said to his sons, "Why do you just keep looking at each other?" 2 He continued, "I have heard that there is grain in Egypt. Go down there and buy some for us, so that we may live and not die."

3 Then ten of Joseph's brothers went down to buy grain from Egypt. 4 But Jacob did not send Benjamin, Joseph's brother, with the others, because he was afraid that harm might come to him. 5 So Israel's sons were among those who went to buy grain, for there was famine in the land of Canaan also.

6 Now Joseph was the governor of the land, the person who sold grain to all its people. So when Joseph's brothers arrived, they bowed down to him with their faces to the ground. 7 As soon as Joseph saw his brothers, he recognized them, but he pretended to be a stranger and spoke harshly to them. "Where do you come from?" he asked.

"From the land of Canaan," they replied, "to buy food."

8 Although Joseph recognized his brothers, they did not recognize him. 9 Then he remembered his dreams about them and said to them, "You are spies! You have come to see where our land is unprotected."

10 "No, my lord," they answered. "Your servants have come to buy food. 11 We are all the sons of one man. Your servants are honest men, not spies."

12 "No!" he said to them. "You have come to see where our land is unprotected."

13 But they replied, "Your servants were twelve brothers, the sons of one man, who lives in the land of Canaan. The youngest is now with our father, and one is no more."

14 Joseph said to them, "It is just as I told you: You are spies! 15 And this is how you will be tested: As surely as Pharaoh lives, you will not leave this place unless your youngest brother comes here. 16 Send one of your number to get your brother; the rest of you will be kept in prison, so that your words may be tested to see if you are telling the truth. If you are not, then as surely as Pharaoh lives, you are spies!" 17 And he put them all in custody for three days.

You saw this coming from a mile away, right?

As famine took the crops of the lands all about Egypt Jacob and his family found themselves in trouble. So Jacob sent his ten oldest sons—the exact group who had sold Joseph into slavery—down to Egypt to buy grain.

Jacob did not send Benjamin, his youngest and the only son of his beloved Rachel remaining to him. All these years later he still remembered losing Joseph. He could not bear to lose Benjamin as well.

Unbeknownst to Jacob or his wayward sons, Joseph was in charge of grain distribution in Egypt and saw his ten brothers arrive. Can you imagine the moment, ghosts of your past appearing before you in the flesh? What a flood of emotions must have run through Joseph: longing, remorse, bitterness, nostalgia, and the love one seems to feel for family even when the experience with them hasn't been good.

As his ten elder brothers knelt at his feet, Joseph remembered his dream long past, that brothers and family would bow to him.

Though Joseph recognized his brothers immediately, not one of them recognized him. They weren't expecting to find him. If they looked for him at all, they'd seek out the garb of a slave, not the robe of a governor.

So many of us only see what we expect to see in other people, even those closest to us. We're quick to pigeonhole, stuffing others in a convenient box and refusing to let them out. We expect the people around us to look, sound, and act as we're accustomed to. If they change, even for the better, it disturbs us. Often we refuse to recognize it.

This is one of the reasons it's hard for families to get over long-standing arguments, or for a single member of a family to reform their lifestyle. When somebody makes an effort to change, the family resists. They're comfortable with one person being the "black sheep", another being the rescuer, another being the disciplinarian, and so on. What good is a disciplinarian without someone to punish? What role does a rescuer have if everyone is healthy? The same people who have been after the black sheep to change their ways all these years feel lost and angry when the black sheep actually does so. We prefer the people we are comfortable with to the people God transforms.

For years groups of middle- and high-school boys have come to my church to play games in the evenings. We have a wonderful time. There's food, candy, and all the pop you can drink. Every one of those gents, no matter what their background or status in the community, has been amazing as long as they've been at our church. I've not had a single discipline problem. Incidents of people being unkind to each other are rare. You'd think these guys were angels incarnate.

When parents of these young lads talk to me they're almost universally grateful, mostly because I'm taking the guys off their hands for a few hours. Often they'll pull me aside and say, "I hope my son has been behaving." When I tell them I've not seen otherwise from any kid in a decade of doing this, they're amazed. "My son? If you only knew…"

I get what they mean, but honestly I do know. None of these kids are perfect. Some of them are quite imperfect. But each has an angelic, responsible side. Not only does the rest of the world not get to see enough of it, the rest of the world is acting *against* it by assuming people are going to be selfish by habit, incredible only by accident. For some of these guys, game nights are the only time they've been given a chance. They've lived up to it too. For a while, at least, they get to wear governor's robes even though everybody else is expecting to see a slave.

Part of our calling as faithful people is to recognize where people are headed, not just where they're standing at the moment. Think of all the Josephs in your life…that family member you've feuded with, the person at work you're holding a grudge against, maybe your own spouse or parent or child. Every one of those people is more than you expect them to be, more than you're willing to perceive them as. This is also true of strangers on the street and most everyone you'll meet. We dare not limit people to our own assumptions about them. We cheat them, the world, and ourselves when we do so.

Your opinion and perception of others do not limit who they really are. What you expect of people is not the sum total of all they have to give. The people around you are more than you realize. Joseph's brothers never got over their errors of perception. Joseph was able to transcend his, as we're about to see. He got over that voice inside whispering that his brothers were defined only by what he had experienced with them. Both he and the people around him were far better off for it.

Not that Joseph let his brothers off the hook easily. He spoke harshly to them at first. Part of this might have been staying in character, not blowing his cover as the Egyptian Governor. Part of it might have been the beginning stages of his plan. Part of it was probably honest anger. But even if the latter comes through strongly, keep in mind that Joseph *could* have done everything he threatened them with in his little sham. Had he seriously accused them as spies, they would have been locked up forever or executed by the Egyptians. Any revenge Joseph wanted was in his power. The lives of his betrayers were in his hands. He did not take them. Instead he asked for something else.

Joseph found a greater desire than justice, a greater need than putting his brothers through exactly what he went through. He wanted to see Benjamin, his full brother and the only one who hadn't sold him down the river.

To make this happen, he questioned his brothers until they admitted that one of their number remained at home. He then proposed to "test the truth" of their claims by imprisoning nine of them and sending one back for the last brother, commanding the missing sibling be brought to Egypt.

"I Told You So"

18 On the third day, Joseph said to them, "Do this and you will live, for I fear God: 19 If you are honest men, let one of your brothers stay here in prison, while the rest of you go and take grain back for your starving households. 20 But you must bring your youngest brother to me, so that your words may be verified and that you may not die." This they proceeded to do.

21 They said to one another, "Surely we are being punished because of our brother. We saw how distressed he was when he pleaded with us for his life, but we would not listen; that's why this distress has come on us."

22 Reuben replied, "Didn't I tell you not to sin against the boy? But you wouldn't listen! Now we must give an accounting for his blood." 23 They did not realize that Joseph could understand them, since he was using an interpreter.

24 He turned away from them and began to weep, but then came back and spoke to them again. He had Simeon taken from them and bound before their eyes.

25 Joseph gave orders to fill their bags with grain, to put each man's silver back in his sack, and to give them provisions for their journey. After this was done for them, 26 they loaded their grain on their donkeys and left.

After three days, Joseph showed mercy on his brothers. His original proposal was to keep them all in jail, releasing one to go and fetch Benjamin. He changed that to keeping but one in jail (Simeon) and letting the rest return to retrieve their brother.

The brothers had no choice but agreeing to the Governor's demand. He could have held Simeon, or any of them, as long as he wished. They stood accused of spying, unjustly but powerfully. They began to see a karmic connection between their treatment of Joseph long ago and the stress they were undergoing at the present time. They hadn't listened to Joseph's pleading, now this governor wasn't listening to theirs.

At this point Reuben pipes up oh-so-helpfully with his version of, "I told you not to do that, guys!"

Before you laugh too hard at him, who among us does not use that same, "Wasn't me!" argument when we quarrel? Never have four more unhelpful words been spoken than, "I told you so".

Thoroughly accused and feeling persecuted, Jacob's sons turned towards home. They would not return empty-handed. With them went the desperately-needed grain. Joseph was doubly generous; unbeknownst to them he gave them back their silver as well.

Odds are it was far more than the 20 shekels they had sold him for.

The Hidden Cost of Selfishness

27 At the place where they stopped for the night one of them opened his sack to get feed for his donkey, and he saw his silver in the mouth of his sack. 28 "My silver has been returned," he said to his brothers. "Here it is in my sack."

Their hearts sank and they turned to each other trembling and said, "What is this that God has done to us?"

Here we see part of the problem with being devious and self-centered. Technically Joseph giving the brothers their money back was a good thing…a windfall for them. But they didn't see it as such. They assumed that in addition to being labeled spies, they would now be accused of cheating the governor out of his money, stealing the grain without payment.

When we do evil we are quick to attribute evil motives to others as well. You know your spouse is having an affair when they constantly accuse *you* of having one. The guy in the conversation accusing everyone else of having ulterior motives has plenty of his own.

Sin clouds our vision, bends us until we only see the world in its terms. We don't have to twist too far before we're not capable of seeing, let alone trusting, goodness anymore. Had Joseph's brothers acted like saints their whole lives, they probably could have come up with 92 good things about getting their money back. Because they saw everything through the lens of their own self-interest, they assumed the governor back in Egypt would be doing so as well. If true, this would have spelled doom for them.

A gift that should have made the brothers joyful instead made them sweat. It's a horrible way to live, one a sane person would want to avoid as much as possible. Practicing generosity and innocence may not seem to have as many immediate tangible rewards as self-centeredness does, but the price you pay for selfishness in the long run dwarfs its benefits.

The Importance of Trust

29 When they came to their father Jacob in the land of Canaan, they told him all that had happened to them. They said, 30 "The man who is lord over the land spoke harshly to us and treated us as though we were spying on the land. 31 But we said to him, 'We are honest men; we are not spies. 32 We were twelve brothers, sons of one father. One is no more, and the youngest is now with our father in Canaan.'

33 "Then the man who is lord over the land said to us, 'This is how I will know whether you are honest men: Leave one of your brothers here with me, and take food for your starving households and go. 34 But bring your youngest brother to me so I will know that you are not spies but honest men. Then I will give your brother back to you, and you can trade in the land.'"

35 As they were emptying their sacks, there in each man's sack was his pouch of silver! When they and their father saw the money pouches, they were frightened. 36 Their father Jacob said to them, "You have deprived me of my children. Joseph is no more and Simeon is no more, and now you want to take Benjamin. Everything is against me!"

37 Then Reuben said to his father, "You may put both of my sons to death if I do not bring him back to you. Entrust him to my care, and I will bring him back."

38 But Jacob said, "My son will not go down there with you; his brother is dead and he is the only one left. If harm comes to him on the journey you are taking, you will bring my gray head down to the grave in sorrow."

The brothers returned home and relayed the story to their father, explaining that they'd lost yet another of his sons and couldn't get him back until Benjamin made the trip to Egypt with them. As they revealed the silver they definitely shouldn't have had, Jacob realized there was a very real possibility that his sons were headed towards disaster. Yet there they stood, begging him to let poor Benjamin go with them.

At this point Jacob figured he was throwing good money after bad and refused to let Benjamin go no matter how Reuben entreated him. Nobody trusted these guys much anymore, not even their father. Nobody believed their assurances, nobody thought they could run their lives right…they couldn't even make a simple shopping trip for grain without bungling it beyond belief. Accused of being spies, losing a son, failing to make payment for the goods…they were just *inventing* ways to mess things up now.

People losing confidence in you is another hidden cost of the self-centered life. Trust is a basic component of every human relationship. Devoid of trust, relationships fill with stress. The moment they turned on Joseph, Jacob's sons all but ensured that kind of relationship with each other. Finally it leeched over to their relationship with their dad.

Trust isn't just a nice idea, it's an ethic. Do our actions help others regard us as trustworthy or do they violate trust? If it's the latter, those actions may not be worth doing in the long run no matter what the short-term gain. The world tells us that we'll be happy getting extra things at the cost of isolating ourselves from each other. We call it "getting ahead" and "distinguishing ourselves". In the end, it all amounts to a really fancy way to be lonely. The more people whose trust we've betrayed on the way, the lonelier we end up being.

Nothing Else Left

43 Now the famine was still severe in the land. *² So when they had eaten all the grain they had brought from Egypt, their father said to them, "Go back and buy us a little more food."*

³ But Judah said to him, "The man warned us solemnly, 'You will not see my face again unless your brother is with you.' ⁴ If you will send our brother along with us, we will go down and buy food for you. ⁵ But if you will not send him, we will not go down, because the man said to us, 'You will not see my face again unless your brother is with you.'"

⁶ Israel asked, "Why did you bring this trouble on me by telling the man you had another brother?"

⁷ They replied, "The man questioned us closely about ourselves and our family. 'Is your father still living?' he asked us. 'Do you have another brother?' We simply answered his questions. How were we to know he would say, 'Bring your brother down here'?"

⁸ Then Judah said to Israel his father, "Send the boy along with me and we will go at once, so that we and you and our children may live and not die. ⁹ I myself will guarantee his safety; you can hold me personally responsible for him. If I do not bring him back to you and set him here before you, I will bear the blame before you all my life. ¹⁰ As it is, if we had not delayed, we could have gone and returned twice."

¹¹ Then their father Israel said to them, "If it must be, then do this: Put some of the best products of the land in your bags and take them down to the man as a gift—a little balm and a little honey, some spices and myrrh, some pistachio nuts and almonds. ¹² Take double the amount of silver with you, for you must return the silver that was put back into the mouths of your sacks. Perhaps it was a mistake. ¹³ Take your brother also and go back to the man at once.¹⁴ And may God Almighty grant you mercy before the man so that he will let your other brother and Benjamin come back with you. As for me, if I am bereaved, I am bereaved."

Jacob and his family delayed the matter as long as possible, as dad still refused to send his last favorite son with those ne'er-do-well brothers. The famine called the question. When they'd eaten through the entire supply of grain they procured from Egypt, they were forced to search for more. The only person who had any was the one person they didn't want to see again, that pesky Egyptian governor.

Jacob was out of options. If he didn't send his sons for more grain, all of them would die, including Benjamin. He couldn't send his sons without Benjamin because the governor would either imprison or execute them, leaving him with no sons and still no grain. Plus Judah was adamant that none of them would go back to Egypt without fulfilling the governor's commands to the letter.

At this point the only response Jacob could muster was, "Why the heck did you tell him you had another brother?!?"

To which his sons replied, "He *asked* us!!! What were we supposed to say?!?"

GARDEN TO DESERT

This family was at the end of their rope.

In the end, all Jacob could do was concede. He prepared his boys the best he could. He loaded them up with gifts for the governor and twice the silver necessary…payment for the last shipment of grain and this one. He prayed desperately that all this was just an accounting error. Then he prayed even more desperately that God would have mercy and let both Simeon and Benjamin return to him. But his last words on the matter were, "If you die, you die." The implication: "There's nothing more I can do about it. It's in God's hands."

Once again, late in life, Jacob experienced a hard truth. God is what you have when there's nothing else left. When power, control, wealth, good health, shelter, companionship, purpose, family…when everything else is stripped from you, only God remains. That is the closest we will ever come to knowing him truly. It's a mark of our fallen world that we meet him most purely in loss and suffering. As long as we're able to grasp at anything else besides God, we will. Only when we lack that power do we understand the fullness of his love and mercy working for us.

The ultimate expression of this phenomenon is the moment of death. I've sat with many people as they've passed from this world. All their preparations ultimately come down to one moment of realization. "I can't do anything about this. Nothing will change it. I guess it's in God's hands now." Ironically enough, that's the way every moment of our lives should be. Instead we spend a lifetime distracting ourselves, pretending we have control, until in the end the realization is forced upon us. We're left with God and trust, that's it.

Sometimes we experience moments that prefigure that ultimate one. That's where Jacob was in this story. He faced the very real possibility of losing his favored son, if not *all* his sons. Death and the powerless feeling that accompanies it were visiting him early. All he could do was throw up his hands and say, "If I am bereaved, I am bereaved." This was another way of saying, "I'm without power. All I have right now is God and trust. I hope that's enough."

God's message to us, shown through scripture and our lives, is the hopeful and assuring answer, "Yes…it will be."

Bags of Treasure

15 So the men took the gifts and double the amount of silver, and Benjamin also. They hurried down to Egypt and presented themselves to Joseph. 16 When Joseph saw Benjamin with them, he said to the steward of his house, "Take these men to my house, slaughter an animal and prepare a meal; they are to eat with me at noon."

17 The man did as Joseph told him and took the men to Joseph's house. 18 Now the men were frightened when they were taken to his house. They thought, "We were brought here because of the silver that was put back into our sacks the first time. He wants to attack us and overpower us and seize us as slaves and take our donkeys."

19 So they went up to Joseph's steward and spoke to him at the entrance to the house. 20 "We beg your pardon, our lord," they said, "we came down here the first time to buy food. 21 But at the place where we stopped for the night we opened our sacks and each of us found his silver—the exact weight—in the mouth of his sack. So we have brought it back with us. 22 We have also brought additional silver with us to buy food. We don't know who put our silver in our sacks."

23 "It's all right," he said. "Don't be afraid. Your God, the God of your father, has given you treasure in your sacks; I received your silver." Then he brought Simeon out to them.

The brothers arrived in Egypt with Benjamin in tow. Instead of being clapped in irons as soon as they appeared, they were invited to dine with the Governor himself. Trusting and optimistic as ever, they took this as a bad sign, assuming that the governor's men were going to jump them at any second.

Sensing they were walking into a trap, they tried to explain their predicament to the governor's steward. They didn't mean to take the money. They had no idea how it got there. They brought it back and then some. Please, couldn't they just make this right?

Then the steward spoke the first reassuring words they'd heard in this whole affair. They didn't have to make it right; somebody else already had. The God of their father Jacob (whom you think they'd know) had been watching out for them. The steward already understood the situation, no harm had come of it. Simeon was free too. The news could not have been any better.

God is the bringer of Good News. Our sins have been forgiven, our lives redeemed, our bondage to the tempter broken. Like Joseph's brothers we try to make right what has already been righted. We offer silver where none is needed, promising to be good and make up for our wrongs. This is not possible. What ransom can we give in exchange for our lives? How do we undo past wrongs? We can imagine compensating for them but we cannot erase them.

God erases them, just as Joseph erased his brothers' debt. We cannot earn this grace, nor pay for it. It comes as a free gift or not at all. Framing it any other way twists and denies God's generosity in favor of our own control.

Sadly, many churches trade on making people "pay" for their sins. They place obstacles before those seeking to understand faith, demand recompense in the form of financial support for the forgiveness God gives all his children freely. Belonging to God's family becomes a privilege for well-endowed "believers", offering dues paid for admission into a carefully-guarded, exclusive club.

This is as silly as claiming Joseph's brothers making good on their grain payment would have made up for them selling him into slavery in the first place. No amount of silver, service rendered, or apologies would have sufficed. Either Joseph would forgive them or he wouldn't. They couldn't buy their way from "No" to "Yes".

Offering gifts and financial sacrifice are important and necessary parts of the life of faith but they are not an economic exchange, us trading money for access to, let alone benefits from, God. Like Joseph's steward, we share God's Good News freely and without restraint. "You come thinking you owe a great debt, but God has filled your sack with treasures instead. You are released…free. You need not relate to the world as if you were still in bondage. Enjoy and share God's bounty instead."

Wasted Opportunities

²⁴ The steward took the men into Joseph's house, gave them water to wash their feet and provided fodder for their donkeys. ²⁵ They prepared their gifts for Joseph's arrival at noon, because they had heard that they were to eat there.

²⁶ When Joseph came home, they presented to him the gifts they had brought into the house, and they bowed down before him to the ground. ²⁷ He asked them how they were, and then he said, "How is your aged father you told me about? Is he still living?"

²⁸ They replied, "Your servant our father is still alive and well." And they bowed down, prostrating themselves before him.

²⁹ As he looked about and saw his brother Benjamin, his own mother's son, he asked, "Is this your youngest brother, the one you told me about?" And he said, "God be gracious to you, my son." ³⁰ Deeply moved at the sight of his brother, Joseph hurried out and looked for a place to weep. He went into his private room and wept there.

³¹ After he had washed his face, he came out and, controlling himself, said, "Serve the food."

³² They served him by himself, the brothers by themselves, and the Egyptians who ate with him by themselves, because Egyptians could not eat with Hebrews, for that is detestable to Egyptians. ³³ The men had been seated before him in the order of their ages, from the firstborn to the youngest; and they looked at each other in astonishment. ³⁴ When portions were served to them from Joseph's table, Benjamin's portion was five times as much as anyone else's. So they feasted and drank freely with him.

Joseph came to see his brothers once more. They gave him gifts in direct contrast to them selling him for riches earlier. They originally got 20 shekels for him. How much did they ended up paying? Sin might offer early profits, but the interest will kill you.

Joseph inquired after their father. In the midst of their constant bowing and scraping (again fulfilling Joseph's prophetic dream) they informed him that Jacob was well.

When Joseph laid eyes on Benjamin he started to lose control. He had to excuse himself and weep in private. When he returned, food was served.

Though Egyptians and Hebrews did not eat together, the brothers were served portions from Joseph's own table. Benjamin got five times as much as the others, a sign of his connection with Joseph. For a moment the siblings were able to relax, eating and drinking freely. This is the way all their meals should have been. This moment had been available to them. Had the brothers spent more time loving each other instead of resenting each other, they would have enjoyed a lifetime full of it. It's a powerful lesson for all of us with less-than-ideal families.

I've always told folks to give up the illusion that they can do everything right, or even be good. Perfect ideals are beyond us. In place of those dreams I usually offer a simpler one: Try to live life so that when you look back on it someday, you don't think it was wasted. Don't wait to be smart or wise. Don't wait to be generous and graceful and do good for others.

So many of us assume age will give us wisdom when with a little bit of love for each other and the world, we could gain insight and peace much earlier. If somebody told us that we could have a million dollars when we were 30 or we could wait until we were 70 to get it, who would choose 70? We could make so many more profitable investments and enjoy the fruits of wealth so much more starting at 30 than starting later.

Forget the million bucks. It won't do you that much good. Grace and mercy, love and faith are another type of riches. Whether you find them at 30 or 70 you still find them...that's the most important thing. As with material wealth, the sooner you pick them up the more you can do with them for yourself and the world around you.

Why did it take a famine and the threat of execution to make Reuben, Judah, and company appreciate what they had? Why did Joseph have to go through slavery and jail and live in a foreign country before they could receive gifts from his hands, before they realized who their brother was and how lucky they were to have him?

God doesn't ask us to be smart, he just asks us not to be so damn stupid all the time...chasing after things that do us no good, holding onto things that wound and impoverish us, cheating ourselves and everyone we know of goodness because we think other things are more important. We're blessed today. We're powerful right now. We have a calling and purpose in this and every moment. The choice between life and death, forgiveness and fear, slavery and freedom shouldn't be hard. It's not a choice at all, really. Yet we keep insisting it is and keep turning down the wrong road just to prove that we can. We call it power…the same power the sons of Jacob felt throwing their brother down a well. It ends up as less than nothing. We miss the life we were meant for chasing a life that ends up meaningless. I cannot think of a sadder epitaph.

Sacks of Sins

44 Now Joseph gave these instructions to the steward of his house: "Fill the men's sacks with as much food as they can carry, and put each man's silver in the mouth of his sack. 2 Then put my cup, the silver one, in the mouth of the youngest one's sack, along with the silver for his grain." And he did as Joseph said.

3 As morning dawned, the men were sent on their way with their donkeys. 4 They had not gone far from the city when Joseph said to his steward, "Go after those men at once, and when you catch up with them, say to them, 'Why have you repaid good with evil? 5 Isn't this the cup my master drinks from and also uses for divination? This is a wicked thing you have done.'"

6 When he caught up with them, he repeated these words to them. 7 But they said to him, "Why does my lord say such things? Far be it from your servants to do anything like that! 8 We even brought back to you from the land of Canaan the silver we found inside the mouths of our sacks. So why would we steal silver or gold from your master's house? 9 If any of your servants is found to have it, he will die; and the rest of us will become my lord's slaves."

10 "Very well, then," he said, "let it be as you say. Whoever is found to have it will become my slave; the rest of you will be free from blame."

11 Each of them quickly lowered his sack to the ground and opened it. 12 Then the steward proceeded to search, beginning with the oldest and ending with the youngest. And the cup was found in Benjamin's sack. 13 At this, they tore their clothes. Then they all loaded their donkeys and returned to the city.

One more scene remains in this little play. Joseph has yet to reveal himself. When he does, the revelation comes with a twist.

Having put his brothers at ease, Joseph prepared one more little test for them. He had his steward put the "Governor's" cup in Benjamin's saddle bags. He let them get a little ways out of town, then sent the steward running after them, accusing them of stealing the silverware.

In a marvelous twist, the brothers actually got to protest righteously. They didn't steal the cup. You can hear sincerity and indignation mix in their response to the steward's accusation. "We may have done a lot of things, but not this! We've done right by you and the governor! We are so confident in this matter that if it's found among us, you can kill whoever has it and we'll all become your slaves."

Naturally the steward found the cup right where he planted it, in Benjamin's sack. And off they all trooped, back to the Governor to face the music, wailing and tearing their clothes in misery all the way.

We live out a version of this story every day as we distract attention from our own faults by pointing out the faults of others. "<u>Sure, I sin, but they _really_ sin</u>. I might have broken one commandment but what about the people who break the other nine?"

"This time I'm innocent" doesn't excuse our wrongdoing. No matter how much we crusade against others, protesting that we don't commit a specific sin that we perceive them committing, the Governor's Cup still sits in our sack. We'd love it if God would punish every type of sinner except the one we are, searching everybody's bags but our own. We quietly assume he'll do just that when we say, "I'm not perfect but I don't think I'm bad enough to go to hell." That doesn't wash. If we dare hope that God will be merciful to us, we must also hope he will be merciful to others.

The actual sin that the brothers were being called in for—stealing a cup—paled in comparison to the infraction they were guilty of: selling their own flesh and blood into slavery. This is also true of us. The sins we acknowledge committing are far less than the sum total of our wrongdoing. We mess up in a hundred ways every day we're not aware of.

This highlights the foolishness of pointing fingers at other people's sins. Demanding to see the contents of someone else's sack becomes far less attractive when we have to show our own as well. Few of us would make that exchange. It's better to admit that we're all carrying baggage, then hope that the Governor will make it turn out OK instead of calling us into account for it.

A Second Chance

¹⁴ Joseph was still in the house when Judah and his brothers came in, and they threw themselves to the ground before him. ¹⁵ Joseph said to them, "What is this you have done? Don't you know that a man like me can find things out by divination?"

¹⁶ "What can we say to my lord?" Judah replied. "What can we say? How can we prove our innocence? God has uncovered your servants' guilt. We are now my lord's slaves—we ourselves and the one who was found to have the cup."

¹⁷ But Joseph said, "Far be it from me to do such a thing! Only the man who was found to have the cup will become my slave. The rest of you, go back to your father in peace."

Standing before the Governor again, the sons of Jacob got a second chance.

Joseph demanded that Benjamin stay with him, likely to keep his brother under his care...the one brother who didn't betray him. Even if everything went horribly wrong, the sons of Rachel would stick together.

But the other brothers insisted upon a harsher penalty than Joseph required. They offered to become the governor's slaves *en masse*, all ten of them together.

This is an exact replay of the moment when those same brothers sold Joseph to the Midianites...a test to see if they've changed. They can walk free with the silver and the grain, back to their homes and families. All they have to do is condemn Benjamin to a life of slavery in Egypt, abandoning him to the "Governor".

Faced with that choice again, will they repeat their heinous act?

Redemption

¹⁸ Then Judah went up to him and said: "Pardon your servant, my lord, let me speak a word to my lord. Do not be angry with your servant, though you are equal to Pharaoh himself. ¹⁹ My lord asked his servants, 'Do you have a father or a brother?' ²⁰ And we answered, 'We have an aged father, and there is a young son born to him in his old age. His brother is dead, and he is the only one of his mother's sons left, and his father loves him.'

²¹ "Then you said to your servants, 'Bring him down to me so I can see him for myself.' ²² And we said to my lord, 'The boy cannot leave his father; if he leaves him, his father will die.' ²³ But you told your servants, 'Unless your youngest brother comes down with you, you will not see my face again.' ²⁴ When we went back to your servant my father, we told him what my lord had said.

²⁵ "Then our father said, 'Go back and buy a little more food.' ²⁶ But we said, 'We cannot go down. Only if our youngest brother is with us will we go. We cannot see the man's face unless our youngest brother is with us.'

²⁷ "Your servant my father said to us, 'You know that my wife bore me two sons. ²⁸ One of them went away from me, and I said, "He has surely been torn to pieces." And I have not seen him since. ²⁹ If you take this one from me too and harm comes to him, you will bring my gray head down to the grave in misery.'

³⁰ "So now, if the boy is not with us when I go back to your servant my father, and if my father, whose life is closely bound up with the boy's life, ³¹ sees that the boy isn't there, he will die. Your servants will bring the gray head of our father down to the grave in sorrow. ³² Your servant guaranteed the boy's safety to my father. I said, 'If I do not bring him back to you, I will bear the blame before you, my father, all my life!'

³³ "Now then, please let your servant remain here as my lord's slave in place of the boy, and let the boy return with his brothers. ³⁴ How can I go back to my father if the boy is not with me? No! Do not let me see the misery that would come on my father."

They will not repeat their mistake.

Instead Judah—the very same Judah who led the charge to sell Joseph, who pulled his brother out of the pit and tossed him to the slave traders—spoke up.

"Please don't kill me for saying this, sir, but I must speak. Our father had a favored wife. She gave birth to two sons before she died. He lost the older one long ago. Benjamin here is the younger, all that my father has left. If my father loses him, the grief will kill him. All he wanted was some grain to keep his family alive. He couldn't bear to lose his dearest son over that. So please, take me instead. I'll stay."

Nothing had changed around Judah. He was still not the favored son. His father doted on another more than him. But Judah himself had changed. Given the chance to make the same choice again, he opted to sacrifice himself to save his brother rather than sacrifice his brother to save himself.

Redemption had arrived. Judah finally discovered that those who seek to save their life will lose it, while those who lose their life for the sake of another will find it. This was moment the sons of Jacob finally became brothers.

The Lightness of Honesty

45 Then Joseph could no longer control himself before all his attendants, and he cried out, "Have everyone leave my presence!" So there was no one with Joseph when he made himself known to his brothers. 2 And he wept so loudly that the Egyptians heard him, and Pharaoh's household heard about it.

3 Joseph said to his brothers, "I am Joseph! Is my father still living?" But his brothers were not able to answer him, because they were terrified at his presence.

When he heard Judah's speech, Joseph had to order everyone else out of the room so the Egyptians wouldn't see their Governor break down in tears. The revelation that his brothers truly had a change of heart, that they weren't the people they used to be, that they actually cared about their family and felt some measure of remorse over their actions…it was everything he had hoped for. Joseph had been prepared to keep Benjamin close to him and jettison the rest of them. Now he got to hold onto all his brothers as a generation reunited.

Joseph's brothers went into shock at the news. Not only was Joseph alive, he was here standing in front of them. The difficulty in reconciling the naïve boy they sold away and this wise, clever governor must have been enormous. Naturally they would have felt the fear of retribution, plus the reality of their own regret now staring them in the face when it had been buried deep. But they need not have worried. This was, above all things, a moment of truth.

Part of that truth was good. The brothers had been willing to sacrifice themselves to save Benjamin. Joseph was not only alive, but doing very well.

Part of that truth was bad...that whole, "Sorry about throwing you in a pit and selling you as a slave, bro!" thing.

As we've seen before in Genesis, good or bad, truth brings its own healing. Their darkest secret was now on display. The brothers couldn't control what happened to them from this point on, but whether reconciliation or punishment was coming, at least they knew it'd be honest. They could stop regretting, denying, and hiding.

Each of us carries a special darkness we keep from the world. For some it's regret over past actions, for others inadequacy, for others pain inflicted upon them by another or a persistent bad habit or a debilitating illness. Whatever form it takes, the darkness keeps us isolated in crowded rooms, fearful in the most secure and loving relationships. We think to ourselves, "If people ever knew, I'd be mortified. I'm the only one bearing this burden."

We don't realize that everyone in the room is thinking the exact same thing. Their darkness might not be the same flavor as ours, but the effects are similar. We all bear burdens we're afraid to reveal.

The world can be cruel. It's not safe to expose ourselves or our darkness indiscriminately. Honesty is not always the best policy. Being truthful about something does not ensure a good outcome. But if we never share it, if the truth never comes to light, our hidden darkness ends up defining us. We assume that it's the most powerful force in our lives, the one that can upset and destroy all others. That's not true. Love and forgiveness are more powerful than any regret, mistake, sin, or wound. But we cannot discover than unless we dare to speak our darkness to someone and hear loving, redeeming words in return.

Sometimes one person who doesn't reject or run from our darkness can lift the burden, helping us to manage its effects and face its consequences from a position of strength and grace instead of bowing to it in secret our entire lives. This is why confession and forgiveness have been a part of the life of faith—and of most worship services—from time immemorial…one of the most sacred trusts of the church and its ministers.

Living gracefully and practicing forgiveness are crucially important. We like to think that showing compassion to others means we're doing good but not showing compassion leaves the people around us in a neutral position…neither better nor worse off. That would be true in a world without sin. With each of us harboring unspoken secrets, lack of compassion isn't neutral. Failing to show grace abandons our neighbors to their internal darkness, condemning them to bear it another day without relief or hope of a way out.

Either we lift others up through our actions or we push them down. Whether we do the latter by evil deeds or inaction matters little, the effect is the same.

With the truth finally revealed and their secret sin on full display, Joseph's brothers experienced this reality. The man they once wounded would now redeem them or condemn them. Joseph would choose grace or destruction. However things went from here, it was time to close the book on their old, hidden life and start a new one.

The Desert Watered

⁴ Then Joseph said to his brothers, "Come close to me." When they had done so, he said, "I am your brother Joseph, the one you sold into Egypt! ⁵ And now, do not be distressed and do not be angry with yourselves for selling me here, because it was to save lives that God sent me ahead of you. ⁶ For two years now there has been famine in the land, and for the next five years there will be no plowing and reaping. ⁷ But God sent me ahead of you to preserve for you a remnant on earth and to save your lives by a great deliverance.

⁸ "So then, it was not you who sent me here, but God. He made me father to Pharaoh, lord of his entire household and ruler of all Egypt. ⁹ Now hurry back to my father and say to him, 'This is what your son Joseph says: God has made me lord of all Egypt. Come down to me; don't delay. ¹⁰ You shall live in the region of Goshen and be near me—you, your children and grandchildren, your flocks and herds, and all you have. ¹¹ I will provide for you there, because five years of famine are still to come. Otherwise you and your household and all who belong to you will become destitute.'

¹² "You can see for yourselves, and so can my brother Benjamin, that it is really I who am speaking to you. ¹³ Tell my father about all the honor accorded me in Egypt and about everything you have seen. And bring my father down here quickly."

¹⁴ Then he threw his arms around his brother Benjamin and wept, and Benjamin embraced him, weeping. ¹⁵ And he kissed all his brothers and wept over them. Afterward his brothers talked with him.

Joseph's true measure comes forth in these passages. Before this we admired him for not giving up despite experiencing horrible betrayals. We appreciated his wisdom while he governed a household, a prison, and a kingdom. We marveled at the perceptive and shrewd way he dealt with his siblings. All of that pales in comparison to his response now.

"Brothers, you are upset and angry because you did something horrible to me. Don't be. Look what has come of it! I was in Egypt at the right time, able to do what was necessary to save you and the world around you. I went where I was needed. God sent me here, not you."

This is incredible. Can you imagine the temptation towards bitterness and revenge? Joseph put that aside and said, "What you did was bad, but it turned out for the good. That good is all I see anymore. The bad holds no power."

C.S. Lewis once speculated that as we step into heaven we'll be able to look back on our lives. He said we'd see that all the places that looked like desert when we were walking through them actually turned out fertile, flood plains in disguise.

God is in the business of turning our mistakes into goodness, our dry places into fountains of life, not just for our sake, but for the sake of those around us. Joseph understood this and held onto it through the worst betrayals imaginable.

When we let circumstances dictate how we feel and react, life becomes a roller coaster. Every up is followed by a down. We can never be secure. When we're on a high, we know a low will follow. We become afraid. When we're down, we suffer.

Joseph found peace in every circumstance. Neither the highs nor the lows ruled him. He experienced them but was not governed by them. He didn't let them dictate how he lived or reacted to others. Joseph was able to show love and mercy despite suffering great injustice. Peace and reconciliation sprang from his hands. The world needs more people like that.

But Joseph's actions did not come from a personal sense of strength or dignity. They came because he trusted in God. He didn't need to step into heaven to know that a desert could become fertile, he saw it happen in Egypt, in front of his own eyes. Knowing this, how could he not share that rejuvenation with his brothers? How could he refuse to let other people see and experience what he had?

The sons of Jacob were human, heirs to the mistakes and shortcomings of our kind. They never perfected their lives or their faith. But in this moment, through the grace Joseph showed them, the deserts of Egypt became the Garden of Eden for them. The 12 sons were together, their sins and errors wiped away. They experienced love and peace the way we were always meant to: strong, indomitable, and enduring.

One person brought this about. The faith of a single individual changed the world around him. We shouldn't miss how powerful Joseph became, not just as Governor of Egypt but as a healer for his people. This mirrors our calling. Each of us becomes so more powerful than we imagine when we stop celebrating our bondage to the world and its circumstances, living instead for the true and important things in life.

Seeking to redeem and protect his loved ones in this time of hardship, Joseph issued an invitation to his family: "Get dad and bring the whole crew down to Egypt. There's plenty of food, I'm in charge, you'll be safe and well." If you ever wondered how the people of Israel ended up in Egypt when Moses saved them in the Great Exodus, now you know. Joseph, one of their own, brought them there to feed and shelter them.

Then the brothers embraced, wept, and talked together. How profound that moment was after all they'd been through. They never expected to see each other again, let alone to be happy together.

People wonder what we'll all do in heaven someday. I'm guessing it'll be for us as it was for Joseph and his family. The postscript to our lives might well be, "They embraced and wept for joy, then they talked together...forever."

A New Invitation

16 When the news reached Pharaoh's palace that Joseph's brothers had come, Pharaoh and all his officials were pleased. 17 Pharaoh said to Joseph, "Tell your brothers, 'Do this: Load your animals and return to the land of Canaan, 18 and bring your father and your families back to me. I will give you the best of the land of Egypt and you can enjoy the fat of the land.'

19 "You are also directed to tell them, 'Do this: Take some carts from Egypt for your children and your wives, and get your father and come. 20 Never mind about your belongings, because the best of all Egypt will be yours.'"

Because he knew and respected Joseph, Pharaoh himself was pleased that his family had arrived. Like Joseph, he invited them all to stay, blessed and sheltered by his hand.

As with many foreign kings we've met in Genesis, Pharaoh would never claim to serve the God of the Hebrews. Yet he becomes a key part of the story because he recognizes God's goodness and strength in Joseph. People of faith are far too quick to claim that God works through them and nobody else. Scripture is full of stories of people bringing grace and redemption into the world without realizing they're doing it. Dismissing people as "non-believers" and discounting the possibility of God working through them is a cheap and tasteless attempt to limit God's work and keep his power for ourselves.

Genesis reminds us repeatedly that the world and its people are broken and mistaken. That applies to *all* of us, people of faith as well as people who wouldn't identify that way. The ways of the world and the ways of faith are quite different, but individual people don't reside in either camp fully.

The strongest people of faith still subscribe to worldly powers. (Think you don't? Take the same test a young man once did before Jesus. Sell ALL your worldly possessions and give them away to the poor. Not gonna do it? I guess you believe they'll keep you secure and give you power.) Conversely, the most worldly among us understand that there's something more to existence than what appears on the surface, even if they wouldn't credit any kind of divine presence as part of that "something more".

I've met many people who don't subscribe to the same God I do, some who don't believe in any God at all. I've met very few people who don't believe in (and respond positively towards) goodness, generosity, and love. If communities of faith spend more time sharing those qualities and less time throwing up walls and protecting their own prerogatives, more people might be willing to admit some level of faith…if not in a deity at least in something beyond themselves.

Joseph spent his entire life working hard in service to others, refusing to let circumstances around him keep him from honoring others and his duty to God. As a result, even the king of worldliness admitted that whatever Joseph had was a good thing and that there should be more of it in the world and, more particularly, in Egypt! Every person of faith should view this as a model. Every second we spend trying to "convert" people is a second wasted. Every day we spend demonstrating love in service to others—*all* others, whether they think like we do or not—is a day we spend doing what God calls us to do.

I cannot speak lowly enough of people who would not have done a thing for Pharaoh because he wasn't a "believer". I cannot speak highly enough of Joseph and people like him who make the world better every day for all God's children. God shines through their faces.

The Good News

21 So the sons of Israel did this. Joseph gave them carts, as Pharaoh had commanded, and he also gave them provisions for their journey. 22 To each of them he gave new clothing, but to Benjamin he gave three hundred shekels of silver and five sets of clothes. 23 And this is what he sent to his father: ten donkeys loaded with the best things of Egypt, and ten female donkeys loaded with grain and bread and other provisions for his journey. 24 Then he sent his brothers away, and as they were leaving he said to them, "Don't quarrel on the way!"

25 So they went up out of Egypt and came to their father Jacob in the land of Canaan. 26 They told him, "Joseph is still alive! In fact, he is ruler of all Egypt." Jacob was stunned; he did not believe them. ²⁷ *But when they told him everything Joseph had said to them, and when he saw the carts Joseph had sent to carry him back, the spirit of their father Jacob revived.* ²⁸ *And Israel said, "I'm convinced! My son Joseph is still alive. I will go and see him before I die."*

Invited by their brother and the king, Jacob's sons returned home with some news for him. "Guess what, dad? That whole 'Joseph's dead' thing was a hoax. He's actually alive and ruling Egypt. By the way, we're moving there because he and Pharaoh invited us. Have you met Pharaoh? Nice guy." When Jacob saw the carts laden with gifts and grain, he knew it was true.

Keep in mind this was the same Jacob who said upon his sons' departure, "If I am bereaved, I am bereaved." He expected nothing but death and mourning from this trip. He knew it was the end. Instead he not only got life, but more life than he dreamed was possible.

This is *exactly* how God operates. He takes our pain, sorrow, and certainty of death and transforms them into life and joy. Jacob got the impossible. The son he had lost was returned to him…along with all his other sons that he feared losing, all the grain he needed, a home for him and his family, and everything he would require to live the rest of his life happily. Plus he knew his children and grandchildren would have the same. At the start of this trip he would have been happy with some sacks of wheat. Look what he got instead!

Jacob represents all of us. We think we know what's possible, that reality extends no farther than our eyes can see. As we age, we grow familiar with the limitations of life. Ultimately we come to understand loss, pain, the certainty of death. Like Jacob, we throw up our hands and say, "There's nothing I can do."

As it turns out, loss and death aren't nearly as certain as God's love for us. We're all going to be surprised like Jacob. We'll be surprised how much our lives ended up meaning; we'll be surprised how much more is in store; we'll be surprised how everything we thought lost is restored to us and multiplied a thousand times over.

THAT'S God's will for us. That's what makes him our God. This is how he's decided to treat us. This is how much we mean to him.

If you've ever experienced getting someone the present they've always dreamed of, then quivered in anticipation waiting for them to open it, you know what God's about. Just multiply that gift by infinity and you've gotten the closest glimpse possible into God's mind.

Imagine Jacob's astonishment, followed by unbridled joy, as the truth of his sons' words sunk in. Joseph was alive! Everything he'd ever hoped about goodness and life was true, and more. Happiness he'd never dared wish for was his.

Forever after in scripture God would be known as the God of Abraham, Isaac, and Jacob. His promise poured over their descendants, to you and me as well. As God turns out sadness to joy we inherit an identity as great as the Biblical titans. If wife-swapping Abraham, favorites-playing Isaac, tricky and bereaved Jacob, and mistreated Joseph can inherit and trust that promise—plus Pharaoh, 10 wayward and misbehaving sons, a couple of constantly fighting sisters and their maids, jealous older brothers, confused servants, and grumpy uncles, to name a few--we call can. We don't receive it because we're smart or good, we receive it because God loves us.

Moving Day

46 So Israel set out with all that was his, and when he reached Beersheba, he offered sacrifices to the God of his father Isaac.

2 And God spoke to Israel in a vision at night and said, "Jacob! Jacob!"

"Here I am," he replied.

3 "I am God, the God of your father," he said. "Do not be afraid to go down to Egypt, for I will make you into a great nation there. 4 I will go down to Egypt with you, and I will surely bring you back again. And Joseph's own hand will close your eyes."

5 Then Jacob left Beersheba, and Israel's sons took their father Jacob and their children and their wives in the carts that Pharaoh had sent to transport him. 6 So Jacob and all his offspring went to Egypt, taking with them their livestock and the possessions they had acquired in Canaan. ⁷ Jacob brought with him to Egypt his sons and grandsons and his daughters and granddaughters—all his offspring.

As Jacob made his final journey, he got one more conversation with God. "Don't be afraid," the Lord told him, "I'm with you wherever you go. Your lost son Joseph will be regained and he'll tend you up until the moment of your death."

Jacob trusted the Lord, experienced the good news firsthand. He took his entire family to Egypt to be reunited with his son. To the end of his days Jacob remained in motion, but every step onward led him closer to goodness.

Reunion

The middle verses of Genesis 46 detail the offspring of Jacob, children and grandchildren. The list is impressive. Then the story picks up with…

²⁶ All those who went to Egypt with Jacob—those who were his direct descendants, not counting his sons' wives—numbered sixty-six persons. ²⁷ With the two sons who had been born to Joseph in Egypt, the members of Jacob's family, which went to Egypt, were seventy in all.

²⁸ Now Jacob sent Judah ahead of him to Joseph to get directions to Goshen. When they arrived in the region of Goshen, ²⁹ Joseph had his chariot made ready and went to Goshen to meet his father Israel. As soon as Joseph appeared before him, he threw his arms around his father and wept for a long time.

³⁰ Israel said to Joseph, "Now I am ready to die, since I have seen for myself that you are still alive."

³¹ Then Joseph said to his brothers and to his father's household, "I will go up and speak to Pharaoh and will say to him, 'My brothers and my father's household, who were living in the land of Canaan, have come to me. ³² The men are shepherds; they tend livestock, and they have brought along their flocks and herds and everything they own.' ³³ When Pharaoh calls you in and asks, 'What is your occupation?' ³⁴ you should answer, 'Your servants have tended livestock from our boyhood on, just as our fathers did.' Then you will be allowed to settle in the region of Goshen, for all shepherds are detestable to the Egyptians."

A family of 70 is impressive by most standards, and this was only the beginning of Jacob's lineage. Eventually his people would number in the hundreds of thousands, their spiritual successors innumerable.

All of the love in the universe was condensed into two people the moment Jacob and Joseph reunited. Israel said to his son in that moment, "Now I am ready to die." Everything he could have possibly wanted had been fulfilled.

Joseph made preparations for his family to live, not just in this generation but far beyond. By emphasizing that they were shepherds, a trade considered undesirable to cultured Egyptians, the Israelites would be given their own parcel of land to settle away from the dominant culture. They'd reside *in* Egypt without becoming *of* Egypt…a critical distinction seen several times over in Genesis, the importance of which would be emphasized even into the New Testament.

Participating in the world and making it better without being mastered by it is a tricky thing, a balance that we never do get right. By segregating his people in Goshen, Joseph tried to make sure that his family had a chance to retain their identity in a foreign land…a plan which would have mixed results.

Settling In

47 Joseph went and told Pharaoh, "My father and brothers, with their flocks and herds and everything they own, have come from the land of Canaan and are now in Goshen." 2 He chose five of his brothers and presented them before Pharaoh.

3 Pharaoh asked the brothers, "What is your occupation?"

"Your servants are shepherds," they replied to Pharaoh, "just as our fathers were." 4 They also said to him, "We have come to live here for a while, because the famine is severe in Canaan and your servants' flocks have no pasture. So now, please let your servants settle in Goshen."

5 Pharaoh said to Joseph, "Your father and your brothers have come to you,6 and the land of Egypt is before you; settle your father and your brothers in the best part of the land. Let them live in Goshen. And if you know of any among them with special ability, put them in charge of my own livestock."

⁷ Then Joseph brought his father Jacob in and presented him before Pharaoh. After Jacob blessed Pharaoh, ⁸ Pharaoh asked him, "How old are you?"

⁹ And Jacob said to Pharaoh, "The years of my pilgrimage are a hundred and thirty. My years have been few and difficult, and they do not equal the years of the pilgrimage of my fathers." ¹⁰ Then Jacob blessed Pharaoh and went out from his presence.

¹¹ So Joseph settled his father and his brothers in Egypt and gave them property in the best part of the land, the district of Rameses, as Pharaoh directed. ¹² Joseph also provided his father and his brothers and all his father's household with food, according to the number of their children.

Jacob and five of his sons got to meet Pharaoh, appearing before the king with Joseph. As Joseph has suggested, they identified themselves as shepherds. Pharaoh agreed to let them stay in Goshen, offering them jobs keeping his own livestock.

When Jacob and the king met, Jacob gave him a blessing. Pharaoh asked how old Jacob was. Jacob claimed himself short-lived at only 130, a mere candle compared to the flame of his forefathers.

With permission from the king, Jacob's family settled in their new home. Joseph provided them all the food they needed. For a moment, at least, everything was good.

This was not to be Israel's final home, though. Jacob's people would remain in Egypt for centuries, but they would return to the Promised Land. This mirrors our own pilgrimage. Whether things are going well or poorly for us, we're not meant to stay in one spot forever. Inactivity quickly becomes bondage; respite turns to indolence, ownership to idolatry. Like Israel, we move constantly towards a greater promise, holding on to the things and places of this world loosely. The food we eat, the shelter over our heads, the possessions we call our own aid us on the journey, but they're not the reason for the journey.

Rising Fortunes

13 There was no food, however, in the whole region because the famine was severe; both Egypt and Canaan wasted away because of the famine. 14 Joseph collected all the money that was to be found in Egypt and Canaan in payment for the grain they were buying, and he brought it to Pharaoh's palace. 15 When the money of the people of Egypt and Canaan was gone, all Egypt came to Joseph and said, "Give us food. Why should we die before your eyes? Our money is all gone."

16 "Then bring your livestock," said Joseph. "I will sell you food in exchange for your livestock, since your money is gone." 17 So they brought their livestock to Joseph, and he gave them food in exchange for their horses, their sheep and goats, their cattle and donkeys. And he brought them through that year with food in exchange for all their livestock.

18 When that year was over, they came to him the following year and said, "We cannot hide from our lord the fact that since our money is gone and our livestock belongs to you, there is nothing left for our lord except our bodies and our land. 19 Why should we perish before your eyes—we and our land as well? Buy us and our land in exchange for food, and we with our land will be in bondage to Pharaoh. Give us seed so that we may live and not die, and that the land may not become desolate."

20 So Joseph bought all the land in Egypt for Pharaoh. The Egyptians, one and all, sold their fields, because the famine was too severe for them. The land became Pharaoh's, 21 and Joseph reduced the people to servitude, from one end of Egypt to the other. 22 However, he did not buy the land of the priests, because they received a regular allotment from Pharaoh and had food enough from the allotment Pharaoh gave them. That is why they did not sell their land.

23 Joseph said to the people, "Now that I have bought you and your land today for Pharaoh, here is seed for you so you can plant the ground. 24 But when the crop comes in, give a fifth of it to Pharaoh. The other four-fifths you may keep as seed for the fields and as food for yourselves and your households and your children."

25 "You have saved our lives," they said. "May we find favor in the eyes of our lord; we will be in bondage to Pharaoh."

²⁶ So Joseph established it as a law concerning land in Egypt—still in force today—that a fifth of the produce belongs to Pharaoh. It was only the land of the priests that did not become Pharaoh's.

Having already done well for his king, Joseph did him one last service, this one farther-reaching than all the rest.

After the famine had wasted away the land for a couple seasons, the only food remaining in Egypt was controlled by Joseph in Pharaoh's name…the stockpile collected in the years of plenty. Without crops, even the Egyptians were starving. First they came to Joseph with all their riches to trade for grain. When they ran out of money they traded away their livestock. As Pharaoh assumed control of all the livestock in Egypt, the importance of his shepherds rose…a boon for Joseph's family.

The famine endured another year and Egypt's people had nothing left to trade. Joseph accepted their lands and their bondage in return for grain, gaining control of Egypt's property and people. Thanks to Joseph, Pharaoh was not just ruler, but owner. Joseph gave the Egyptians grain to plant in their fields but he required 1/5 of each harvest thereafter go into Pharaoh's coffers, guaranteeing that the royal family would remain enormously wealthy in perpetuity.

The only people exempt from this exchange were the priests, who already lived off of Pharaoh's bounty and did not have to sell themselves or their land for grain. Even working for a foreign king in a foreign land, Joseph did not end up meddling with foreign religion or getting rich off of its deities.

A Last Request

²⁷ Now the Israelites settled in Egypt in the region of Goshen. They acquired property there and were fruitful and increased greatly in number.

²⁸ Jacob lived in Egypt seventeen years, and the years of his life were a hundred and forty-seven. ²⁹ When the time drew near for Israel to die, he called for his son Joseph and said to him, "If I have found favor in your eyes, put your hand under my thigh and promise that you will show me kindness and faithfulness. Do not bury me in Egypt, ³⁰ but when I rest with my fathers, carry me out of Egypt and bury me where they are buried."

"I will do as you say," he said.

31 "Swear to me," he said. Then Joseph swore to him, and Israel worshiped as he leaned on the top of his staff.

As Jacob prepared to pass from the world, he extracted a promise from his son. He did not want to rest in Egypt's soil forever. He asked to be carried back to the land of his fathers, the land promised to him by God. Joseph agreed to do this.

Though Jacob was an old man, leaning on his staff for support, he still worshiped the God who walked him through his tumultuous, but ultimately fulfilling, life. This was a poignant statement of faith. Jacob would not stop short of his goal, nor would he let any infirmity stop him from clinging to the God whom he once wrestled. To the end, Jacob held on.

Adoption

48 Some time later Joseph was told, "Your father is ill." So he took his two sons Manasseh and Ephraim along with him. 2 When Jacob was told, "Your son Joseph has come to you," Israel rallied his strength and sat up on the bed.

3 Jacob said to Joseph, "God Almighty appeared to me at Luz in the land of Canaan, and there he blessed me 4 and said to me, 'I am going to make you fruitful and increase your numbers. I will make you a community of peoples, and I will give this land as an everlasting possession to your descendants after you.'

5 "Now then, your two sons born to you in Egypt before I came to you here will be reckoned as mine; Ephraim and Manasseh will be mine, just as Reuben and Simeon are mine. 6 Any children born to you after them will be yours; in the territory they inherit they will be reckoned under the names of their brothers. 7 As I was returning from Paddan, to my sorrow Rachel died in the land of Canaan while we were still on the way, a little distance from Ephrath. So I buried her there beside the road to Ephrath" (that is, Bethlehem).

Genesis 48 describes an interesting blessing. Knowing his father was about to pass, Joseph took his two sons, Manasseh and Ephraim, to see their grandpa. A visit from his favorite boy was enough to rally Jacob to sit upright in his bed.

When Joseph entered, Jacob wanted to speak to him about his sons. Though they were a product of Joseph and an Egyptian woman, Jacob insisted that they would be regarded as his own children, no different than his own sons to him. Once upon a time God promised to increase Jacob's numbers,to make his family large. It was large enough to include these two boys. Their names would be recorded in the official family lineage. They would inherit Jacob's land and promise. Any children that Joseph had thereafter could inherit also, but the primary place and right would belong to Manasseh and Ephraim.

Communities guard their lineage jealously. Long-term members are regarded with reverence. Status is defined by who you're related to as much as who you are. Unsure of the future—and in many ways the present—we canonize our history and family trees, weighing most heavily the things we can best describe and control. People connected to our past are insiders; new, odd, disconnected people are treated with suspicion. Churches fall prey to this line of thinking far too easily.

Our faith hinges on the concept of adoption. Scripture is rife with stories of seemingly disconnected people being grafted onto God's story, leading God's people in ways that the firmly entrenched could not manage. We divide people into categories then try to measure how closely they relate. God doesn't care about our divisions; when he looks at us he still sees one family.

Unless we're Jewish, our only access to Genesis comes through our adoption into God's story through Jesus. Had he not made us his own by suffering, dying, and rising again, we'd have no part in these passages except being condemned. We are the outsiders, Gentiles (meaning non-Jews or outsiders) brought into the fold not because of our merits, experience, or tenure, but because somebody loved us. Yet when it's our turn to adopt others, we retreat into suspicion and ask why we should.

Churches grow in sedimentary layers, like rock formations. Elderly members comprise the bottommost layer. They've seen plenty of changes during their lifetimes, forced to adopt practices and people far different than they grew up with. They layer right beneath them belongs to people in their fifties, the first generation adopted by the older members as times changed. Though their access to the church came through adoption, this generation doesn't like to adopt others in return. They see strangers as threats, potential siblings in competition with them for attention and control. They want to be the center of the family. They tend to be rigid, rule-bound, excluding others. Instead of serving the church, they define themselves as the church and assume everyone else will serve them. When God brings someone new with vibrant ideas into the family, they do everything they can to downplay, ostracize, and keep themselves as the only "true" members.

Jacob did not have to give land to Joseph's sons. He didn't have to elevate them alongside their uncles, bringing them closer to him. He chose to do so freely, that he might bless them just as God had blessed him. Our purpose is similar. We should not ask who we should give to. God answers that question when he sends folks across our path. Did you meet them? Then you're intended to do good for them. "How should I do the good I am meant to do with this person?" should dominate our thoughts.

If we spent less time picking and choosing who to show grace to and more time actually showing it, the people around us would understand God's story and their place in it more clearly. That adoption is such an uphill battle in communities of faith shows how disconnected we are from the Word of God we claim to follow. Our churches lose touch with the Creator and Savior, becoming temples of our need to supplant him. Adam and Eve's sin echoes loudest in our most sacred places.

Breaking With Convention

8 When Israel saw the sons of Joseph, he asked, "Who are these?"

9 "They are the sons God has given me here," Joseph said to his father.

Then Israel said, "Bring them to me so I may bless them."

10 Now Israel's eyes were failing because of old age, and he could hardly see. So Joseph brought his sons close to him, and his father kissed them and embraced them.

11 Israel said to Joseph, "I never expected to see your face again, and now God has allowed me to see your children too."

¹² Then Joseph removed them from Israel's knees and bowed down with his face to the ground. ¹³ And Joseph took both of them, Ephraim on his right toward Israel's left hand and Manasseh on his left toward Israel's right hand, and brought them close to him. ¹⁴ But Israel reached out his right hand and put it on Ephraim's head, though he was the younger, and crossing his arms, he put his left hand on Manasseh's head, even though Manasseh was the firstborn.

¹⁵ Then he blessed Joseph and said,

"May the God before whom my fathers
    Abraham and Isaac walked faithfully,
the God who has been my shepherd
    all my life to this day,
¹⁶ the Angel who has delivered me from all harm
    —may he bless these boys.
May they be called by my name
    and the names of my fathers Abraham and Isaac,
and may they increase greatly
    on the earth."

¹⁷ When Joseph saw his father placing his right hand on Ephraim's head he was displeased; so he took hold of his father's hand to move it from Ephraim's head to Manasseh's head. ¹⁸ Joseph said to him, "No, my father, this one is the firstborn; put your right hand on his head."

¹⁹ But his father refused and said, "I know, my son, I know. He too will become a people, and he too will become great. Nevertheless, his younger brother will be greater than he, and his descendants will become a group of nations." ²⁰ He blessed them that day and said,

"In your name will Israel pronounce this blessing:
    'May God make you like Ephraim and Manasseh.'"

So he put Ephraim ahead of Manasseh.

²¹ Then Israel said to Joseph, "I am about to die, but God will be with you and take you back to the land of your fathers. ²² And to you I give one more ridge of land than to your brothers, the ridge I took from the Amorites with my sword and my bow."

Noticing that Joseph's two boys were there that day, Jacob offered to give them his blessing directly.

Jacob's failing eyes in verse 10 immediately recall those of his own father, when the near-blind patriarch inverted Jacob and Esau's blessings in a tent long ago. Just as his father did, Jacob passed his blessing to Joseph's two sons in reverse order. Ephraim, the younger, was blessed with the right hand, considered the primary blessing. Manasseh, the elder, received the left, the subordinate blessing.

Joseph objected to this but Jacob claimed it was intentional. He secured both boys in the lineage, passing on his name and his God. He blessed both to be able to "increase greatly on the earth". Yet Ephraim was destined to be remembered first, increasing in the greatest ways. Future generations would remember Joseph's sons in the order Jacob blessed them.

Why Jacob did this, we are not told. He might have had a soft spot for younger brothers. Perhaps the early events of Joseph's life (symbolized by Manasseh, "I Forget") were meant to be remembered second to his eventual prosperity (Ephraim, "Doubly Blessed"). All we know is that custom demanded he do it the other way and he didn't.

God seldom hews to convention. Ritual and tradition are necessary parts of the human experience. They bring order and familiarity. They help us comprehend things that would otherwise be too big for us. We're incapable of interpreting meaning until it's channeled and bounded, abstractions broken down and made relatable.

How many people understand urban traffic planning? Compare that to how many people actually drive on city streets. Drivers don't need to see the whole picture in order to relate to each other and their environment. They need to know that red means stop and green means go. As long as everybody sticks to that convention, all will be well. The combined decades of study and labor accumulated by the traffic engineering committee can be reduced to a single moment when a driver sees a red dot and presses his foot down on the correct pedal. The light contains our collective wisdom. As he views and follows it, our driver becomes as smart as the PhD who put it there.

But those conventions can, and should, be broken upon occasion. An ambulance driving a patient to hospital, a driver trying to avoid an accident, and your average right-turner can all pass the red light validly. In other contexts we can see red lights without stopping at all...as when watching them blink on a Christmas tree. In all cases the red-light rule is meant to serve the good of the people, not the people to serve the rule. Red lights are helpful but not universally binding.

This is also true of our faith symbols. None of our paintings or sculptures of Jesus actually look like he did. Without them we couldn't understand that God once walked among us in human form. So we stick the same image of Jesus onto every window, painting frame, and TV show we can find, putting up with the surface inaccuracy so we can grasp the bigger truth.

Is this inauthentic? Sure. Every representation of God's story is. That's usually a good thing. Imagine a Sunday School Christmas Pageant with the true-to-life odor of Manger Cow Poop wafting across the pews. The distracted congregation would miss the point entirely. Omitting that detail is not only permissible, but necessary. Paintings and pageants, too, are helpful but not universally binding.

We get into trouble when we can no longer change our not-completely-authentic representations...just the same as if we could not pass any red light without stopping. If we get offended when someone suggests that Jesus looks different than our stained-glass window or the Christmas Pageant can be portrayed in different forms, we've left the path of faith and fallen into the ditch of convention. For this reason breaking patterns from time to time is important, even if those patterns are old and even if the new way is just as flawed as the way we've become used to.

Our understanding, even when fondly repeated and taken as gospel, does not equal God's There's nothing wrong with *expressing* infinity in a particular way, but when we *limit* infinity to that particular expression, we end up worshipping the symbol instead of the God it's meant to connect us to.

Jacob showed a willingness to break with convention when necessary. This annoyed his father Isaac, his brother Esau, and his son Joseph. They all expected things to go differently than they did. But their expectations did not govern the universe, nor do ours. God's ways are bigger than we can imagine, covering far more ground than we expect them to. Following something so vast is bound to frustrate and disappoint us, but the second we refuse to be frustrated, disappointed, or change our minds we have ceased following God and begun leading him.

We don't get to order the world to our liking. Like Joseph, Ephraim, and Manasseh, we're called to put up with it when things don't go our way and try to find the goodness in things that are different than we expect. Jacob blessed the boys backwards. The entire family had to put up with it. That's life.

Many Blessings

Genesis 49 details Jacob's visions for his sons. The blessings have several layers. Some reflect a *personal* interaction between Jacob and his offspring, stemming from the stories we've read in Genesis. Some carry a *prophetic* aspect, foretelling the destinies of Jacob's descendants. There's also a *historic* aspect to the blessings. These men lent their names to the tribes of Israel. Things happened to those tribes in the time between Jacob's words and the time these passages were written down. Those events may be reflected in Jacob's blessings…prophecy to him but history to the authors of the book.

49 Then Jacob called for his sons and said: "Gather around so I can tell you what will happen to you in days to come.

2 "Assemble and listen, sons of Jacob;
listen to your father Israel.

3 "Reuben, you are my firstborn,
my might, the first sign of my strength,
excelling in honor, excelling in power.
4 Turbulent as the waters, you will no longer excel,
for you went up onto your father's bed,
onto my couch and defiled it.

5 "Simeon and Levi are brothers—
their swords are weapons of violence.
6 Let me not enter their council,

let me not join their assembly,
for they have killed men in their anger
   and hamstrung oxen as they pleased.
⁷ Cursed be their anger, so fierce,
   and their fury, so cruel!
I will scatter them in Jacob
   and disperse them in Israel.

Joseph may have forgiven his brothers, but dad had a long memory. This was made clear in his first "blessing". Reuben, the eldest son, was strong and powerful. He would be robbed of that power because he slept with his father's wife.

Similarly Simeon and Levi would be undone by their own actions. They tended towards violence. Jacob would not claim them, nor credit them with any contribution to the family besides leading it astray.

At the end of Genesis we learn the same lesson taught at the beginning: sin has consequences. We can forgive, alleviate, and compensate for them, but we cannot undo them. Only God has that power, and it will not be expressed fully until all things are unmade and made new again. Though beloved and still claimed as family, patterns of wrongdoing would follow Reuben, Simeon, and Levi.

⁸ "Judah, your brothers will praise you;
   your hand will be on the neck of your enemies;
   your father's sons will bow down to you.
⁹ You are a lion's cub, Judah;
   you return from the prey, my son.
Like a lion he crouches and lies down,
   like a lioness—who dares to rouse him?
¹⁰ The scepter will not depart from Judah,
   nor the ruler's staff from between his feet,
until he to whom it belongs shall come
   and the obedience of the nations shall be his.
¹¹ He will tether his donkey to a vine,
   his colt to the choicest branch;
he will wash his garments in wine,

> *his robes in the blood of grapes.*
> *[12] His eyes will be darker than wine,*
> *his teeth whiter than milk.*

Here we find the first beneficial blessing, and what a prediction it was! Not only would Judah have the respect of his brothers and conquer his enemies, he would rule until the time came for a greater ruler yet, the long-intended king. Judah's brothers would bow down to him; all nations would bow down to the One who was to come.

The New Testament lineages of Jesus trace his family back to Judah. Imagery of donkey, vine, wine, and blood in Jacob's blessing for Judah conjure images of the Christ. No blessing could have been more special.

One wonders if Judah would have thought it so if he realized that thousands of years would pass before the blessing flowered fully, with thousands more (and counting) before its full fruits could be enjoyed? We all assume that God's plan will be expressed during our lifetimes…another way of saying that we're the center of everything. This is why "end of the world" scenarios become so popular.

If Abraham's descendants were like grains of sand, then by definition we're a grain, neither the whole beach nor the master of it. Each grain does its part. Only together, seen in relationship to each other with an impossibly long view, does the role of each grain become apparent in relation to the whole.

Everybody dreams they'll change the world. The world doesn't change much, nor for long. Technology changes; cultures and nations change. Each successive generation puts a new spin on old sins. We get where we're going faster but with no more power to stop it than the ancients in these Genesis stories had.

And yet, grain by grain and blessing by blessing, the beach builds into something more than any individual grain could achieve. Somehow the seemingly-endless cycle culminates in something beautiful.

If we are the center, if the world starts and ends with us, then the beach becomes impossibly small and crumbles into meaninglessness. If we are a small part of a large story that goes on through us, but also around (and in some ways despite) us, we become larger and more enduring than we ever imagined.

The smallest part of Judah's blessing pointed to what would happen to him. The greater part was contained in what would happen *through* him, even long after he was gone from the earth. So it is for all of us.

13 "Zebulun will live by the seashore
and become a haven for ships;
his border will extend toward Sidon.

14 "Issachar is a rawboned donkey
lying down among the sheep pens.
15 When he sees how good is his resting place
and how pleasant is his land,
he will bend his shoulder to the burden
and submit to forced labor.

16 "Dan will provide justice for his people
as one of the tribes of Israel.
17 Dan will be a snake by the roadside,
a viper along the path,
that bites the horse's heels
so that its rider tumbles backward.

18 "I look for your deliverance, Lord.

19 "Gad will be attacked by a band of raiders,
but he will attack them at their heels.

20 "Asher's food will be rich;
he will provide delicacies fit for a king.

21 "Naphtali is a doe set free
that bears beautiful fawns.

The next sons got mixed blessings. The people of Zebulun would live by the coast. Issachar would live in pleasant lands but somehow become subjugated to them. Dan's people would be just but also clever like snakes. Gad would find trouble with raiders but would persevere. The people of Asher would become chefs. Naphtali would have beautiful children.

You can see where certain characteristics, stereotypes, and historical events may have played into these prophecies. They sound very much like us when we say, "Folks from the East Coast are fast-paced and businesslike, folks from the South are good cooks." None of us springs fully-formed into the world. We are products of where we came from, influenced by our culture and surroundings. These are not destiny, but they shape how we see and interpret destiny. This puts a great burden on us to create environments that foster positive things. We work not just for ourselves, but for those who come after.

> 22 *"Joseph is a fruitful vine,*
> *a fruitful vine near a spring,*
> *whose branches climb over a wall.*
> 23 *With bitterness archers attacked him;*
> *they shot at him with hostility.*
> 24 *But his bow remained steady,*
> *his strong arms stayed limber,*
> *because of the hand of the Mighty One of Jacob,*
> *because of the Shepherd, the Rock of Israel,*
> 25 *because of your father's God, who helps you,*
> *because of the Almighty, who blesses you*
> *with blessings of the skies above,*
> *blessings of the deep springs below,*
> *blessings of the breast and womb.*
> 26 *Your father's blessings are greater*
> *than the blessings of the ancient mountains,*
> *than the bounty of the age-old hills.*
> *Let all these rest on the head of Joseph,*
> *on the brow of the prince among his brothers.*
>
> 27 *"Benjamin is a ravenous wolf;*
> *in the morning he devours the prey,*
> *in the evening he divides the plunder."*

28 All these are the twelve tribes of Israel, and this is what their father said to them when he blessed them, giving each the blessing appropriate to him.

After all the years, Joseph was still Jacob's favorite son. His blessing wasn't as theologically profound as Judah's but he got plenty of good stuff. He would resist his enemies, have the help of God, plus blessings of sky, earth, and fruitful reproduction as well. All that Jacob had he bestowed upon Joseph, the "prince among his brothers."

Benjamin didn't get all that, but he would hunt like the wolf, devouring prey and dividing their plunder. He would be able to take what he wanted…a little like getting a gift card from dad instead of a defined present.

Many of these blessings would be reflected in later books of the Old Testament as the various tribes contributed to the life of Israel and interacted with the people around them.

Last Words

29 Then he gave them these instructions: "I am about to be gathered to my people. Bury me with my fathers in the cave in the field of Ephron the Hittite, 30 the cave in the field of Machpelah, near Mamre in Canaan, which Abraham bought along with the field as a burial place from Ephron the Hittite. 31 There Abraham and his wife Sarah were buried, there Isaac and his wife Rebekah were buried, and there I buried Leah. 32 The field and the cave in it were bought from the Hittites."

33 When Jacob had finished giving instructions to his sons, he drew his feet up into the bed, breathed his last and was gathered to his people.

After blessing his sons, Jacob made his final request, to be buried physically where he would soon reside spiritually: with his forefathers and foremothers. The bond between Jacob's family and their land transcended economic or property considerations. Jacob saw himself bound to the Promise, and therefore bound to the land it encompassed. Being buried "back home" was not just a sentimental wish for him, but a theological imperative.

Americans, in particular, have a hard time understanding this viewpoint. We're mobile, raised in the culture of pioneers and immigrants. We're always looking outward, valuing exploration, taking our God with us over the next undiscovered hill. Jacob wandered his whole life, but he never considered anyplace home except the land God had promised to him. His descendants would spend centuries trying to get back to the place that his blessing made their birthright.

Whether this is good or bad is immaterial. It's part of the human condition. We all see God through the lens of particular promises, evidenced in dearly-held aspects of our life. Some associate God with land or property, others with relationships or causes, others with churches or ways of thinking. We experience joy and suffering as we seek God in the fields in which we've planted him.

Whenever I hear, "Why do those people associate God so much with a particular piece of land?" I always want to respond, "Why do you hold so dearly to your farm and family?" What seems crazy from the outside makes perfect sense on the inside; what seems strange when other people do it seems normal when we do it ourselves.

Most people take this to mean that nobody's really crazy. "Walk a mile in their shoes," the old saying goes, "And you'll understand them." I go the other way. Walk a mile in other people's shoes and you're going to find that all of us are crazy. Insanity just comes in different flavors.

Our main goal in life isn't to be sane, it's to be crazy in the best ways for the best things. I've had strangers knock on my door to say they're hundreds of dollars short in rent and I've written that rent check on the spot. To most people that seems crazy, and I agree! But it's just as crazy to think that holding back the money is going to get me somewhere or make my life more fulfilling somehow. I'd rather be the giving kind of crazy than the selfish and fearful kind of crazy…mostly because that's the kind of crazy God asked me to be.

You have to be a *little bit* crazy to die on a cross to save the exact people who put you up there in the first place. That the ultimate self-giving, loving sacrifice seems impossibly insane to us while our own behavior and assumptions seem normal shows what poor judges of sanity we are.

All Jacob knew in the end was that he wanted to be home, with his family and people, so he wouldn't be alone for eternity. Seeing as how he'd be dead and wouldn't know differently, that was kind of crazy too. But the basics of his desire, even if expressed inadequately, revealed part of God's design for us. Everything he asked for—rest, peace, belonging, reunion with our loved ones--is exactly what God gives us in our return to the Promised Land...not some dusty cave in the Mideast, but paradise restored.

Our insanity manifests itself tragically when we confuse any part of earth with heaven, any relationship or tradition in this broken life with the way things were meant to be. But when we stop assuming we're the sane arbiters of reality and start understanding we're crazy, suddenly that crazy voice calling us to be something more than we design or desire doesn't seem so odd anymore. Trips to lands we haven't seen, trust in dreams that haven't come true yet, prosperity and wholeness coming from the worst of circumstances seem more normal. We realize that, as the crazy ones, any voice of real sanity is going to sound abnormal to us. Instead of fearing things that are different than we expect, we learn to trust things because they *are* different than we expect: life from death, salvation from a cross, freedom from following and trusting instead of choosing and directing.

We can never choose to be sane, at least not entirely. Our only choice is whether our craziness will serve a greater purpose or whether it will point to and justify itself alone. Will we admit we're crazy, accepting and learning from each other accordingly, or will we insist we're the only ones who aren't and point fingers at everybody else, fighting over patches of dirt and pieces of colored paper until our insanity comes to a merciful end?

Am I justified because I think I'm sane or am I justified because I trust that the only sane Being in the universe loves me enough to speak through me and make something come of my insanity? Do I want to be "right" by my own terms, living alone as master of my own universe, or do I want to be crazy for something beyond myself and be together with all the other crazy people I've known and loved and who have loved me in return?

"Hey, mixed up sons," said Jacob, "Bury me with my people, back in the cave we bought from those mixed-up foreigners. Our family wasn't perfect, but we loved each other. That's where I belong and that's who I belong with."

Thus says the whole family of God.

Faith is Kindness

50 Joseph threw himself on his father and wept over him and kissed him.² Then Joseph directed the physicians in his service to embalm his father Israel. So the physicians embalmed him, ³ taking a full forty days, for that was the time required for embalming. And the Egyptians mourned for him seventy days.

⁴ When the days of mourning had passed, Joseph said to Pharaoh's court, "If I have found favor in your eyes, speak to Pharaoh for me. Tell him, ⁵ 'My father made me swear an oath and said, "I am about to die; bury me in the tomb I dug for myself in the land of Canaan." Now let me go up and bury my father; then I will return.'"

⁶ Pharaoh said, "Go up and bury your father, as he made you swear to do."

⁷ So Joseph went up to bury his father. All Pharaoh's officials accompanied him—the dignitaries of his court and all the dignitaries of Egypt— ⁸ besides all the members of Joseph's household and his brothers and those belonging to his father's household. Only their children and their flocks and herds were left in Goshen. ⁹ Chariots and horsemen also went up with him. It was a very large company.

¹⁰ When they reached the threshing floor of Atad, near the Jordan, they lamented loudly and bitterly; and there Joseph observed a seven-day period of mourning for his father. ¹¹ When the Canaanites who lived there saw the mourning at the threshing floor of Atad, they said, "The Egyptians are holding a solemn ceremony of mourning." That is why that place near the Jordan is called Abel Mizraim.

¹² So Jacob's sons did as he had commanded them: ¹³ They carried him to the land of Canaan and buried him in the cave in the field of Machpelah, near Mamre, which Abraham had bought along with the field as a burial place from Ephron the Hittite. ¹⁴ After burying his father, Joseph returned to Egypt, together with his brothers and all the others who had gone with him to bury his father.

So Jacob, the boy who had started his life by helping to divide a family, was mourned as a great man by two diverse nations whom he helped unite. Joseph and all the family of Israel gather to fulfill his last request, to be buried with his forebears. Jacob was heir to all the fear and misfortune of humanity, but also heir to an even greater promise. In the end the promise won out. His life, even the less admirable parts, had brought him and his family to a place of honor and redemption.

15 When Joseph's brothers saw that their father was dead, they said, "What if Joseph holds a grudge against us and pays us back for all the wrongs we did to him?" 16 So they sent word to Joseph, saying, "Your father left these instructions before he died: 17 'This is what you are to say to Joseph: I ask you to forgive your brothers the sins and the wrongs they committed in treating you so badly.' Now please forgive the sins of the servants of the God of your father." When their message came to him, Joseph wept.

18 His brothers then came and threw themselves down before him. "We are your slaves," they said.

19 But Joseph said to them, "Don't be afraid. Am I in the place of God? 20 You intended to harm me, but God intended it for good to accomplish what is now being done, the saving of many lives. 21 So then, don't be afraid. I will provide for you and your children." And he reassured them and spoke kindly to them.

Even now Joseph's brothers worried about his feelings towards them. Had he been holding back until their father died, waiting to take his revenge? Whether Jacob actually left the instructions they say he did is up to debate. They certainly felt the reminder was needed, lest Joseph turn on them.

They need not have worried. Joseph meant what he said. He had forgiven them and credited any harm that might have come to him as one of the necessary prices of living out God's plan in a fallen world.

Joseph's question in Genesis 50:19, "Am I in the place of God?" reflected the one Adam and Eve asked way back in Genesis 3. Every character in between wrestled with it in one way or another. This was humanity's great sin, trying to take the place and power of their Creator, putting the self at the center of all things and judging the universe thereby.

Joseph bookends Genesis by implying a negative answer to the question. "I am not in the place of God. I will neither be your master nor your judge." In promising to feed them and their children he actually reflected God in the way that matters: providing, caring, nurturing, and serving.

Joseph's response caused a theological reversal. They made up for the whole world getting broken. "Speaking kindly" to his brothers was the corrective that fixed the world, as humanity showed forth the image of God once more.

Most of us have been raised to think of God as a white-bearded man in the sky who smites you if you do something wrong. We know a just God, an angry God, a judgmental God. We've not been lied to—those are all aspects of God's being—but we've been misdirected.

Respect towards God and his power is wise. Fear of the Lord is the beginning of wisdom. But respect and fear are neither the end of our relationship with God nor the sum total. They filter out most of the wrong ways we're tempted to view him, but they don't give us the right way to relate to him any more than respecting your earthly father is sufficient to describe that relationship. Fearing or respecting God isn't goodness in itself, it sets the table for goodness.

Focusing so much on the table-setting, we miss the meal. God's enduring attribute is kindness. This is why God sticks with us through our sins. This is why God still sustains the world today, through generation after messed up generation. He's kind. He loves us. He looks at our sin-misshapen lives and chooses to see beauty instead.

God didn't wipe the world clean and start anew after Adam and Eve broke it because he loved them and wanted to be kind to them. God hasn't brought about the end of the world yet because he was waiting to be kind to you, too. He'll probably wait to be kind to your children and grandchildren. For all we know he might let us create new people to be kind to until the sun explodes a few billion years from now.

When we are kind to each other we come as close as possible to representing God and living out his will on earth. Everything else you've heard or read or watched about God and his people should be viewed in that light.

The faith, the church, and the world have seen enough of people who preach respect and fear but lack kindness. They set the table in God's name but slap your hands away from the perfectly-placed silverware when you pick it up to eat. They're in love with their own creation, not God's feast. Better to eat with your fingers than end up eternally hungry, eternally fussy, deriving your self-worth from making other people miserable. Tax collectors, prostitutes, and sinners will sit down to eat with Jesus before those jerks.

As I've just demonstrated, kindness does not mean refusing to stand against evil. (Yes, preaching respect for God but omitting kindness is evil…all the more so because it's being done in God's name.) The purpose for standing against evil is neither self-justification nor righteous anger. We stand against evil because it crowds out kindness. We try to rid ourselves of evil so that we can be kind.

When we abandon kindness in favor of righteous indignation or judgement, we assume a role that God had the right to take with us but didn't. He is the ultimate Just Judge. He is offended more than anyone else by our sin. But God did not come to earth to condemn, but to save. When we refuse to be kind—even for reasons we consider righteous—we usurp God's place and God's will, assuming we can make a better decision than he. As we do so we repeat the exact sin that made us unrighteous in the first place.

After all they had said, after all the wrong they had done to him, Joseph still spoke to his brothers kindly. May all God's saints have the courage and faith to do the same to their brothers and sisters.

From Garden to Desert and Back Again

22 Joseph stayed in Egypt, along with all his father's family. He lived a hundred and ten years 23 and saw the third generation of Ephraim's children. Also the children of Makir son of Manasseh were placed at birth on Joseph's knees.

24 Then Joseph said to his brothers, "I am about to die. But God will surely come to your aid and take you up out of this land to the land he promised on oath to Abraham, Isaac and Jacob." 25 And Joseph made the Israelites swear an oath and said, "God will surely come to your aid, and then you must carry my bones up from this place."

26 So Joseph died at the age of a hundred and ten. And after they embalmed him, he was placed in a coffin in Egypt.

At the end of his life, Joseph extracted the same promise from his brothers that they gave to their father. He had lived a long life and was content. He knew God would continue to watch over his family. He wished to return to the place where God's promise led: the Promised Land. He asked to be buried there.

Jacob and Joseph had amazing vision but they couldn't see forever. They could only connect God's promise with what they knew: the land in which they had grown up. When we die, we make the same request that they did. "Please, let me remain forever in the Promised Land." Our vision doesn't extend beyond the end of our lives.

Because of events that unfolded thousands of years after Joseph—because of the savior that would come from the line of Abraham, Isaac, and Jacob—we now understand God's promise in a different way. No longer is it connected to a particular patch of earthly property. No longer does "forever" mean "buried as bones under the ground". We receive a living promise of life eternal with God and our loved ones that Joseph and his brothers could only guess at. We do not ask to lie resting next to our family, we hope to live in joy and peace forevermore with our family and all of God's children.

The characters of Genesis, from Adam and Eve through Noah and all of Abraham's children, lived by something they could not understand or see, but that they trusted in anyway. They provide examples for us, but not because they were "good people", as we were taught in Sunday School. They were just as mistaken and fallible as any human. As they trusted and followed, these imperfect people became far more than even they understood.

The story of Genesis is that of a garden becoming a desert, then a desert becoming a garden again. Where sin dried and parched, God walked with his people and watered. He continues to walk with his children today, with the spiritual heirs of the characters we've read about as well as their family by blood. The great take-away from Genesis is not that we're better, richer, more powerful, or less mixed-up than anyone else, rather that we're blessed because someone cares for us so much that he's willing to transform heaven and earth to make our lives what they were always meant to be.

EPILOGUE

And there you have it, a tremendous, tragic, yet hopeful story that boils down to two things:

1. We're imperfect and cannot find our way back to perfection.

2. Someone loves us anyway and is so committed to that love, and to us, that no power in the universe will stop him from making things right.

The particulars of each story vary, but in one way or another they all point to these twin truths. We dare not claim to understand why God would do this for us, let alone to merit it. All we can do is be thankful and trust.

I suspect that many will argue with or tumble over some of the things I've presented. That's good. I'd be disappointed if you found nothing in this book true, but I'd be equally disappointed if you took it as the single, infallible interpretation of these scriptures. The point of the book is not to provide answers for all time, but to open up the possibility that these words hold more potential and meaning than we realize or could ever discover...that scriptural exploration is worthwhile because it's fascinating and the overarching message is very, very good.

You, too, have permission to talk, to explore, to wring every bit of juice and meaning from God's Word as it will give you, which is an infinite supply. One of the greatest joys of our journey together is getting to share these things. Thank you for sharing this with me.

Until next time, God bless.

ABOUT THE AUTHOR

David Deckard has served as an ordained pastor in the Evangelical Lutheran Church in America for 17 years. The views expressed herein are his own, have not been vetted or approved of by the ELCA, and do not necessarily reflect the stance or positions of the denomination or any member thereof.

David is also the Managing Editor of Blazersedge.com, fulfilling a life-long passion by writing about basketball and the Portland Trail Blazers. He lives in the Pacific Northwest with his wife, two children, three cats, 400 board games, and the means to make caramel espresso drinks whenever he wishes.

Made in the USA
San Bernardino, CA
13 March 2016